COMMUNICATION
AND SOCIAL SKILLS

SCHOOLS COUNCIL COMMUNICATION AND SOCIAL SKILLS PROJECT

COMMUNICATION AND SOCIAL SKILLS

Towards a Theory and Practice of Audio-visual Language and Learning

Carol Lorac
Michael Weiss

Wheaton

A Division of Pergamon Press

A. Wheaton & Company Limited
A Division of Pergamon Press
Hennock Road, Exeter EX2 8RP

Pergamon Press Ltd
Headington Hill Hall, Oxford OX3 0BW

Pergamon Press Inc.
Maxwell House, Fairview Park, Elmsford, New York 10523

Pergamon Canada Ltd
Suite 104, 150 Consumers Road, Willowdale, Ontario M2J 1P9

Pergamon Press (Australia) Pty Ltd
P.O. Box 544, Potts Point, N.S.W. 2011

Pergamon Press GmbH
Hammerweg 6, D-6242 Kronberg, Federal Republic of Germany

First published 1981

Project Evaluator: Lewis Owen

Graphics: Bill Timms
Photography: Michael Weiss and Barry Smith

Printed in Great Britain by A. Wheaton & Co. Ltd, Exeter (DT)
ISBN 0 08-026426-3 flexi
ISBN 0 08-026427-1 hard

Contents

Acknowledgements

We should like to thank the following:

Our Evaluator, Lewis Owen, who worked in conjunction with us on Chapter 10 and edited the draft manuscript.

Our Chairman of Consultative Committee, Ernest Goodman, for his advice throughout the Project and his contribution to Chapter 1.

Our Curriculum Officer, Maurice Plaskow, for his inspiration and invaluable guidance.

Our Consultative Committee, whose concern for the development of our work led to a detailed study of our progress at every stage:

Dai Davies (representing the Schools Council Professional Committee), Headmaster, Christopher Whitehead Boys' School, Worcester.
Arthur Dews, Senior Education Adviser, Durham Local Education Authority.
Maurice Edmundson, Her Majesty's Inspectorate.
M. Pauleen Gilbert, Headteacher, Seaton Hirst County Middle School, Ashington.
Malcolm Glenn, Schools Council Field Officer for the North East of England, now Head, Coulby Newham Secondary School, Middlesbrough.
Ron Johnson (representing the Schools Council English Committee), Chairman of the Cheshire County Advisory Staff.
Toby Procter, Project Editor, Schools Council.
Douglas Proctor, Deputy Head, Tomlinson Middle School, Rothbury, now Head, Cramlington No. 4 School, Northumberland.
Leslie F. Ryder, Director of Learning Resources, Inner London Education Authority.
David Smetherham, Principal Research Officer, Schools Council.
Ron Smith, Teacher Adviser for Curriculum Development, Northumberland County Council.
Tom Stabler, Headteacher, Kingsley Primary School, Hartlepool, now Adviser, Cleveland County Council.
John Storey, Schools Council Field Officer for the North East of England.
Anne Tighe, Teacher, Boynton Comprehensive School, Middlesbrough.
Joan Walmsley, Head of German, Brinkburn Comprehensive School, South Shields.
Norman Willis, Assistant Director, Council for Educational Technology.

The many teachers and pupils without whom this book could not have been written, in particular the headteachers of the schools described in the case studies and the teachers directly involved in the work:

Ann Beresford, Ian Blacklock, Pamela Brown, Bob Calvert, Cathleen Galbraith, Malcolm Gerrie, Sheila Graber, Michael Harris, Tony Hodgson, Ted Liddy, Bill Parker, Eric Peel, Ken Riddle, Joan Walmsley.

Our gratitude is also due to:

Durham Local Education Authority, Northumberland Local Education Authority, South Tyneside Local Education Authority, Gateshead Local Education Authority, Sunderland Local Education Authority, Centre for Information and Advice on Educational Disadvantage, New College Durham, Huddersfield Polytechnic, Brighton Polytechnic.

Preface

In March 1976 the Schools Council accepted a proposal to examine the effects that the production of television, film and tape-slide programmes by pupils themselves would have upon their learning. The work was to be carried out with pupils of secondary age of all abilities and for a wide range of curriculum subjects. The proposal grew out of previous work undertaken by the authors which suggested that careful structuring of such activity could encourage the development of many different communication and social skills as well as providing a useful method of learning the subject itself. The proposal was for a four-year study in which the first two years would test the feasibility of such activity in a variety of contexts and the second two years develop teaching materials.

The specific aims of the Project were:

1. To extend methods which had been successfully developed for use by pupils of television, film and tape-slide, and to define the contribution that this work could make to the teaching of communication and social skills.
2. To define the contribution that such methods could make to pupils' learning over a wide range of curriculum courses.
3. To investigate the kind of support, in terms of training and resources, that teachers would need to carry out this work.
4. To investigate the resource materials that pupils would need.

The authors were given a half-time secondment by Durham Education Authority to direct and carry out the first two years' activity. This enabled work to be developed on a local scale involving five authorities in the northeast of England. The work was based at New College, Durham.

Ten schools were selected on the basis of ensuring a wide range of subjects, pupils' ages and abilities, and where necessary the teacher was trained by the Project team in an initial two-day course followed by school-based support. Information on the progress of the work was collected in visits by the Project team and their evaluator, which involved over four hundred hours of observation, a programme of interviews with teachers and pupils, and the video and sound recording of sixty hours of class-room activity.

Twenty teachers and thirteen subject areas were involved. Each teacher adapted part of his teaching programme to take account of the suggestions offered by the Project team. As a result, for part of his teaching time he helped pupils to respond to the subject under study by making a television programme, film or tape-slide. In most cases this involved the pupils in discussing and researching a topic, writing an outline programme plan, producing and rehearsing what was to be seen and heard, and recording and critically appraising the final product. Pupils were encouraged to work in small groups and to be largely responsible for the organization and execution of the necessary work.

This book describes the first phase of the Project. The main part describes the work undertaken by the teachers, which has been organized into a series of case studies (Chapters 2–9) each of which includes a brief evaluation by the teacher of his own work. Each case study is presented in an individual style in order to recreate something of the different atmosphere produced by each class and its teacher. It is hoped that the reader will be able to gain useful information from the whole range of case studies, in addition to the one or two specifically concerned with his own specialism. Anonymity of the teachers and schools has been preserved throughout, although a list of the teachers is provided in the Acknowledgements.

Chapter 1 was written jointly with the chairman of the Project's consultative committee and provides a general introduction to the rationale of the Project. Chapters 10–12 give a detailed evaluation: Chapter 10 relates the Project's findings to current educational thinking; Chapter 11 summarizes the main changes in organization and attitudes necessary to implement the methods developed by the Project; Chapter 12 demonstrates how many of the most significant learning gains resulted from the use by pupils of recorded sound and vision to organize and express their learning. Chapter 10 was written in conjunction with the Project's evaluator.

In 1978 the Project was granted a further £65000 by the Schools Council to complete its second phase – that of producing class-room materials to support teachers wishing to introduce the methods described here into their teaching programmes. For this phase the Project moved to Brighton Polytechnic and the directors were able to work full time. At the time of going to press, the directors have done a considerable amount of work on developing stimulus starter packs for use by teachers and pupils. These packs give the necessary technical information, enable users to translate specific subject-matter into sounds and images of various types, and enable users to organize these sounds and images into audio-visual statements. This material has been thoroughly tested on groups of pupils of various ages and abilities. It was discovered that certain methods and skills are crucial to success in this work (see Appendix 1, page 188), and material for developing these has been incorporated in the packs.

CHAPTER 1

An Introduction to the Project

The growing complexity and sophistication of the modern world make heavy demands upon the understanding and abilities of all young people, no matter what their academic potential might seem to be. Indeed, the gap between these demands and the capacity of young people to respond to them confidently seems to have widened in the post-war years, partly because society requires an ever wider range of personal and social skills. It is also becoming clearer that, unless these skills receive sufficient and expert attention, serious stresses can develop within the individual, inside schools and in society at large. Particularly dangerous are those stresses and conflicts which are due to, or are deepened by, the inability of individuals to communicate adequately. People also need a firm understanding of their dependence on each other, and must be able to form empathic relationships with others in a complex variety of social settings.

This inadequacy of communication and social skills reveals itself not only in social conflicts such as discord between generations, but also in the classroom, where it greatly reduces both teaching and learning potential. Many teachers are aware of these problems and are deeply concerned about their own responsibility in preparing pupils for creative participation in society.

It has long been realized by educators that communication abilities are critical, and both the language used by young people to communicate within their peer groups and with others, and their social behaviour have received considerable attention. However, the form and direction of almost all the work that has been done have been shaped by a number of assumptions which are overdue for close re-examination. One of these is the notion of the almost total supremacy in the learning process of verbal (particularly written) and numerical languages. Another is the view that learning proceeds most efficiently through overwhelming attention to logical thought, analysis, sequential reasoning and abstraction. Both notions place a premium upon the learning of a body of knowledge and related intellectual processes through *individual* activity and skills, and by implication diminish the importance of not only the social context in which learning and action take place, but also the development of the social skills necessary for the effective participation in society mentioned earlier.

There is good recent evidence[1] to support the view that there are important

[1]R. Ornstern, *The Psychology of Consciousness*. San Francisco: W. H. Freeman.

modes of response and learning other than the verbal, the numerical and the sequential, and that to ignore these other modes at best narrows children's understanding and at worst warps it or makes it impossible. In addition there is a pressing need to facilitate some form of *achievement* for those children who can achieve little in the conventional verbal/literacy/mathematical modes. Without some form of self-recognized and externally approved achievement, the downward spiral of deteriorating self-image and inability to cope with the conventional modes destroys the individual, alienates him from these conventional modes and makes almost any form of constructive learning or skill acquisition very difficult indeed. The most fundamental requirement of the learning environment is that it must establish firmly the worth of the individual, and this means recognition of the full range of abilities that pupils may possess.

Those who have worked constantly with young people over a long period know how important to them are the non-verbal modes of response, knowing and communication – particularly those of visual form, sound, gesture and movement. These are languages in constant and powerful use in the modern world yet their importance is still not generally acknowledged in education, because of the relative importance assigned to cognition and the narrow interpretation of this term. The broader view[2] implies that it is possible and important to know the world visually, auditorily and kinaesthetically. If so, then many youngsters who find it difficult to learn about the world by means of verbal and mathematical surrogates may find this much easier if they are given opportunities to explore the world visually, auditorily and kinaesthetically.

Although a lot of work has been done on harnessing technological developments to education in the shape of audio-visual aids, these aids have been mainly used as teaching supports, to transmit information for verbal and mathematical modes of learning, and not as media through the production of which children experience creative learning directly.

Because children vary so much and because subject-matter is so diverse, all teachers look for a variety of modes of learning. This book offers only one approach to learning – the opportunity to explore the world of learning through an unusually wide range of modes of understanding. It also allows pupils to extend their concrete experience of the world, to engage in group activities demanding collaboration and decision-making, and to use the products of educational technology actively and creatively as tools for exploring learning rather than as means of passive learning controlled by the teacher.

The work described suggests that the educational gains possible through intelligent use of this approach are diverse, but special attention is given throughout to gains in the development of communication and social skills, which, as suggested earlier, are crucial to satisfying and effective operation in the world.

Communication Skills

The term 'communication skills' is used advisedly, as 'language skills' carries for most people narrow connotations of verbally based skills. These are, of course, of major importance, and much of the evaluation of the Project has been in this area. Communication skills, however, cover skills relevant to all

[2]For further development see Elliot W. Eisner, *The Role of the Arts in the Invention of Man.*
Paper delivered to the 23rd World Congress of I.N.S.E.A., August 1978.

modes by which information, about facts, feelings, judgements, concepts or whatever, is passed from one person or group to others. It will naturally cover verbal language but it must also cover such powerful forms of communication as visual images and patterns of sound. Equally important, and central to the work described, are the significance and effects of using a number of these modes together. This aspect is explored throughout the book, but particularly in Chapter 12.

It would be inappropriate to attempt at this stage to write an exhaustive list of communication skills, particularly as those which are specially encouraged by the present methods are revealed in later chapters in the contexts in which they were observed, and in Appendix 1 (p. 188). However, it is suggested that the following might be important:

The ability to achieve precision in the communication of facts.

The ability to recognize and eliminate confusion and irrelevancy.

The ability to move from simple to more complex structures.

The ability, where appropriate, to express feeling sensitively.

The ability to seek out, consider and select evidence or material to support or amplify a statement.

The ability to relate the medium to the message, i.e. to match what has to be communicated to an image, sound or words according to which is most effective.

The ability to enrich communication by the use of intonation, emphasis, timing, volume, rhythm, lighting, focus, angle, composition, etc.

Social Skills

Social skills are taken to be all those skills which facilitate effective relationships within groups. They certainly involve the flexibility necessary to adapt to changes in role arising from changes in the composition and activities of groups. They also include the important ability to cope with the rejection of one's own ideas. A longer list of social skills is also to be found in Appendix 1 (p. 188).

The Project directors had for several years been exploring what happened, in terms of educational outcomes, when pupils learned through making television programmes, films and tape-slide sequences. The work was collaborative, active and creative. Although it might well have had a valuable spin-off in developing in the youngsters a more informed and critical attitude to the media, this was a side issue. It was *most important* that this work was *not* seen as 'media studies', nor was it a new 'subject', one to be added to an already full curriculum. Rather it was offered as an alternative, but very important, *method* of learning – to be applied to any part of the existing curriculum. What is more, it was assumed from the beginning that teachers using the method would be primarily interested in improvement in their pupils' learning of school subjects.

The Project directors had been excited to find that when young people were encouraged to learn by shaping and recording presentations in the medium of sound and vision (in history, biology or whatever), certain gains seemed to follow, and pupils often began to display talents and potential not previously revealed by more orthodox methods. In the first place, motivation to learn seemed to strengthen, and this seemed to outlive the early period when the novelty of the methods and equipment could have been thought to be strong contributory factors. Children's capacities to communicate orally became more sharply developed, and it was discovered that a number of children had talents in this mode which had hitherto been completely unsuspected. Both oral and written work seemed to benefit from the increased clarity of understanding and purpose required by the necessity to select images, speech and sounds appropriate to the ideas being illustrated, and by the necessity to communicate as clearly and convincingly as possible with others. Because of the nature of the audio-visual medium the finished product could be shown, with benefit, to a wide range of audiences. This had a marked effect on pride in workmanship, and on the pupils' tenacity of purpose.

The collaborative nature of making a programme in sound and vision in this way seemed in itself also to have decisive benefits of a social nature. Perhaps because everyone had a part to play and the end-product could be viewed critically by others, the principle of shared responsibility was accepted. Leaders emerged or were elected as the need arose, and these would vary with the task in hand. Pupils indeed began to learn to accept the rejection or modification of their own ideas without bitterness or undue dismay. Another important development was that teacher/pupil relationships became more collaborative, because they were based upon the need to pool special expertise rather than upon authority.

There was no attempt by the Project directors to impose any particular order of importance as far as the aims of the teacher were concerned and teachers agreed to engage in the work for a variety of reasons. In some cases recorded sound and vision were seen as means by which pupils could bypass their difficulties in writing. In others the hope was to motivate reluctant readers and writers. Certainly there was widespread interest in discovering what effect this change of approach would have upon subject learning, and most of the teachers valued the idea of their pupils working collaboratively and shaping their work through group discussion.

It is worth mentioning that, although the trials mainly covered the age range 11–16 years, the considerable interest shown in this work by teachers in further-education establishments has been reflected by the inclusion of Chapter 9, a case study of work with students aged 16–19 years in a college of further education.

Pupil groups organized, researched and recorded their work in each subject and the Project team, led by the authors, provided support in the shape of information and advice about class organization, media techniques and evaluation. It was inevitable that the activity and the collaborative aspects of the work would lead to practical problems: such things as class organization, monitoring the progress of an individual working within a group, and teachers adjusting to more advisory roles. The handling of the equipment also presented difficulties. Where these and other problems arose, the Project team provided support.

As teachers gained experience, they began to extend their original work to other parts of the curriculum, classes and ability levels and to meet new aims. Some built their work into examination syllabuses. Because new kinds of learning gains took place, teachers modified the work on the basis of these, so that the rationale underlying the work became both wider and more convincing.

As the work progressed, it was subjected to very close observation and monitoring in a variety of ways: through many hours of observation by the Project team and by independent observers on the basis of the categories outlined in Appendix 1, by the frequent and systematic interviewing of teachers and pupils and by the recording of pupil and teacher activity, which was then analysed by the methods described in Chapter 10.

It would be wrong to pre-empt the evaluation in this opening chapter. Suffice it to say that the hypotheses formed by the authors on the basis of their earlier work seem generally to be upheld. There was general agreement about increased pupil motivation. There seemed to be a significant increase in the pupils' constructive use of speech, and they often displayed unexpected skill in relating to each other in the complex group situations generated by the work. Some pupils obviously found it possible to organize and express thoughts about subjects in a way that they had failed to achieve through writing alone, and teachers were generally in no doubt as to the greater richness and completeness of the learning experiences made possible by these new methods. It is also important to note that the energy and interest of teachers and pupils seemed to be maintained over the whole period.

It was felt strongly by all concerned that large-scale, quantitative methods of evaluating the Project were impossible in view of the Project's scale, and inappropriate in view of the qualitative nature of the inquiry. This is not to say that ultimately this sort of work might not profitably be subjected to certain kinds of quantitative/qualitative analysis so as to offer insight not yielded by methods already used. One needs to know, for example, the differing probabilities of learning gains throughout the ability range for a specific technique, and how expensive in terms of time and equipment these gains are. But to be in any degree precise this would require far more time and resources than were available to the Project team. In spite of these limitations, we feel that Chapters 10–12 have considerable importance for educationalists of all kinds wherever children's enthusiasm and understanding are sought, rather than their resigned involvement, and wherever a rich, holistic learning is desired.

This book was written primarily for practising teachers as a guide to the method. Thus, in the interests of length, it does not include a review of the examination by the Project team of the literature in the field, nor a full evaluation of the theoretical implications of the work. It is hoped that interested teachers will find valuable information, guidance and encouragement in the following chapters.

SHARING

RESEARCHING

SCRIPTING

READING

SPEAKING

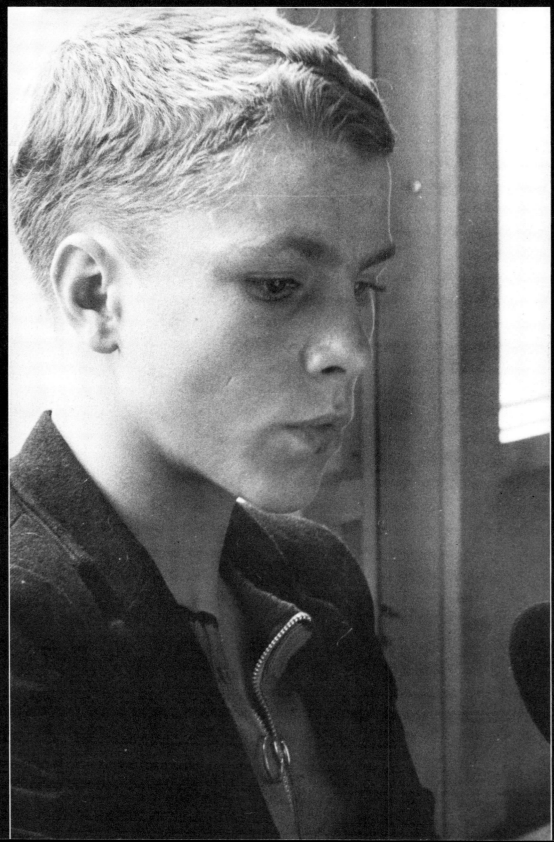

LISTENING

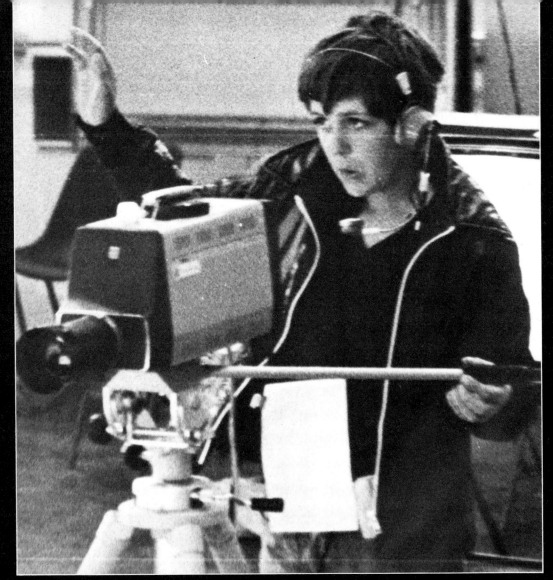

CONTROLLING

VIEWING

Case Studies

School

Form entry	7
Catchment area	Mainly council estate plus small area of private housing
Buildings	Early 1960s
Situation	Urban
Size of sixth form	80

Class

Number	History: 30
	Drama: 25
	Life studies: 26
Boys/Girls	Mixed in each case
Streaming	History: low band, mixed ability
	Drama: top band
	Life studies: low band, mixed ability
Age	History: 2nd year
	Drama: 5th year
	Life studies: 4th year
Time per week	History: 4 × 35 min plus 2 × 35 min citizenship
	Drama: afternoon
	Life studies: morning
Examinations	CSE

Teacher

Training	B.A., P.G.C.E.
Subjects taught	History, humanities
Years teaching	4
Special responsibility	Head of audio-visual resources
Sex	Male

CHAPTER 2

History : Television

History

This teacher taught history and humanities in a seven-form-entry comprehensive school. When introduced to the Communication and Social Skills Project he decided to work with a second-year mixed-ability group. He saw this class for both history and citizenship, six lessons in all per week.

After discussions with the Project team, the local adviser and his headteacher, he decided to teach the four history lessons in the normal way, but to adapt the two citizenship lessons for the methods outlined by the Project. The general aim of the citizenship course was to provide the pupils with the knowledge and skills required for participating in our democratic and civil processes. It seemed to him that the Project's audio-visual methods (which can so readily be based on groups negotiating democratically) were ideal for this purpose (especially as they could generate the need to seek out sources of relevant information from the environment). In addition the teacher welcomed the opportunity to offer the pupils greater responsibility for their own learning and felt that the group activity that could result would be useful in developing the pupils' language skills in a range of situations.

He felt that this activity could be achieved by dividing the class into small work groups, each producing an audio-visual statement on a carefully selected topic from the history lessons. Accordingly, he provided background reading and illustrative material for the selected topics, and rearranged the desks into working surfaces of four desks each.

In using the Project's audio-visual methods and requesting pupils to work towards an audio-visual statement, he had to sensitize the pupils to a number of general areas of learning and activity. Like all the teachers involved in the Project, he had to develop a way of teaching the pupils how to use recording equipment; he also had to guide them on ways of organizing and accomplishing the various tasks that the making of audio-visual statements would require; and finally he had to help them to visualize and to represent in sound ideas and information contained within the subject under study.

The recording medium for this particular school was video. The school possessed a video camera and videotape-recorder, and could borrow portable video equipment from a local college or a further small mobile studio (two video cameras and a mixing panel) from the local education authority.

To begin with this teacher used the school's television equipment, which consisted of one camera and one videotape-recorder but with no editing facility (to be found in 20% of English secondary schools according to a Central Office of Information survey in 1977). He wanted to start with audio-visual formats that the pupils could easily grasp and so decided to begin with sequences of still pictures and an occasional live presenter. The still pictures were drawn by the pupils or taken from books or magazines.

Because this school did not have an editing facility, and initially because the pupils were working with one camera, the simplest production technique which was suitable for these programmes and this equipment was to set up a series of scenes and then to shoot these one after another to produce a smooth final product. The scenes had to be linked in some way, and five simple techniques were offered to the pupils:[1]

1. Set out a series of pictures on a board, then simply record these in sequence, moving smoothly from each one to the next with the camera.
2. Make the screen blank by covering the lens (with, for example, a hand or piece of card) between each shot.
3. Create an interesting effect between pictures by covering the lens with something like a piece of net curtain.
4. After recording one picture, defocus the camera lens, move the camera to the next picture and refocus.
5. Add a presenter (speaking directly to the camera) who links the pictures with talk.

The pupils were asked to select pictures from books or work packs. They were also encouraged to draw pictures (they could have been shown how to take and use their own photographs as well). An interesting development was the making of a model of a Victorian house, whose interior they were able to show in a series of close-up shots (this simple technique can be used with all sorts of models).

They were now shown four types of sound component:

1. A voice speaking as an accompaniment to the still pictures or scenes.
2. Music.
3. Music and speech together.
4. A presenter giving 'live' information.

When they had developed sufficient understanding of what they were to do and how to do it, they were split into work groups of four to six each. These groups set to work on their chosen history topics: they discussed their

aims and devised work methods; they read and they selected pictures; they recorded their findings in the form of notes and sketches.

The next stage, where they adapted their ideas directly to the medium, was critical. They mounted their selected pictures in sequence on a board or arranged them in order of presentation. Then they devised a speech and/or music accompaniment – an intricate and fairly technical process. Contrary to his expectations, during this stage the teacher noted a high level of motivation, and the appearance of many interesting ideas. The pupils wrote their own scripts, and tested them by reading aloud. They often wrote and rewrote these scripts five or six times, with undiminished interest. This stage lasted several weeks, and it threw up serious problems of resource provision and class management the teacher had never encountered before.

Because the final programmes were to be presented to an audience, there was a need for great accuracy and detail in the historical content of the programmes, and also for good visual and sound material in the presentation. The groups soon found that their history textbooks were inadequate. To resolve this the teacher brought into the class-room a great deal of written and visual material from the school library and elsewhere, finding packs such as the Jackdaw wallets of particular value.

The organization and management of the class became increasingly difficult as each group sought the teacher's help. Progress would slow down as two or more groups simultaneously sought advice or found themselves simultaneously ready for recording. The teacher resolved these problems by breaking down both the traditional history and the audio-visual work into their elements:

1. Listening to the teacher giving information.
2. Making notes or writing essays on the basis of the teacher's information.
3. Writing answers to questions set by the teacher or by the history textbook.
4. Reading around the topic.
5. Seeking the teacher's advice.
6. Discussing and organizing the material which had been gathered.
7. Writing scripts.
8. Recording.

---

[1]To make the case studies easily accessible, wherever possible we have avoided the use of technical terms associated with audio-visual recording. Eventually teachers will wish to introduce these terms to pupils, and to aid this, reference has been made in the Bibliography to a series of books that will adequately cover the need. Useful organizations are also mentioned in Appendix 2.

Because there were six groups, the teacher devised a six-week plan. This plan was put up on a chart on the wall and each group (allocated a letter from A to F) was able to see exactly what its commitment was. The work plan consisted of five processes and was preceded by a review by the teacher of the period of history to be studied:

1. Write up notes from teacher's talk.
2. Make notes on appropriate sections of the textbook.
3. Answer questions set by the teacher and questions from certain pages of the textbook.
4. After discussion and research write the script and record the sound.
5. Video-record the programme.

Each group was free to organize itself within the broad outlines of the programme. Thus if, for example, they were held up because the teacher was working with another group, they could switch to some other part of the plan: this took the pressure off the teacher and the other resources, and the pupils enjoyed the exercise of planning and taking responsibility for their own work programmes. Within the plan, each group was allocated one week when it had first claim on the television equipment.

Apart from his support and advisory function, the teacher developed his own programme of activities throughout the six weeks. Early on, he realized the difficulty the pupils would have in translating their ideas into sound and vision, so he led a general discussion on television techniques, from which emerged the concept of a 'story-board' as a method of recording the developing programme. He found that a story-board helped the pupils to think clearly and logically about the sequence of their visual and sound ideas.

Next the teacher formally introduced the pupils to a method of writing a script, then finally he demonstrated how to use the television equipment. This demonstration went particularly well. The children were disciplined and constructive, and learned the techniques easily: they learned how to focus the camera, how to tilt and how to pan; they learned how different kinds of light affect the picture; and they learned to be careful with the equipment, especially the camera and the video-recorder.

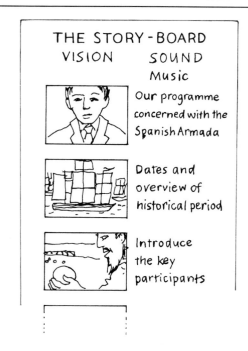

As the time for final recording of the programme drew near, they were helped to try out their scripts and to experiment with titles: at this stage they mostly opted to televise the titles as they were projected on to an overhead-projection screen. On the overhead projector, using a roll of transparent acetate, they were able to move the titles smoothly, which created a very professional effect on the videotape.

The climax of the six-week cycle of activity was when the whole class watched all the completed programmes. The ensuing discussions were full of intelligent and constructive criticism, including much self-criticism.

The Teacher's Viewpoint
The teacher felt that this kind of work combined well with academic work:

'If a child is really going to get anything out of history he has to develop a feeling for it. . . . This kind of activity will give him a much better feeling for the period than simply studying history in the normal way. . . . Also it fits in well with our Schools Council History Project. We introduce this to children to give them the idea that history is like detective work.

'We tend to give third forms a broad grounding in several different periods of history, in order to build a foundation for the more specialized work in the GCE and CSE syllabuses. This means that their feeling for any one period of history tends to lack depth. If we can link the broader-based studies with this kind of deeper work (as I have done here) then this will make a better preparation for the examination years.

'What is more, normally the children don't develop any overall sense of the period until they've finished a year's work. But if they set about this project and you make sure that the first few weeks of it are simply groundwork, give them all the possible sources and get them started with simple books, then you can go through the entire period rapidly. They don't lose interest because they need to have this broader view in order to make their very specific programmes.

'This class is a mixture of bright and not-so-bright pupils. What I particularly noticed was the way the television work enabled the lower-ability pupils to express themselves much better. For example, there was a group doing a programme on the Fire of London. In it there were two rather dull girls and one dull lad. They have extreme difficulty in academic subjects so they're not good at putting things down in words. However they got quite enthusiastic about this work. They got to the stage where they had sorted out the script (quite a lot of it in the form of words and ideas from Pepys' diary). When I asked them how they were going to put this over visually, they had wonderful ideas of the feeling of what it must have been like. They chose that lovely painting of the people running from St Paul's as it's burning. In all their ideas they were able to express their feelings about the events. They did a lot of their own drawings and had very good ideas for sound effects. In terms of the emotional approach to history it was very very good. Also, we've been able to get a meaningful bit of history out of them without their having to worry too much about hand-writing and spelling – they usually become disheartened by their lack of ability to write.

'We have one or two disruptive pupils in the class. When I gave them jobs to do, like work-ing the videotape-recorder or pulling captions, they got really involved. They were very enthusiastic about their own work and whenever they were not busy they helped other pupils.'

General Studies

During the early part of the same term the teacher, along with the school's drama specialist, was asked to teach a group of twenty fifth-form girls who remained in school whilst the rest of their year had games. He was to be with these girls for one afternoon each week. His intention was to use the same equipment as was used with the history group, exploring a range of subjects with them.

The two teachers devoted the first afternoon to showing the class how to put a television programme together. They demonstrated the movement of the camera and the controls of the videotape-recorder, showed the pupils a simple television script and demonstrated the camera techniques of panning across the pic-ture and using a hand to cover the camera lens between pictures. Then, in order to demon-strate all the techniques in operation, the teachers made a short programme.

They placed a number of printed pictures taken from a resource pack in an order pre-scribed in a prepared script. Whilst one teacher read a poem the other handled the camera and changed the pictures. After this they were able immediately to replay the piece thus recorded. The children saw the entire process from start to finish. According to the teacher:

'They were captivated. Despite running twenty minutes after the final bell, they were still willing to stay behind and discuss and criticize.'

During the year these children went on to make a number of programmes, developing techniques for expressing their reactions to various topics and themes presented to them. One of these was their interpretation of the witch scenes from *Macbeth*. After discussing the scenes, three of the girls made costumes and choreographed a series of movements whilst three others practised reading the lines. Their programme consisted of the words of the scenes being spoken to the visual accompani-ment of a combination of shots of hands, faces, costumes and movement. Added to this was a montage of suitably eerie background music and effects.

Commenting on this and the other projects the class had undertaken, both teachers noted a change in their own role in the class-room.

They reported that the pupils were very active; they themselves responded to pupils' requests rather than directing their activity:

'We were providing technical advice whether helping with the speeches, the shots or the costumes. The children were taking decisions and shaping their responses to the text and medium offered. We only outlined suggestions when approached.'

Life Skills

During the following academic year the history teacher teamed up with an environmental-studies specialist and began work with a fourth-year option group for one morning a week on part of a life-skills programme. This time, working with the whole class as one group, they made a programme detailing the development of their town from a coal-mining community to one dominated by light industry.

Their studies began with a traditional presentation of historical information about the locality, followed by an introduction to the proposed method of working. In this an analogy was drawn between documenting their work as a series of recorded sounds and pictures and documenting it in written form (supported with drawings and pictures). It was explained to the pupils that they could visit locations important to their studies, record interviews, and record people and places (the school had now borrowed a 'portapack' and a portable two-camera studio which the local authority loaned to schools on a half-termly basis). Also they could record pictures, music and the spoken word in their own class-room.

The teachers split the class into four groups, giving each responsibility for specific aspects of the work:

Group 1 was to be concerned with the part of the programme dealing with coal mining.
Group 2 was to be concerned with the part dealing with light industry.
Group 3 was to deal with technical matters and form the technical recording crew.
Group 4 was to be responsible for the collection and production of still pictures and graphics.

The plan of activities was as follows:

Week 1   Class discussion of ideas and development of an overall plan of action. Division of class into two groups: Group A, consisting of Group 1 and half of Groups 3 and 4; and Group B, consisting of Group 2 and the other halves of Groups 3 and 4. Discussion in groups of mining sequence (Group A) and local-industry sequence (Group B). Recording the developing plans in the form of a story-board.

Week 2   Groups 1 (mining) and 4 (graphics) visit local records office to research development of mining and to look for useful pictures and documents. Group 2 (light industry) visit factory in local industrial estate, talk with managers and plan sequence of shots inside the factory. Group 3 (technical) remain at school to gain practice with the recording equipment.

Week 3   Talk at school given by the education officer from the records office to the whole class covering: the construction of a talk on local history and the organization of material; the use and value of visual material; how to conduct a recorded interview (she played an example); the necessity for and role of humour; the development of an overall shape and structure. Application of these techniques by the pupils to their own script-writing.

Week 4   Group 1 (mining) visit local pit to arrange location shots. Group 2 (light industry) revisit factory to tighten up factory sequence. Half of Group 3 (technical) with Group 1 and half with Group 2. Group 4 (graphics) develop pictures and graphics at school.

Week 5   Group 1 (mining), with the portapack, do all the location shots at the local pit and interview the manager. Group 2 (light industry) work on television studio sequences. Half of Group 3 (technical) with Group 1 and half with Group 2. Group 4 (graphics) work with Group 2 on the two still-picture sequences.

Week 6   Group 1 (mining) review their portable location videotapes and finalize television studio sequences. Group 2 (light industry), with the portapack, do all location shots inside the factory and interview the personnel officer and an ex-pupil of the school who works at the factory. Half of Group 3 (technical) with Group 1 and half with Group 2. Group 4 (graphics) work with Group 1 on the television studio sequences.

Week 7   All groups review the separate parts and edit them together in sequence to produce their final programme.

The plan had just been formulated when the Project was approached by Yorkshire Television. The educational advisers of the company had expressed interest in the methods and inquired whether the Project could provide examples of its work with groups of pupils making a study of local industry for a series of programmes concerned with the 'Transition to Work'.[2] After a series of discussions between the television company, the Project team and the teachers it was decided to film the work of this class and also that of a class from another school who were using tape-slide production to study the milk industry.

A professional film crew was organized and filmed the process that the pupils went through. The pupils were filmed discussing their ideas, visiting the local records office and interviewing the local pit manager, a personnel manager and a worker at a local factory. The film crew followed them scripting and selecting appropriate music, and filmed them at work producing pictures and graphics to complement those that they had discovered at the records office. The pupils were shown how to use the television equipment and were filmed working as a team to produce the various sequences of their programme. Finally the class and teacher were filmed viewing and discussing their finished work.

The Yorkshire films succeeded in capturing both the process and at least part of the confidence newly displayed by the pupils. It is this development of confidence that is the subject of the following character study written by one of the Project directors after a visit by the Project team to watch the pupils in action.

A Portrait of the Pupil Director

A shy, gangling boy sat in the middle of one of the groups, watching what was happening. Different pupils were taking on the various roles required for recording their final programme in their class-room studio. The teacher and a couple of pupils who were going

to be acting out the dramatized sequence left the class-room to find a number of props.

'O.K., John, you direct for the moment.' John rose to his feet and moved into action. He quietly checked the various components, the still pictures, the music; he checked the various people playing the different roles. Everyone was ready for a run-through. 'Let's start,' he said, and a run-through began.

John stayed as the director and he became a leader and a tower of strength to the team. A caption-puller was flapping; he had mislaid a still picture. There was John immediately reassuring him and setting the wheels in motion to find it. An actor needed black make-up for a scene down a mine: John was rounding up the girl responsible and checking that it was done properly. John developed a certain standardized language and a ritual that all the crew could react to: 'Stand by, studio; roll VTR; cut camera one.' He cued the presenter to start speaking with a movement of his hand. Instructions to the boy on the record-player – 'bring it up now; more; hold it; take it down slowly, slowly' – were all communicated by decisive, calm hand signals. The boy on the record-player kept his eyes glued to John. John was in control and was co-ordinating all the various activities; John was trusted. John grew in confidence and stature. His voice was clear and decisive, and his handling of his crew sympathetic and quiet but disciplined. He developed such confidence that a marvellous moment occurred when the Yorkshire Television crew was televising them and moved one of their lights into a position for their own filming. John went up to the Yorkshire Television director and said, 'You can't put your lights there. They will alter the type of effect we are trying to create down the pit in this scene.' The director explained his action and John went thoughtfully back to his own crew to prepare them for the beginning of the filming. John has great difficulty in reading and writing, and although these basic skills are fundamental to his development, he had bypassed his two biggest weaknesses and difficulties. He had succeeded both in communicating with his fellow crew members and, by his key role in the making of the final product, in communicating with an audience outside the class-room in a form that was permanent and could be replayed and learned from.

[2]These programmes are available from the Project. See Appendix 2 for address.

THE PUPILS' PROGRAMME

Introductory music

Voice-over Presenter: In the nineteenth century there were many small mines in the area, and in the pit villages . . .

. . . coal affected all aspects of life, from housing, clothing, education, religion and politics, down to the daily routine of life.

There was no escaping the shadow of the mine. It was the only future open to lads. Coal always came first. What was life like for a miner?

He would often rise before dawn, according to his shift, . . .

. . . and prepare himself for a working day that would often last between twelve and fourteen hours.

His wife would rise before him and prepare his food, or 'bait' as it's known, usually only bread and dripping.

Wages were very poor. A man was paid according to how many tubs he filled with coal. But if there was any stone in the tub he received nothing.

He would sometimes work a full shift for only a few pence.

His house would be owned by the mine and part of his wages would be paid in tokens that could only be spent at the pit shop.

When he went down the mine he would frequently have to walk and crawl several miles to reach the coal face, where he would stay for the rest of the shift, even eating his bait crouching in the oppressive heat and flickering candlelight.

He would return home dirty and exhausted to a hot meal, a bath and a prospect of the next day's labour. Death and injury were frequent and a constant fear.

Music

Voice-over Presenter: In a pit village, the pit was your life from birth to death.

A lad would work down the pit from an early age.

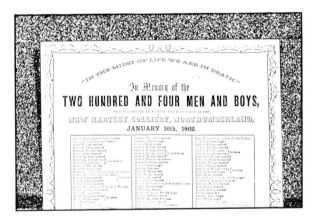

When we visited the Records Office, we discovered this list of pitmen who died in the Hartley Disaster.

Adam Macey, aged 22; John Macey, aged 55; Robert North, aged 25; George North, aged 10; John North, aged 14; Alexander North, aged 12.

Times have changed. The lads who go down the pit from this school will find very different conditions today.

Interviewer: Can you tell us how mining has changed over the last two hundred years?

Manager: Well, mining has changed quite considerably, Kim, in the past hundred years. All the coal is machine mined now and because of that, and because of the systems of support we use, we're much more efficient than we used to be and we're much safer.

Voice-over Presenter: Light industry is increasing in Blyth and we asked Linda Raffle what it was like working in one of the new factories.

Interviewer: What time do you start in the morning?

L: Quarter to eight.

I: What time do you finish at night?

L: Monday to Thursday five o'clock, and on Friday quarter to one.

I: What do you work as?

L: I work making gents' and ladies' raincoats on a Sobar system, which involves five people. It's getting the work from the cutting room, booking it on to the production floor, fusing it, which is to strengthen the parts of the coats, putting it on to the fusing press, which is to shrink parts of the coats, then giving it a Sobar, which is just giving it a number so it doesn't get lost on the floor, and then the job I actually do is parting it off with the tickets so it doesn't get mixed up and lost on the floor.

Voice-over Presenter: Next year we'll be leaving school. Some of the lads will go down the mine. Most of the girls will go to a factory. But unemployment is high in Blyth. We wonder what the future holds for us.

School	(I)	(II)
Form entry	6	7
Catchment area	Cross-section	90% council estate
Buildings	1972	1950s
Situation	Urban	Backs on to rural area; fronts on to housing estate
Size of sixth form	200 (trad.)	None (11–16 yr)

Class	(I)	(II)
Number	32	18
Boys/Girls	Girls	Mixed
Streaming	Mixed ability	Low ability
Age	3rd year	5th year
Time per week	1 h	4 × 35 min
Subject	Art	Health and leisure
Examinations	GCE/CSE	Non-exam

Teacher	(I)	(II)
Training	N.D.D., A.T.D.	Teacher's certificate (mature entrant)
Subjects taught	Art	English, careers
Years teaching	17	3 (20 yr in industry)
Special responsibility	Head of creative arts	None
Sex	Female	Male

CHAPTER 3

Art / Science : Animated Film

Cine-animation is the creation of the illusion of movement from normally inert objects or pictures and relies on the use of a single-frame device. In normal filming the film passes through the gate of the camera at a rate of 18 or 24 frames per second; in animation the film is exposed one frame at a time, each frame recording the object or drawing in a slightly different position, so that on projection objects or lines appear to have a life of their own.[1]

In object animation the camera is fixed firmly on a tripod and a model car, for example, is placed on a well-lit table approximately 14 in. from the camera lens. Two frames of film are exposed using the single-frame release then the car is moved forward $1/4$ in. and two more frames exposed. This procedure is repeated until eighteen frames have been exposed. On projection the car will appear to have moved forward approximately 2 in. under its own steam.

Object animation is only one of the methods possible. Paper cut-outs, drawn animation and speeded-up live action are a few of the other methods in common use, and they all give teachers and pupils considerable scope to explore their chosen subject in a new and creative way.

We have found the following equipment useful in the production and showing of animated films (obviously these items can be varied to suit individual needs):

1. A Super 8 camera with a close-up lens and single-frame device.
2. A Super 8 sound-projector.
3. If the faster Ektachrome 160 Super 8 Cassette film is used then the only lighting needed is an ordinary 150 W bulb with reflector.
4. A tripod.
5. A simple home-made animation rostrum with hinged glass and peg bars.
6. If cell animation is considered then a simple light-box can be made.
7. 'Stripe' sound-track can be either striped on to a film by a laboratory or produced by pupils in school on a home-made striper.

All other materials will be readily available in any art room, apart from cells (acetate sheets used in drawn animation). These can be cut from a roll of overhead-projector material or, more cheaply, purchased.

Here the teacher was an art teacher whose experience with animation was extensive. She had already worked very successfully for several years with various groups of pupils in an after-school animation club. Because of this success she was eager to discover what could be done with animated film in the normal curriculum, where the groups would be large, the atmosphere more formal and where all the children would be involved, not just enthusiasts.

As an art specialist, her main concern in

---

[1]In the Bibliography we have suggested several books that might be useful to anyone wishing to embark on cine-animation.

animation work was to extend the visual awareness of her pupils, but she realized that there were exciting learning possibilities if this could be linked to the conceptual learning required in other subjects. Consequently, with the agreement of the headteacher, she decided to work with a second-year mixed-ability class during their art lessons on topics taken from biology – one of the school's biology teachers had expressed interest, and the time-table had been rearranged for him to teach this class. By chance, he was free during the art period and was available then for consultation. A music teacher also expressed interest and volunteered to help with the creation of soundtracks to accompany the films.

Before the team-teaching with the biology specialist could take place, it was necessary to train the pupils in animation techniques. Lessons were devoted to animation for two weeks at the end of the summer term to allow the films to be processed in the vacation so that the class could start the new school year by seeing examples of their own work.

In these first lessons, the class divided itself into groups, each group appointing a leader, who was required to co-ordinate the work of the group. Sometimes this worked very well, but it depended on the calibre of the leader. The techniques of animation were discussed and illustrated with the help of films made in the after-school club. Each pupil was then allowed twenty-four frames of film for an animation whose subject was the human body. Each individual planned a 2 second film, and the class watched, fascinated, as the films were made. In the next exercise each group planned and filmed a 10 second programme.

At the beginning of the new school year the processed films were viewed by everybody, and this was sufficient to make them enthusiastic to press on to the next stage. Each group was now set the task of making a film to introduce themselves by name. They were free to choose their own methods for doing this, and were provided with materials such as plasticine, plastic letters, paint and paper. As the group discussed their work, they recorded their plans in story-board form.

Contrary to the teacher's expectations, when offered a change of activity to painting or pottery the pupils insisted on sticking to the animations. She was worried because the work felt less organized than her usual art work. She was accustomed to setting exercises which each child tackled in his own way, and which enabled her to see every individual's progress at each stage. She was used to a quiet atmosphere, with occasional chatter and not much movement. Now she found herself forced into a change of teaching style. In this work each small group was tackling a different set of problems and each individual was making a unique contribution. The atmosphere could no longer be quiet: indeed, general chatter indicated intense commitment.

This initial insecurity (she could no longer control and monitor each small stage in a child's development) gradually gave way to confidence in her new teaching style – moving from group to group, offering guidance and monitoring progress in a different manner. By the time the pupils had completed the animation of group names she had mastered the new style. There was also pressure within the groups for re-forming, and this she encouraged. The result was that groups now had a membership varying from two to six, while one pupil worked alone on a specialized animation technique. Despite not being able to see any results of the current term's filming until the very end of the term (processing takes some time) they were eager to work on the next stage. In fact this enthusiasm grew throughout the term. The final project of the term was 'Animate the life of . . . .'. The teacher gave the example of a ruler that was born an inch and grew to be a foot.

The teacher made a number of observations at the end of this term:

1. Motivation had been very high, considering there had been no feedback in the shape of processed film until the end of term.
2. The achievements of the less able had been comparable with those of the more able, whereas in painting there had always been a considerable difference.
3. The more able were distinguished by setting themselves challenges that enabled them to stretch themselves.
4. The pupils showed some sophistication and sensitivity in group discussions, and used technical concepts easily.
5. The pupils generally showed far more responsibility and social skills than normal.

6. They were 'more themselves', and she felt she had got to know them as well by that point as she would normally expect to after four years.

7. They were using a considerable amount of artistic planning in relation to colour, shape and composition, comparable with what she would normally expect from fourth- or fifth-year pupils.

8. The cost of the materials was considerably less than it would have been for painting and pottery: they used so little and used it so carefully.

Learning Biology through Animation

With a term's experience behind them the pupils began their attempts at animating topics taken from their biology course. The following extract is from a report written by a member of the Project team after visiting the class when it was well into this process.

The art room in which the work takes place is spacious, light, and opens into the pottery room. The individual tables have been moved together and groups of varying sizes sit around them. There was a sense of industry in the air as each group discussed and evaluated what was being done. Next to the door I entered by a group of three was working on the movement of an earthworm. In the far corner of the room a group was working on pollination in plants. I asked them to explain what they were doing.

'We've got to the bit where we've labelled all the parts of the flower, so that when the first years do this sort of thing Mr A (the biology master) will be able to show them the film. So they will find it easier, so that they will not have the trouble like we had last year. We made all the flowers and everything and we put roots on them and we showed at the start of the film a tiny little seed growing up into a great big plant. [Turning to another member of the group.] Where's the bee? [The second pupil pointed to a small painted cut-out.] Yes, over there. The bee comes along and it disappears into the centre of the flower. Then we zoomed right in and we went into the centre of the flower and we showed all the parts of it, and the fertilization, and the bee coming down. He rubs against the anther when he comes for the nectar down the flower and he carries all the pollen off. So when he went to another flower he would rub against the anther again and the pollen would go off him on to the female part of the flower. Then all the pollen would go on the pistils and it would fertilize all the seeds and then all the seeds would burst out of the ovary, and the bee would fly off to find another plant.'

The group told me that the first time they tackled this film they felt quite confident as they had already covered the topic in their biology lesson. They took out their biology notes and studied the carefully drawn diagrams. At this point they believed that they had a firm grasp of the subject. However it soon became apparent to them that they did not. The teacher explained their difficulty:

'On pollination. We were trying to do self-pollination. I looked at the book and couldn't work out the process. They were trying to animate it: "The pollen goes here", "This happens here". The nice thing about animation is that if you don't understand the process in detail you can't animate it.' She told me that at this point they called on the biology teacher for advice. He welcomed the opportunity to help them. He also welcomed the fact that this was a further method of monitoring their understanding of concepts and processes.

The pupils were patient throughout the teacher's intervention but clearly wanted to continue their description of their work. They told me about the problem they had with their cut-out bee:

'We got to this bit with all the pollen and everything. We didn't know how to get it [the bee] out, so he flew out upside down – he went in the right way up and said "buzz" and he came out upside down and went "zzub".'

'You see,' they explained, 'the first years will remember. You see, that's the whole point of it. That's why we tried to get a bit of humour into it as well, so they will remember.

'We did the whole thing in cut-outs. I think they are much better, much easier, and you get some kind of excitement when you are making them. You are thinking of how you can do it. You break it down into steps. Like, start with the easiest and work your way to the hardest. So once you understand one [cut-out] you can work out the next one, and so on. Come and see the bits of it we've got back from the processing firm. We haven't edited it together in order yet.'

We moved from the art room to the pottery room. In one corner there was an 8 mm projector and screen. We waited while another group finished viewing its work and discussed the next part of its schedule. The pollination group then showed the pieces of the film that had been completed.

They talked about the film as it played: '. . . there you've got the different parts of the female and the top, see that, that's the stigma. And that's the style, and then the bottom, see, where the yellow eggs are, that's the ovary, and the ovary's opened and the two peas at the top, that's the pollen, they're going to go down there, see.'

I asked them how they had achieved the effects that we had viewed:

'Oh well, we are just doing double frames [I looked questioningly]. We use two frames of film on one scene, then we move the scene a bit and take two more frames. Eighteen frames make one second. Everything then looks as if it's moving. Had a bit of a job getting the lamp set up [this was used to illuminate the object being filmed] because Jill had it with a sort of light on the top and it was dark at the bottom. We had to keep pushing it around. You remember those eggs growing. Well, we got some yellow paper like this [pointing to a piece] and we cut out the eggs. Then we cut them out a bit bigger and then [even] bigger. Then we took two pictures of the smaller ones, removed them and put the bigger ones in their place and then you get them growing on the film.'

I felt that at this point I should move on to another group and accordingly I thanked the pollinators and left them discussing the editing of their film sequences.

Across the room I could see five girls grouped around a full-size human skeleton. I learned from a girl nearby that they were attempting to make a film on bone movement. I joined the group, introduced myself, and proceeded to ask a number of questions:

Question: Does it always work, your first idea?
Answer: No.
Q: What do you do when it doesn't work?
A: Start thinking again.
Q: What's been the most difficult part?
A1: Getting everything ready.
A2: Making the story-board.

Q: Did one person do the story-board or did you work as a group?
A1: We worked together.
A2: Yeah, we shared the work completely.
A3: Then we split it up into different bits, like the title.
Q: What are you trying to show?
A1: How it moves.
A2: How the joints work.
A3: We're not sure how to do it.
A1: Yeah – could be right and it could be wrong.
A2: You, you move yourself and the others could watch – yes, that sounds like a good idea – and see if it was right.

I left the group to explore this latest idea. As I moved away I took a final glance at their progress. One girl was holding the skeleton's arm in a flexed position imitating another girl who had her arm in a similar position. The rest of the group were offering advice and busily evaluating the whole procedure.

Moving back into the art room, I came across a girl working on her own. She was engrossed in painting cells (cellophane sheets) with a biology textbook open before her. She was working on a film to demonstrate the circulation of blood in the pumping heart.

The teacher told me that this project had met with great difficulty through no fault of the pupil. The girl had worked very hard studying the text and diagrams on the movement of blood through the heart, but she had finally called on the teacher for help as she could not visualize the blood movement. The

teacher studied the diagram, then the text, then the diagram again, but could not see how blood could flow in the way described. Next the biology teacher was consulted. After studying the book for a few minutes, he announced that there was a valve missing in the textbook diagram. I wondered how many pupils across the country use this book, copy the diagram and learn it without ever really understanding it. Indeed I was forming the impression, not just from animation but from all audio-visual work, that translating oral or written information into visual images forces pupils to think very carefully about the subject under study. As when translating from one language to another, they are forced, in order to produce adequate results, to achieve a deeper and more precise understanding. I began to wonder of my own teaching how much of what I marked correct indicated understanding and how much merely memory. Indeed I must admit my guilt on occasions when I have deliberately encouraged the latter in order to help a pupil pass an examination in a subject he did not fully understand.

On completion of the first set of biology animations many of the pupils asked whether they could make animated films about other school subjects. Accepting this request, the teacher found herself advising groups working on domestic science, physical education and mathematics. Others wanted to remake earlier films, eliminating technical errors in focusing, lighting, drawing and movement.

For each new subject, a subject specialist was approached and in all cases enthusiastically agreed to advise. One such project was by a group of four girls whose intention was to make an instructional animation on the preparation of an apple pie. The film that they planned and made took the viewer from measuring ingredients, through cooking to the final pie.

The Teacher's Viewpoint

'I'd like to think that in art classes pupils get the chance to do things the way they want to, but the very fact of thirty children sitting at thirty desks and concentrating on one concept such as composition means that this is not often the case. In the animation classes, however, the pupils can draw on a much wider

variety of material, and because something like composition is far more open to variation, they do have a wide choice. As a result they have all produced things which are much more personal.

'I took them in the first year for conventional art lessons and I thought they were getting on pretty well; I thought I knew them pretty well. But this year they have developed in completely different directions from those I had thought them capable of, and have shown in many cases that they can do much more than I had thought. Clearly animation offers them a much greater opportunity to express themselves. With normal art work it's probably the fifth year before pupils have really mastered the materials and can get over what they want to say. With a piece of animation they can grasp the basic skills in half an hour. Also, there is no obviously accepted tradition that they have to live up to; they don't have to feel they're competing with skilful artists.

'In animation the pupils focus on what they are trying to make the pictures *do* and *say*. Strangely enough this makes their drawing and painting of figures and animals much better; their drawing is not as inhibited, because it is not an end in itself. If they have a genuine problem with co-ordination or the ability to handle a pencil, for example, they are held back in art whereas in animation they are free to try something else, such as plasticine, figures or objects cut out of magazines. There are several ways of putting the idea across, and this develops their confidence and artistic sense. They can then combine animation with painting to the benefit of each.

'Also, because you know the children better you're much more likely to make the right assessment and give the right help. You see, they talk more about their work, much more about their painting. They normally have a lot of problems in talking about composition, colour schemes or tone. It takes a long time to learn to use this language, but it's a language they have got to learn, to be confident with. Whereas they don't usually master it until the third or fourth year, with animation they do so immediately. They might not know the technical word at first, such as composition, but you hear them saying "Shall we have it here? No, we'll have it there. It feels better when we have it nearer the centre", and so on. They very quickly learn aesthetic appreciation, and the technical language is then much easier for them to acquire.

'I don't mind spending art time on animations based on other subjects such as biology. For my purpose the subject-matter is immaterial; it's what you do with it in art terms, the artistic expression and skill, that counts.

'If we extend this work there will be a time-tabling problem. At the moment, by chance, the home-economics area is next door and the teacher has been prepared to advise pupils making animated films on aspects of home economics, and to have a small group of these children filming in part of her home-economics area when required. Teachers of other subjects come along at four o'clock and offer help and advice. The pupils stay behind to ask questions and get feedback on how well they are expressing the subject. I hope that time could be set apart when this could be done. It certainly works because we have seen it working, but the administration is complicated.

'For some reason the material the pupils use matters more to them when making a film. In the second year, the choice of material for a subject tends to be a bit arbitrary, but with animation the pupils think what will work best in a particular situation – you can hear the comments and discussion as they work out solutions. They may try out something on paper and see that it doesn't work, then try it out in plasticine and perhaps discover they can get their ideas over more clearly. They find it easy to discriminate like this because they are clear about what they want to say. It is usually very difficult to get an idea across in one picture but it is simpler in a film because it can be gradually built up through a sequence of pictures. What is more, the children are aware of their audience for a film, rarely so for a painting. They ask, "How will they take that part in?", and so on. A really good painting requires a great deal of planning and forethought. These children find that hard to do as individuals, but here a great deal of planning goes on within the group; they refine their thinking during the creative process because each new 'scene' is a logical development from the last.

'When I had become more confident in this new style of teaching, I found I could get my teaching points across as they arose *in situ*. I could also see pupils attacking art problems I would have thought beyond them. This insight allowed me to build up far higher expectations of what sorts of art they could produce. Because they had more control over what they were doing they developed responsibility for their own work. They were highly disciplined in the way they organized themselves, handled each other, took decisions and solved problems. Undoubtedly the discipline comes from the requirements of the medium. There were heated discussions but they realized that differences had to be resolved if the film was to be made: the commitment to what they were trying to say in the film generated the need to resolve discussions quickly. They did not expect the teacher to take the decisions. They often sought my opinion, but this was treated within the group as a contribution equal to anybody else's.

'I thought that this keenness might wear off, that the cameras were a novelty whose interest would pass. But the attraction seems to be being able to make inanimate objects move about and do anything you want them to do. Otherwise I think they would have got sick of using the equipment by now, because such a lot of time has been spent in preparation rather than using it. I offered them a change of activity but they would have none of it. Certainly the power of this type of communication held them.

'Looking at the specifically artistic concerns, I found a real difference in the visual thinking of the pupils, especially in the areas of time and movement. At first they were totally engrossed in making a shape and were not thinking how it would move, because they were not sure about this anyway. If I asked what it was going to do they would tell me. But if I then asked how it was going to do this, I found that they hadn't thought that out. So the difference between this and a picture was that they were going to make it move, which opened up a whole new dimension. They started to ask questions: "How am I going to move this from A to B?", "Should I use a bit of string?", "Should I use this and try it out?" They were thinking for themselves. Time was another factor – they could move forwards and backwards and all continuous activities had to show some sort of passage of time.

'Visual problem-solving and spatial-reasoning came to the fore and resulted in an exceedingly rich activity. It was interesting to see in the mixed-ability group a couple of little girls from the remedial section working as members of a team with some of the brightest pupils. They had never worked as part of a team before and had had little real contact with the brighter pupils. But you knew they were part of the team and working together and I think this thrilled them to bits. They had their jobs and their roles and they were exceedingly proud of their parts. The brighter ones could rush ahead with ideas because it is such a versatile medium, but in the end the whole group was involved and each member played her part. With this form of sharing they could all achieve something.'

A Second Case Study of the Use of Animated Film

The local authority in which the previous teacher worked encouraged the development of audio-visual work with pupils. It lent a range of equipment to schools and organized a number of courses for interested teachers. One such course was led by the previous teacher and the present case study describes the work of a teacher who attended that course and went on to develop animation work in his own school.

The second teacher worked with a group of fifth-year leavers for one afternoon each week devoted to options. The pupils were required to select one option from a range which included shooting, riding, football and this particular option, health and leisure, which used film-making techniques. The pupils were offered a wide range of topics within this subject and explored their chosen topics by making animated films.

The teacher worked in his normal classroom and moved the desks from their rows into groups of four and six in order to provide larger work surfaces and to facilitate communication within the groups of pupils. The animation equipment consisted of an 8 mm camera, a home-made animation stand, a board with an editing-viewer attached and a projector. In addition, the teacher provided an assortment of basic art materials – plain paper, pencils, crayons, scissors, etc. – and an extensive collection of magazines, colour supplements and *Reader's Digests*, which he particularly recommended.

The basic technique consisted of the animation of cut-out pictures, most of which were culled from the magazines made available by the teacher. Each group of pupils discussed its chosen theme and recorded its findings on a story-board. When the story-board was complete they began to search for appropriate pictures. Often new ideas were suggested by the search itself and agreed ideas abandoned if the search revealed that no appropriate pictures

1. *Finalizing next cut-out*
2. *Positioning previous cut-out*
3. *Exposing film*

were available. Some groups started with only a general idea of what the final visual statement would look like, and developed and refined it during the search itself. Some groups drew and coloured their own visuals and then cut them out.

As each group completed the preparation of a sequence it would move to the animation stand and film. Occasionally, several groups were ready to film at the same time. Then one would be selected to film while the others went on with preparing their next sequence until it was their turn.

The animation stand was simply a retort stand to hold the film camera, a board on which the visual work could be placed and a table lamp positioned to illuminate the board. The camera had a cable release for exposing each frame of film.

The children became skilled at envisaging the final visual effect of the movements they created by filming their cut-outs. Placing their cut-outs on the board, they arranged them for the first shot and then, using the cable release to prevent the camera from jogging, exposed two frames of film (having already checked the focus and exposure details). They then moved their cut-outs to the next position and again exposed the film twice. This was continued until the whole of the sequence had been filmed.

The return of processed film was always eagerly awaited. When it came, the first priority was to project everything for everybody to see. Then work on editing the film began. First the film was cut and each group's pieces were reassembled into their finished sequence. Only one pupil could work on the editing-viewer at a time, so everybody else went on to plan or research further work.

Group 1 worked on an animated film on dental care. They started by making two lists, one of bad things to eat, the other of good. They were offered a range of visual resources by the teacher and selected a poster about tooth decay which contained a large colourful picture of a witch. Two girls made a traced cut-out of the witch and cast her as their central character. Then, using cut-outs of sweets, they animated the witch to eat gradually a plateful of sweets, with the result that she suffered from terrible tooth decay. This was followed by cut-outs of lips closed, partially open and fully open and cut-outs of whole carrots and partially eaten carrots disappearing into the moving mouth, likewise apples and other good foods. The pupils then decided to animate the drinking of a bottle of milk. This presented a technical and conceptual problem. The shape of the milk bottle was cut out of a large piece of yellow paper. A piece of white paper was placed behind the bottle-shaped hole and there was a full bottle of milk. By gradually pulling down the sheet of white paper from behind the cut-out bottle, the milk was slowly made to disappear to reveal, unfortunately, the desk! After quite a heated discussion the group saw that, because they had cut the milk-bottle shape out of a piece of yellow paper, they needed a yellow background so that when the milk disappeared the bottle would become transparent and yellow would show behind it. So a large piece of yellow paper was put behind the white paper. The teacher commented that the problem-solving and decision-taking required to tackle animated-film work is one of its most important educational aspects.

Group 2 produced a film about wild-life parks which encouraged families to take their children, explained that walking in the fresh air is important to good health and suggested that the attraction of the wild life would encourage this physical exercise. Their persuasive message was conveyed by a number of slogans: for example, 'Instead of "lion" around, come to Lampton Lion Park and see a real lion'. Also, guidance was given about behaviour and safety. The filming again presented a number of conceptual problems and the pupils employed a wide range of ideas in their solution. The group showed a good deal of ingenuity in tackling these problems, each individual taking great pains to explain his idea to the group.

Group 3 made a film about the hazards of alcohol. They were surrounded by cut-outs of bottles, glasses and someone drinking from a glass. They prepared their own drawings of his brain and nervous system and hoped to animate them so as to show that alcohol could gradually take over these control centres. They also made their own posters showing the dangers of alcohol, which they were going to film and then animate.

Group 4 made a film on road safety. They

planned to use small models of cars as well as a painted background and cut-out figures. One sequence filmed was a painted background showing a street, with houses and shops. A cut-out pedestrian was gradually moved across the road, each movement being given two frames of film. A model car moved along the road and knocked down this pedestrian. The pupils went on to develop and film a series of such sequences illustrating careful and careless behaviour, each with an appropriate result.

The Teacher's Viewpoint

'At the beginning none of these children had ever used even a normal camera, so I had to explain what the cine-camera could do, and how to perform techniques they had seen in films, such as fading in and out and animating. I also had to explain the need for thorough planning and organization.

'The work has created enthusiasm. The children enjoy working in groups, which I think is important because most of them will be working in big factories and they need to learn to work together, to discuss as groups and to reach decisions democratically. They are low-ability children and usually gossip in class, but here their talk was always concentrated on the task, so they inevitably developed skill in using sophisticated technical language. One boy had to explain to a lad who joined the group late how to edit film. This developed his own linguistic skill and his confidence. His feedback was to watch the new lad editing while he instructed.

'I persuaded one girl who was good at filming to stay on and take CSE English. I take her for English and noticed an improvement in her essay-writing. In film-making, the children have to think out the whole story in a logical sequence. They see the need to plan because they have to decide what materials to get and what actions to take, in what order. Whereas this girl used to 'plunge in' when writing an essay, she has now started to plan her essays as she would a film.

'All the children are learning to express ideas although most of them normally find great difficulty in written expression, the traditional mode. Of course there have always been discussions, but these often inhibit certain kinds of children. I have found in this work that even the very shy children contribute a great deal to discussion and writing, simply because of the necessity to do a good job.

'The children work actively as a group as if I wasn't there. When I have had to leave the room for a few minutes, I have returned to find them working uninterruptedly (probably not even having noticed that I had left the room). I feel that I got to know them as people much better than I do examination classes. I would like to take my exam classes for one extra lesson a week on film animation. It would help me to get to know them and resolve their academic difficulties. I believe this work would help their vocabulary and competence in oral language. In fact the Head of English thinks that we might incorporate this work into the English curriculum as part of a Mode 3 CSE.'

School

Form entry	8
Catchment area	Very large cross-section
Buildings	Part 1800s, part 1966, part 1971
Situation	City outskirts/centre of established private housing estate
Size of sixth form	120 (some new sixth)

Class

Number	32
Boys/Girls	Mixed
Streaming	Lowest ability
Age	5th year
Time per week	5 h
Subject	Rural studies
Examinations	CSE Mode 3

Teacher

Training	Cert.Ed., Dip.Ed.
Subjects taught	Woodwork, technical studies, English, local studies, rural studies
Years teaching	21
Special responsibility	Senior Teacher, also Head of Technical Studies with responsibility for curriculum development for slow learners
Sex	Male

CHAPTER 4

Rural Studies :
Television / Tape-slide

The teachers, a slightly larger than average class-room and an aging school bus formed the major resources for teaching rural studies to the fifth year. The course itself had developed out of the particular interest in agriculture of the school's Head of Technical Studies and was based on an educational philosophy that placed a high value on direct experience. Pupils were regularly taken into the surrounding country to study aspects of geography at first hand. These visits were recorded by the pupils in writing with drawings and entered into a loose-leaf file. The idea of recording the studies with television cameras on videotape was new to teachers and pupils alike.

The first introduction to the television recording machinery was a visit to a television studio at a nearby college. The studio was used by a number of Project schools as well as by lecturers at the college itself. It consisted of three television cameras on movable tripods, a videotape-recorder, a vision-mixer (a device for switching or fading from camera to camera), a sound-mixer and microphones. Each camera had connected to it a set of headphones with a microphone attached which allowed communication between the cameramen and the director. The pupils' first visit was for a 2 h session.

On arrival they were given a short introductory talk. This talk described the stages they would need to go through in order to prepare for a television recording:

Discussion of the topic
Research to find related material
Planning the programme (script-writing)
Making any pictures planned in the script
Rehearsing any drama or spoken lines planned in the script
Recording

The talk also included a simple classification of aspects of sound and vision that might help them to translate their chosen topics into television programmes:

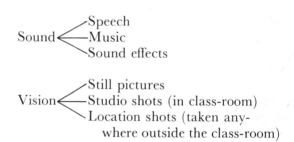

Next the children found out how each piece of equipment was controlled. Whilst half of the group was helped to work on the control panel, the other half worked the cameras or improvised in front of the cameras.

At the control console they were introduced to the idea of changing the picture from one camera to another. They were offered two ways of doing this: either as a cut (sharp change) or a mix (slow change). The two alternatives were demonstrated and they were shown which controls to use.

One pupil (acting as director) instructed another pupil (acting as vision-mixer) using the control box, while the rest watched. He checked visually that the vision-mixer produced the effect called for. Each pupil was

encouraged to take a turn at both the director's role and the vision-mixer's role. In addition, all pupils were encouraged to use a microphone and earphones to communicate with the cameramen, requesting camera movements and checking the response on the appropriate television screen (monitor).

Meanwhile, in the main body of the studio the other half of the group was familiarizing itself with the camera movements and controls and responding to instructions received through the headphones that they wore. The teacher made sure that each pupil had some experience of camera work before the two halves of the class changed places.

After about half an hour, the pupils had been introduced to the concept of recording their ideas on television, shown the television machinery and given a chance to explore its use. At this point they were drawn together again and introduced to the prepared script that they were to televise.

The class teachers had previously allocated the various practical roles necessary for televising the script. These roles were explained and the pupils decided which of the three cameras should film each item on the script. The youngsters then went to their various positions and rehearsed and recorded the scripted programme.

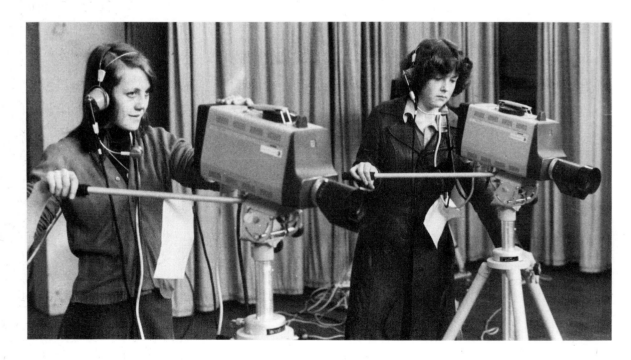

Shot	Camera	Vision	Sound	Monitor
1	F.U. 1	Capt. TV	F.U. music	
2	Mix 2	Capt. Old people		
3	Super 1	Capt. Title	Fade music	
4	Mix 3	M.S. Presenter	Good evening. Tonight we are looking at the situation confronting human beings as they face old age.	
5	Mix 2	Capt. Old face	V.O. If a man does not keep pace with his companions perhaps it is because he hears a different drummer. Let him step to the music he hears, however measured or far away.	
6	Mix 1	Capt. Old face	V.O. Man dwells apart, though not alone; he walks among his peers unread; the best of thoughts which he hath known, for lack of listeners are not said.	

7	Mix 2	Capt. Old face	V.O. Happy the man, and happy he alone. He who can call today his own. He who, secure within, can say, 'Tomorrow do thy worst for I have lived today.'
8	Cut 3	M.S. Presenter	I have two senior citizens with me in the studio. Let's see what old age means to them.
9	Cut 1	3s Presenter and two interviewees	*Presenter:* Good evening, can I begin with Mrs Daniels on my right? Can you tell me what old age means to you?
10	Cut 2	First interviewee	For me it means not being able to get about as much. I also have a problem with food: I don't feel like cooking for just myself, yet I've got to eat and I can't afford some foods that I really like.
11	Cut 1	Second interviewee	The bits o' bairns skit yer. [The children make fun of you.]
12	Cut 3	M.S. Presenter	Perhaps old age is really just a social condition inflicted on a section of the society by the environment in which they live – or is it?
13	Cut 2	Dramatic sequence	

GLOSSARY

F.U. — Fade up picture or sound

Mix — Fade from one picture to the next

Super — Superimpose one picture over a
second

Capt. — Caption, usually followed by
identification

M.S. — Mid-shot

V.O. — Voice-over – speech heard without the
speaker being visible

3s — Three shot – shot of three people

Programme Making

After this valuable and skilled introduction to the methods of making television programmes, the teachers decided to divide the class into four teams, each of which would work on its chosen topic in rural studies. Each team set to work to produce a script ready for recording on the afternoon when the college equipment would be available.

Team 1: 'Bacon and Eggs – the Great British Breakfast'

When the portable equipment arrived from the college, the team was ready. They had prepared a script in which all the words to be spoken had been worked out precisely, they had decided on the location for each sequence, they had selected each member's role, and they had planned the afternoon's recording down to the last detail.

First they were to film at a local farm, describing how pigs are bred for slaughter, then they would return to the school hen-house to film the way chickens are cared for. They would then collect and pack some of the eggs, and finally record a typical English breakfast scene 'on location' in the domestic-science room. In the following weeks they would edit these recordings and synthesize them in their final order as well as scripting a short sequence to be recorded in the college studio and added to the final programme.

While the teacher was parking the bus at the farm, the pupils organized themselves into their various roles (director, cameraman, sound technician, presenter and two assistants) to discuss the filming of the first sequence. They identified the first lines to be spoken in the script, where the scene would

take place, where each team member would stand and what help they would need from the farmer. By the time the teacher arrived with the farmer not only was everything ready but the team had had a rehearsal. The lad selected to read the script suddenly encountered real problems in the live situation. While the crew was absorbed with camera angles, positions and so on, the director became a real director and teacher: he coached the script-reader through his lines, despite all sorts of false starts and much embarrassment. Although the team could have chosen a more proficient reader (they were, after all, very pressed for time), they instead chose to help him through the task with a combination of advice and encouragement.

It was the first time that the cameraman (considered to be semi-literate by the school) had used a hand-held camera. At first his shots were inevitably static but he quickly developed the ability to follow movement, or to introduce visual movement into a static scene by moving himself. In fact he became remarkably competent in the half-hour spent at the farm. This was the more surprising since the team had given the technical roles to its least-able members.

The crew filmed a small piglet, a weaning pig, the weighing of the pig, the pigman and the stalls. In the bus on the way back to school a 'script meeting' ensued spontaneously. It consisted of an evaluation of the activity that had taken place in the light of their objectives, and a mutual briefing session on the filming to take place at the school.

At the edge of the school playground, alongside the school building itself, stood a 3 m by 2½ m hen-house in which were kept twenty Rhode Island Reds. The schoolchildren were responsible for feeding and watering these chickens and for cleaning the hen-house. This hen-house, the chickens, the various cleaning implements and two actors comprised the next scene.

While the audience was informed of the need to clean the hen-house regularly, and to water and feed the chickens, the camera peered into the far distance, showing the perimeter of the school grounds, and the squeaking sound of a moving wheelbarrow was heard coming closer. After a short time the wheelbarrow, loaded with cleaning

implements, and the actor had moved sufficiently close to be clearly defined by the camera lens. The cameraman followed the boy and
wheelbarrow until they stopped in front of the
hen-house. He then moved closer as the door
of the hen-house was opened, and followed the
boy's movements as he shovelled out old wood
shavings into the barrow and then emerged,
hen under arm, to face the camera and said:

'This, this is a Rhode Island Red and it is a
favourite with the housewife as it lays brown
eggs.'

The hen was then replaced in the hen-house
and a second pupil entered with a large metal
bucket and proceeded to explain that on the
left of the hen-house were to be found the
nesting-boxes, on the right perches and on the
floor sawdust and food. The camera was
moved to capture each of the items mentioned
and then returned to the nesting-boxes as it
was explained that the eggs were collected
each morning. The camera followed the boy's
movements as he explored each nesting-box
for eggs, which he put in the large bucket.
Clearly under great pressure from being
filmed, the boy neglected to look carefully
enough as he pushed his hand into the last
nesting-box and received a sharp and
unscripted cue from a brooding hen.

When they had returned the barrow, closed
the hen-house door, replaced the lens cap on
the camera and wound up the microphone
wire, the team walked towards the school
entrance. Near the entrance they stopped and
discussed what to do next, with the aid of their
script:

First Boy: Right. Next. Next bit we're in the
class-room and the narrator says, 'Almost
every day peoples. . . .'
Second Boy: We've done that.
First Boy: We haven't done that.
Third Boy: We have, man.
Second Boy: We have [pointing at the script].
First Boy: Oh.
Third Boy: We've put that up the front now.
First Boy: Right, that should have been at the
beginning, like. That should have been done
in the class-room.

As they all concentrated on the script to see
how the mistake could be rectified the teacher
caught up with the group.

Teacher: I tell you what I've got, lads. I've got
the bucket in there [points to the class-
room] with all the eggs and a couple of
empty cartons.
Second Boy [recognizing part of the script]: Got
to get eggs in the box.
Teacher: Aye. You've got to get eggs in the box
so that the people doing the cooking can
take them out again. Come on, we haven't
got long.

In the class-room the pupils filmed a scene in
which eggs were taken from the bucket and
placed in cartons.

The final scene was recorded in a domestic-
science room. The scene was set: whilst one
pupil found a frying-pan and matches, another
looked for plates, cutlery, teacups and a
teapot; the actors rehearsed their lines and
reminded each other of the sequence of acting;
the cameraman positioned the microphone
and then himself. Panting, the last member of
the group arrived carrying a packet of bacon
he had bought at a local shop. Somebody said
'Action!' and the script-reader began:

'Almost every day British people eat bacon
and eggs but they do not know how it comes to
be there or think where it comes from.'

Having decided that they had completed
the location shooting, the team turned their
attention to the planned studio sequences.
They were to show a presenter who would
explain the different cuts of bacon. After his
first few words they would change to a shot of
a diagram of these different cuts, and as each
one was mentioned, they would point the
camera at it. Although this sequence could
have been recorded quite adequately with the
portable camera, the studio visit had been
planned in advance and the teacher believed
that the studio activity offered its own educational benefits, so was keen for the pupils to
keep to the original plan.

The following week the pupils concerned
with 'British Breakfast' joined the rest of the
class for a joint viewing session during which
all the programmes made by the groups were
shown. The class was transfixed. The run of
programmes exhibited novelty, humour, accuracy, drama and many other qualities.
Although no one programme could be said to
have reached a professional standard, it was
abundantly clear that the limiting factor was

the teacher's lack of knowledge of the techniques and logic of recorded sound and vision, and not the pupils' lack of ability. Indeed, over the next two years, as the teacher developed his knowledge and understanding of these media, what the pupils were able to achieve also grew. Consequently, the last venture in which we were involved with this teacher was a fairly sophisticated tape-slide sequence detailing the industrial production of milk. However, before describing that project we shall return to the work of the other three teams that made up the original class.

Two of the teams were boys, the other girls. Like that for 'British Breakfast', the work of each of these teams was complex and exhibited the stamp of the personalities involved. Where the teams differed significantly was in the degree of planning and in the stages at which the pupils organized their material into a coherent statement. This, in turn, affected the type of language they tended to use.

Team 2: 'Litter'

Whereas 'British Breakfast' was the result of a carefully written and carefully executed script, 'Litter' resulted from a script which gave only the location in which each scene was to be recorded and the subject of each scene. The pupils had planned to use the portable television camera, and proceeded fairly quickly from their initial discussions to the first location for the actual filming.

Armed with the camera, recorder and microphone and a general idea of what they wanted to convey, the pupils arrived at the school playground after break. At one edge of what was a surprisingly clear playground lay the object of this team's attention: a small piece of waste ground on which lay scattered a number of empty crisp-packets. The subject-heading in their script was 'Corner of school playground – eyesore', so the camera was used to survey the scene whilst one pupil commented on the carelessness which it typified. The pupils then rewound the tape and replayed their recording, commenting on the success with which both the camerawoman and the narrator had executed their roles. Then, satisfied, they moved to the next location: the school tuck-shop.

On arrival they surveyed the scene and discussed how they could link the shop to the litter problem they had identified. They decided to show four pupils walking away from the shop eating an assortment of sweets. As they turned a corner and mounted two steps into a school corridor they were to deposit their sweet-wrappers on an otherwise immaculate floor. As this was taking place, a narrator would comment on the irresponsibility of this action and the work for others that it would cause. In the event, the scene was quite successful and the pupils deposited a fine array of wrappers with a convincing degree of abandon.

Other scenes followed a similar pattern. The pupils would arrive, survey the location, discuss how they would illustrate the point they wished to make, record with an improvised commentary, replay, modify if necessary and then progress to the next scene. They used short dramatic pieces as described above, impromptu interviews with the school caretaker and a class-mate, and scenes inside and outside the school. They even managed to capitalize on an unexpected visit by the Headteacher to the class-room by even more unexpectedly turning the camera on to him and asking him to say a few words on the general problem of litter.

This act was symptomatic of the spiralling confidence exhibited by the team. It was noticeable, with each scene, that the pupils' reaction to the replayed tape was one of delight, mild surprise at their own achievement and, most of all, pride. It was this pride that, as each successful scene was completed, added to their growing self-confidence.

Team 3: 'Pollution'

This team abandoned the idea of scripting altogether. The result of their initial discussion was to ask the teacher to suggest places where they could see examples of pollution. The teacher responded by organizing a visit to a world-famous polluter of County Durham – the steelworks at Consett, which have been depositing red dust on the town for decades so that the roof-tops and streets are now all a pale shade of rust.

The group decided that they would complete their visit before deciding what to say in their programme. What they would do would be to record visually all the examples of pollution they saw and then on returning to school replay them and improvise a commentary whilst watching. Thus, after playing the recordings through once and discussing their significance, during the second replay they began to speak:

Pupil A: This is the scrap-yard at Consett with derelict buildings.
Pupil B: Why hasn't it been pulled down?
A: Council must have never bothered.
Pupil C: It's an eyesore to people passing through!
Pupil D: Should clear it up.
Pupil E: Attracts rats.
C: It's just standing there right in the way.
D: There'll be diseases in it.
A: The smell round there, it's horrible.
C: There's a lot of smoke.
E: How do people live round there? Must have something to put up with, all the smoke.
D: Why?
E: You only wash on certain days cos of the dust an' that.

Team 4: 'Ferreting'

The pupils involved in 'Ferreting' used a certain degree of scripting, with locations and general ideas noted on paper, but without details of the commentary or vision. In this case, however, the early discussion was quite full and the plan of activity was clear in each pupil's mind. The script or list served as a reminder and no more.

Where the pupils did cover new ground was in the structure of the programme itself. It was to be a dramatic piece. Unlike 'Litter', where a number of the scenes were simple dramatic illustrations of everyday occurrences, here the pupils filmed a drama in the full sense of the word, with a development to a climax and a resolution – in this case a tragedy (at least for the rabbit). A pupil explained the overall structure of the programme:

'First we're gonna get the ferrets, then we're gonna look for the holes. Once we've found the holes we'll show how to place the nets down. We'll have a lad explain the action as it takes place. Like the dog has found some sets running up a hill and two lads are running up looking at the sets, inspecting it, then looking round for the other. After the nets are put down there's an argument about whose ferret will go down. Then one's put down. But no good. Then the other. We're gonna tell about ferreting while we wait for the ferret to come out again. We'll show the rabbit being caught at the end where he drives on the net. Hope we get that bit right.'

The work took place on a rainy day in late winter with pupils and teacher trudging through six inches of mud to reach the agreed location. It was the mud and rain that occasioned the following comments from the teacher:

'They'd have gone through anything because they wanted to do it, and these are the so-called "problem children". On a nice sunny day, what a lovely nature walk it would have been. It was a lousy day today.'

'Your Daily Pinta'

Two terms after this initial television work the teacher, now working with a new group of fourth-year boys, set out to produce a much more sophisticated piece of work, again in rural studies, but this time as a tape-slide sequence. The intention of the programme was to show how milk is produced from 'udder to doorstep'. The finished programme uses music and voices, lettering and location shots, and purely visual sequences. It is quite beautifully paced. What is of greatest interest is the way in which the pupils organized their thinking in planning the programme. Here the teacher introduced a new development not present in any of the previous examples: the pupils went through two distinct planning stages. First they discussed the overall shape and content of their programme, identified each location they felt they should visit and specified the people they would like to interview. They decided on some of the questions they wanted to ask in these interviews but by no means all. Finally they identified what they considered to be the most important pictures in story-board form.

The places were visited, people interviewed (using additional questions that seemed relevant at the time) and photographs taken. The second planning stage arose on return to the class-room. The pupils had gathered a massive amount of taped information and were faced with the task of assimilating the new information, deciding what should be included, and deciding what should be summarized and what should appear in the form of interviews in the final programme. This process, which involved a great deal of subject learning, resulted in a programme which was an interesting mixture of summary and interview.

The Teacher's Viewpoint

Whereas in a normal three-hour session the teacher found that these low-ability children could not concentrate for any length of time, he was astonished now to find them concentrating on one thing for extraordinarily long periods of time.

'The motivation produced by the equipment itself, never mind the end result, was tremendous. We found that even the least motivated children responded. Pupils who had not been signficant before suddenly became significant because every single cog was necessary for the machine to function. Once this had happened, everybody produced written work, not just the few who usually did. Initially a plan was made, but the plan took three lessons, and they had to write three essays. But because there was a real, urgent purpose for their essays, they did them well.

'They succeeded with writing because they had to think this thing out step by step, so their final statement had been thought out step by step. The equipment provided another medium for teaching them this logic.

'The sheer quantity of purposeful talk increased dramatically. Before this I had been particularly perturbed by the middle group, who were usually very reluctant to talk, and very inarticulate. But, because they had specific jobs to do which required communication, they practised oral language much more frequently. They started by making programmes for themselves, in order to conquer the medium, but then they felt the need to explain to and communicate with an audience. It is said that the best way to learn something is to try to teach it. What is more, the content of the learning was so close to the children. It was their school, their film, their hive, their pig, their visit, not someone else's book or film. Also, the audience was captivated because they could identify with their friends who had taken the pictures.

'Usually the children don't do a lot of group work. They all study an area and produce an individual report which may contain pictures, charts or writing. When a videotape or tape-slide sequence was made the end-product was a group product. All members of the group contributed even to the script-writing. This must have helped the slower learners. What I feel is now important is to find out how to assess the individual contributions to the end-product, and how to monitor the development of language skills.

'Different leaders appeared. I thought that I had identified the leaders in the class – those who normally spoke up – but several lads reacted like George. Although he was usually very quiet, not a domineering boy at all, talking livened him up; he became a leader, and very strong-willed.

'Some people would say, "Why bother trailing down to the farm or getting the school bus organized when you could have done the topic in half the time at school?" The phrase "done it" is the key. The children have not been taught the topic, they have literally "done it", so they understand it.

'I don't think introducing the Project's methods intruded much. It is a two-year course and this work was ideal at the end of each topic as a recap, because areas could be swiftly covered for a new reason. It was integrated into our usual work: we got much better results, and we taught better because the equipment was there.

'I shall always remember that boy who played the old man in the introductory programme. At first he was sitting as a fifteen-year-old boy, then the interviewer asked, "What do you think about old age?" There was a terrific pause while he sat in silence and grew older, first thirty-five, then fifty-five until in the end his face was seventy-five. The cameras were running, everybody was poised and waiting, then at last it came: "The bairns skit y." (the children take the mickey out of you). I thought that was marvellous. He really had put sixty years on himself and he knew exactly how these people were feeling. His expression was there. He had really experienced and understood.'

The chapter ends with extracts from the final versions of the five programmes mentioned. Each of these extracts illustrates one relationship between language and the different approaches to audio-visual statements: the effect of the order in which commentary and vision are recorded on the final programme and resultant communication with the audience.

1. 'BRITISH BREAKFAST'

A planned and completely scripted programme:

Almost every day British people eat bacon and eggs for breakfast but they do not know how it comes to be there or think where it comes from. In this programme we intend to show this to the people.

When the piglets are born they are put in a farrowing-pen. They are kept there until they are ready for weaning. The pigs are then put into their fattening-pen, when they are fattened to be ready for butchering.

2. 'LITTER'

A partly planned programme with commentary and vision developed on location:

People who get . . . crisps and what not from the tuck-shop, when they open the bags and eat the crisps and sweets they throw the bags down without thinking that somebody has to come round to pick the rubbish up. Some people throw it down and forget all about it, and they are too lazy to put it in the bin. Sometimes when litter-bins have been filled up people come along and kick them down and then people start kicking the bags about and it makes the place look very untidy.

Not only do the people put the litter in the school yard but they also put it in the school desks. It makes it very untidy. People can't put their books and bags and what not in. Take this for an example. . . .

3. 'POLLUTION'

A commentary recorded after the visual sequence was recorded:

This is a slag-heap. This is slag from Consett Steelworks.

The trees, they would be lovely if it wasn't for the pollution of the slag-heaps.

Kills all the plants round there.

The slag-tip burning behind it – behind the hill.

It's always there – it's always burning. It looks a mess.

Doesn't make much of a place for the kids to go, does it?

When you walk past there it smells, makes you cough. Gets down your throat. You cannot see all that good.

Why don't the people move from Consett?

Why, that's where most of the work is.

Employs half of the population in Consett.

4. 'FERRETING'

A dramatic creation:

Ferreter 1: Fetch it out. Fetch 'im out. Go on. Dig, dig, dig. Go on.
Commentator: Er, the dogs looking for the rabbits.
Ferreter 1: That's it if you get that one there.
Ferreter 2: O.K.
F1: Hang on.
F2: Good, good. Fetch [to dog].
F1: Here, I'll put mine in.
F2: No, divn't.
F1: Why?
F2: This is small, man, if that gets hold of the rabbit. . . .
F1: Nah.
F2: It'll kill it. It's got no chance.
F1: It only nips in and bites it.
F2: Why, look at the size of this – you wait till next year for it. [Long discussion ensues on merits of ferrets.]
F1: Why, aye it is, man, look at it. It's ready to go down.
F2: Well, which one shall we put down?
F1: I'll tell you what, we'll flick up.
F2: Aye, toss a coin.
F1: Have you got one?
F2: Aye. Heads mine ganns down. Tails yours does.
F1: Go on [to ferret – he won toss].
F2: Better catch one.
F1: Oh ah.
F2: What's happening?
F1: It's stopped. It's coming out.

5. 'YOUR DAILY PINTA'
Live interviewing and post-location commentary:

Narrator 1: Southside Farm is situated in central Durham ten miles from Durham City.

Narrator 2: Mr Gibson has been the tenant of Southside Farm since 1951.

Boy Interviewer: Good morning, Mr Gibson, can you spare a few minutes to give a brief history of your farm, please?

Farmer: Yes. We came here in 1951. In those days we farmed 370 acres. There were no cows on the farm; it was mainly a potato and an arable farm. We introduced cows in 1954. In those days. . . .

Narrator 1: Before a cow can have a calf it must be mated with the bull.

Narrator 2: The bull we saw at the farm weighed 18 cwt.

Boy Interviewer: Do you have much trouble with him?

Farmer: Well, you see he's in a bull pen. We have a service pen which we. . . .

Narrator 1: The milk travels along a pipe from the milk tanker to the storage house called a silo.

Narrator 2: A lot of milk still arrives in churns, but this we were told is an inefficient process and will be stopped next year.

Milk Marketing Board Manager: The milk which comes into the dairy here comes in two different. . . .

School	(I)	(II)
Form entry	10	6
Catchment area	Cross-section	Council estate
Buildings	Early 1960s	Post-war
Situation	Semi-rural	Declining mining village
Size of sixth form	40 (half new sixth)	15

Class	(I)	(II)
Number	18	24
Boys/Girls	Boys	Mixed
Streaming	Below average, band 2 remedial	Lowest stream
Age	15 yr	14–15 yr
Time per week	Afternoon (4 × 35 min)	$3/4$–1 h
Subject	Humanities	English
Examinations	CSE Mode 3 (eight sat exam – gained grade 4; four were not up to standard of exam; six left at Easter, before exam)	Non-exam

Teacher	(I)	(II)
Training	M.A.	Cert. Ed.
Subjects taught	English	English
Years teaching	20	26
Special responsibility	Deputy Headteacher, Head of English	Head of English
Sex	Female	Male

CHAPTER 5

Remedial English : Television / Tape-slide

This chapter outlines the way in which two schools used the Project's audio-visual methods to help pupils in remedial English classes. In both schools the work was taken on by an experienced member of staff who also encouraged a younger member of staff to try out these methods with his classes. The chapter will concentrate on the methods used by the experienced teacher, but will comment briefly at the end of each section on the involvement and experiences of the younger teacher.

School I

Here the teacher was working with the lowest-ability fourth-year group and took them for a complete afternoon. The top part of this lower-ability group was attending the local technical college, sampling various crafts, while the middle range, unable to cope with the technical course, was at a local farm, sampling agricultural work, so readers may be able to visualize the remainder of the group, who were the youngsters this teacher was trying to help.

Her main aim was to motivate these eighteen pupils towards increased effort in practising the spoken and written word. Since the school had an audiotape-recorder, a television camera (without a viewfinder), a videotape-recorder and a monitor, she decided to use television to aid her literacy programme.

To explain the class-room activity we shall describe nine lessons, each representing an afternoon's work. This example describes the use of television as a stimulus, the resources used, and an integration of audio-visual methods with more traditional methods familiar to teachers.

LESSON 1

The teacher did not say at first that television would be used. She started by explaining to the class that she wanted them to consider the topic of violence. The children were easily able to draw on their own experience or on vicarious experience, and therefore a lively discussion developed. This ranged over – Dad hitting Mum when he came home drunk, older brother hitting younger brother, gang violence in the streets in the evening, the inevitable brush with the police, and violence on television and in films. The teacher taped this discussion and at the end of the lesson played the tape to the class. She said that the children were very excited at hearing themselves speak and displayed an enormous amount of pride in how they performed.

LESSON 2

To introduce the medium, the teacher played a videotape which had been made by another class in the same school. The children were fascinated by what their fellow-pupils had done and were delighted when they recognized the face or voice of a particular friend. The teacher then explained that they would make a videotape that afternoon and that the audiotape of the discussion that they had had the previous week would form the sound-track. She then produced a number of pictures (some from the Schools Council humanities curriculum pack *Law and Order*, Heinemann) from which the pupils could select those which they felt illustrated each part of the discussion. The pictures formed the vision, the discussion tape the sound-track. The result was simple but effective.

The teacher said that the children had learned to express their opinions and ideas (on violence in this case) and were aware of their own achievement.

LESSON 3
Continuing with the same theme, the teacher read the pupils the story *Seventeen Oranges*, by Bill Naughton. This gave the class the opportunity to consider someone else's experience. They now had further evidence for group discussion. The teacher asked them to construct a short piece of improvised drama based on the situation presented in the story.

LESSON 4
The pupils built upon the work of Lesson 3 by drawing pictures and scripting their improvisation. They then made a video-recording of the pictures accompanied by a commentary, followed by a video-recording of the dramatic work.

The teacher was very pleased with the pupils' reaction: 'Without any prompting they had recognized a need to *write* a short script for the drama and had then set about the task.'

The pupils read aloud the first part of the Bill Naughton story as their introduction.

LESSON 5
The group was taken to a local magistrates' court to observe court procedures. On returning to school the teacher gave them newspaper reports of the local court proceedings and helped them to relate these to what they had observed. At the end of the lesson she asked the pupils to watch 'Crown Court' on television and to relate that to what they had seen in court.

LESSON 6
The pupils found the language of the humanities curriculum pack too difficult so the teacher had to abandon this except for the pictures, which she did find useful. She substituted the Macmillan pack *You and the Law*, from which she took 'The Jarvis Case' (about football hooliganism). The pupils read the case, discussed it and began to dramatize it. Possibly as a result of their experience at the magistrates' court, the case became very real to them.

LESSON 7
The pupils continued to develop their dramatization of 'The Jarvis Case'. The roles included a magistrate, a clerk, a prosecuting council, a council for defence, a police constable, Jarvis and some football witnesses. The dramatization was televised and then viewed.

The pupils were very pleased with their final product. According to the teacher, they thought it was marvellous. They never criticized themselves but they did find small faults with other pupils' contributions. The teacher was impressed with their development and use of formal court language. She noticed that they used a number of special phrases they had heard during their visit to the court.

LESSON 8
This lesson was devoted to a talk by a local policeman. The talk and the discussion that followed were videotaped by the class.

LESSON 9
The pupils were encouraged to write poems or short stories on some aspect of violence. They were then asked to select or draw pictures which would illustrate what they had written. The pupils read their poem or short story aloud and recorded it on audiotape. They then used this as the sound-track. For the vision they used either still pictures, or the face of a pupil looking into the distance as though his thoughts were being spoken, or a mixture of both techniques.

Tape-slide
Later in the same year the teacher used the school's mediaeval fair as an opportunity to experiment with making a tape-slide programme. During the year she had been helped by a fifth-form boy who was studying for a CSE examination. He had joined the teacher for each of her lessons which involved use of the school's video equipment and had acted as a technician and general aid. He intended to write up his experiences as part of a project for CSE. On this occasion, he used the school's camera to take a selection of slides of the various activities at the fair.

When the slides had been processed the pupils viewed them, selected those they considered the best, placed them in order and scripted a commentary. The teacher encouraged each pupil to take responsibility for the commentary on at least one slide. She was pleased that a number of the pupils tried really hard to emulate the more sophisticated language of one of the more capable members of the class.

The pleasure that the pupils quite obviously took in viewing their finished programme was enhanced when the programme was shown to the most able group of their year and they were congratulated by their more academic peers. Later the pupils received further confirmation of their achievement when their programme was shown at a parent/teacher meeting.

Towards the end of the year the teacher discussed with the pupils their course for the following year. Among the possibilities open to these pupils was a practical study of motor-car maintenance. The class showed great interest in this idea, but when they were informed that it was an alternative to their humanities course, they rejected it in favour of a further year's course structured in a similar way.

During the remainder of the year the teacher and class went on to produce a further tape-slide and a number of short pieces of television. The work has continued for two years and it is planned to retain it in future work programmes for this type of group.

Pupils' Comments

The following comments have been taken from an interview with the class at the end of their second term of work.

Interviewer: Do you enjoy school?
Pupil A: Nah.
I: Why not?
A: Hate it. Don't like English.
I: You don't like English. What don't you like about English?
A: I just don't like English, like writing and that, cos I can't think of nowt to write.
I: Do you enjoy humanities?
A: Aye.
I: But you keep thinking of things to write there?
A: Aye, I can there.
I: This isn't English but do you think that you are doing anything connected with English in this?
Pupil B: Yeah. You talk better and getting your words out better.
I: You think that's happened to you?
B: Yeah.
I: What have you found the most difficult thing?
Pupil C: Keeping a straight face on television. You get embarrassed when you start laughing.
I: So you try and keep a straight face on television. Anything else you find difficult?
C: Speaking without getting your words tangled up.
I: Have you improved, do you think?
C: Yes, since I've started.
I: You are not doing too badly now.
C: Well, I'm used to talking on a tape-recorder now.
I: Do you agree with him?
Pupil D: Talking?
I: That it has helped your talking.
D: Yes.
I: Have you noticed any improvement? Can you think about how you talk, and can you tell me specifically the little pieces of improvement you've seen?
D: Talking too fast.
I: When do you know you're talking too fast?
D: I can't think of the words to say. I start a sentence but I can't finish it.
I: And do you notice this when you're actually speaking to the television camera or do you notice it when you see it back?
D: When I see it back.
I: And has that improved?
D: Yes.
I: What goes through your mind when you're talking to a television camera? What are you thinking about? Are you thinking about what you look like? Are you thinking ahead to what the next words are?
Pupil E: I'm thinking about the sounds of the words I'm saying.
I: You've never been on a programme? Have you been there when they've been making one?
Pupil F: Sometimes.
I: What do you think about it? Would you like to be in one?
F: No, cos I always laugh.
I: You always laugh. You don't think like our

friend over there that you might overcome that?

F: No, I start laughing.

I: Well, what have you contributed? What have you given the group?

F: The answers to some of the questions.

I: You worked out some of the answers and someone else spoke them?

F: Sometimes, aye.

I: Were you pleased with the way they spoke them?

F: Yeah. It's good.

I: What was the first programme like? What did you think about it?

Pupil G: Well, I didn't think it was very good when I saw it.

I: Why?

G: Because everyone was slow in their answers.

I: Why do you think that was?

G: Nervousness, I suppose.

I: Did it improve?

G: Yes.

I: Was it better the second time? Did they improve?

G: Yes.

I: Yes. So what was the difference?

G: Well, he knew what he was going to say before he said it.

I: Oh, I see. So what about other people? You've seen them?

G: Yes, they do improve I think.

I: They do improve. What bit improves?

G: They answer quicker and, er, give more intelligent answers as well.

I: Anything else?

G: I think it was because we didn't rehearse it, we didn't rehearse it much before we done it, we just . . . half the films we just done in an afternoon. We didn't write them up or nothing before. . . .

I: Tell me, what do you think about this work?

Pupil H: It's much better with the telly.

I: Why is that?

H: Cos you see yourself on telly and gives you more pleasure; it's more pleasant working with cameras and that.

Finally, the following interesting comment was made in an answer to an examination question at the end of the fifth year, a year and a half later:

'To make a film we find a subject that everybody wants to do then we write up how we are going to do it like; who does the camera, who speaks and who plays the different parts. Then we get on with it; we switch on the videotape and then start whatever it is we are doing. From doing this we have learnt that if you help each other you can make a lot of progress.'

The Teacher's Viewpoint

The teacher was asked whether she thought that pupils had learned anything specific as a result of the use of audio-visual methods.

'They have said themselves that if they know the tape is running they hate to dry up. They keep going, and this, I suppose, means that they are stretching themselves. They do have blank moments, like anyone else, and they get very embarrassed when that happens. When it does we switch off the videotape. If it happens too often there is an element of irritation at doing the same thing over and over again. They get quite annoyed with each other for spoiling what they see as the end-product, so I suppose that pressure must extend them.

'I think that discussion in class can be a bit nebulous. If it is on tape, either ordinary tape or videotape, it becomes something you can pin down, show again, come back to and perhaps revise. From that point of view it has been quite useful. It probably does focus their attention. For example, if we are doing a particular programme it makes them realize that we have not got time for irrelevancies and therefore have to be much clearer. We have to check more carefully what we are aiming at so there has to be a process of selection. However, that process does not emerge until we are making the programme.

'These boys need success and this seems to be a way in which they can get a measure of success that they would not otherwise achieve. That, to me, is the main justification for this method, because if you give them success you will change their attitude to lots of other things.'

The Younger Teacher

This teacher was working with the top stream of the third year on a Dickens project. She hoped that using television would help the pupils to 'rediscover Dickens in an active and participatory way'.

To help the pupils overcome the novelty of using television she encouraged them to watch and listen to themselves on television at an early stage. They worked the machinery and talked freely in front of the cameras. They then saw and heard themselves, which they thoroughly enjoyed. The teacher was surprised that the girls in the class showed a much greater ability to handle the equipment than did the boys.

After the pupils had read *David Copperfield* the teacher made a selection of passages from the book and asked the pupils to write their reactions in both verse and prose form. They were then asked to script short dialogues among some of the characters. Using the poetry, prose and dialogues and working in groups, the pupils developed a sound-track. The groups then selected or drew pictures to accompany their sound-tracks and went on to record these combinations. The results were viewed by all the children, who criticized each piece.

On splitting into groups the usually well-behaved class became noisy, boisterous and argumentative, each pupil attempting to assert his own opinion. The teacher said that the pupils had great difficulty in working in groups.

The children compared their end-result with broadcast television and were a little disappointed. After discussion the class felt that they and the teacher should watch 'Blue Peter' as an example of an appropriate format for their own work.

The pupils found the televising of dramatic scenes to be relatively unsuccessful but the more formal situations of interviews and debates worked well. The teacher felt unable to provide a structure for the more than adequate flow of ideas from the pupils.

School II

One of the children in this school had had writing difficulties for many years. He had been given remedial classes in English but had made no progress. All the help given had been aimed directly at the written word.

As part of the Project this pupil became involved in writing a small piece of a television script. After he had written it no one could understand it so he was asked to read exactly what was written down and this was recorded. By listening to the tape, rather than referring to the written form, he could now recognize where he had made mistakes. He then went back to the written work and tried to correct it. He also *asked* for help from the teacher.

The More Experienced Teacher

This teacher adapted the Project's suggestions to work with the bottom stream of the fourth year, whose English work was almost entirely remedial. He hoped that offering these pupils the opportunity to work in another medium (one with which they were familiar and one from which they gained so much pleasure) would remotivate them. The children were bad readers, experienced great difficulty in reading aloud, found it difficult not to shout in class discussions, wrote with difficulty and did not punctuate their writing. It was the development of skills in these areas on which the teacher intended to concentrate.

The teacher and pupils visited the television studio at the local college. They were introduced to the equipment and a simple script which, during the following hour, they made into a short television programme. The production of the script involved the pupils in the following:

Reading – the cameramen, vision- and sound-mixers, caption-pullers, etc., all had to follow the written script.

Reading aloud – three of the programme's sequences required reading aloud of voice-over parts, three the reading aloud of poetry and one reading aloud by an interviewer and two interviewees.

Discussing and giving instructions in a controlled and fluent manner – to co-ordinate the various practical activities.

It was hoped that in the development of their own scripts the pupils would find it necessary to *write* and to *punctuate* in order that every member of the production team would be able to read and follow the script, whether they were reading it aloud or using it as a plan around which to organize other activities.

Early on it became clear that, although the teacher's aims were being largely satisfied, the use of television disguised these basic activities from the pupils, who were simply aware of being able to make a television programme, to operate television equipment and to see themselves on television.

After this introductory session, the teacher chose a short story by Sid Chaplin as the basis for the class work.

'Blackberries'

Back in the class-room, the story was read to the pupils, after which they began to discuss and write their television adaptation. This turned out to involve a sensitive mingling of narrative for a story-teller and dialogue for dramatic scenes.

The television programme opens with the story-teller reading the story directly to the audience. As she reads, her picture gives way to a series of still pictures which blend into one another to illustrate the unfolding story. The story-teller's voice then gives way to a dramatization using the voices of three lads who took the parts of various characters already introduced by the story-teller. It is at this point that we wish that readers were able to see and hear the programme that these pupils produced.

We can show a still picture of the story-teller and the pictures drawn by the pupils[1] but we shall have to ask readers to imagine the various expressions and emotions passing across this girl's face as she begins reading the story. We must also ask readers to imagine each still picture merging into the next, to achieve continuous visual movement, and to visualize some pictures being slowly panned across. For instance, the camera moved slowly from left to right across Picture 4 to give the impression of moving along the road. In other pictures the pupils slowly zoomed into an interesting or relevant spot or started in a small area of interest and gradually opened out to show its context. Finally, we hope that readers will be able to imagine from the printed script what the sound-track actually sounds like: young, developing voices (and developing readers) struggling to achieve the dramatic intonation required by the dialogue, and the crystal-clear, slightly jerky sound of the young story-teller as she beautifully weaves her tale.

[1]The pictures had been drawn and painted during the class's art lessons.

Story-teller: One day three lads went brambling. It was bright and sunny and the bushes were thick with blackberries. The place had once been a wood.

Far below was the river, coiling like a snake and spanned by the Jubilee Bridge.

Vic was eating as many as he picked. John was carefully picking his. Ray was not interested in blackberries, he was more interested in spiders.

John: Be careful when you're picking them cos they squash in your hand. They'll make a good pie for tea tomorrow.

Vic: Look at Ray – he's looking for spiders instead of picking blackberries. He'll never get his bag full. By, there's some big uns here.

Ray: Hey, look what I've found!

John: I'm not going to look at your spiders.

Ray: They're not spiders. I've found some birds. I think they're dead though. They look like partridges.

Vic: How do you know they're partridges?

Ray: I've seen pictures of partridges in a book at home.

John: I know what we'll do with them. Let's take them home. I've heard you can eat them.

Story-teller: They lay in the long grass, limp with blood on them. There were six of them. The boys took two each and set off for home. Through the bracken they swished, climbed over the fence and on to the road.

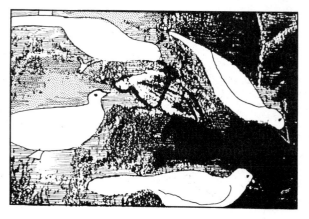

A car passed them, an old Ford. The driver looked at them as he went by. After twenty yards or so his brakes squeaked and the car came to a halt.

The man, who looked like a farmer, jumped out.

Driver: Hey, what's that you've got there?

Ray: We weren't doing anything, mister.

Driver: I asked, what have you got there?

John: We found them, mister, when we were picking blackberries.

Vic: We never killed them. We just found them lying there in that field.

Driver: All right there. I believe you. Tell you what – those birds are poor eating, not worth carrying! Put them under the front seat of the car and I'll give you a ride in the car.

Ray: Ta very much, mister. We've never been in a car before.

Story-teller: The car shook and began to move. A little needle pulsed on a kind of clock-face on the bonnet of the car. The wind beat against their cheeks. The hands of the driver were steady on the wheel.

Down the hill they went, around the bend and over the bridge.

They whizzed past a slow farm cart drawn by a weary horse.

The boy seated on the front of the cart saluted them enviously.

His collie dog sat with lolling tongue and looked at them with shiny eyes.

It then gave an agonized howl as the car brushed past with only inches to spare. The driver turned and grinned.

At last they rushed up a short steep bank shaded by trees and turned a corner.

The car slowed down. They passed a row of houses and came out into the market square.

The car drew up beside a pub and the driver got out.

Driver: This is where I have to stop, lads. Got some business to attend to.
John: What time will you be going back?
Driver: Oh, about ten o'clock tonight!
Vic: How are we going to get back home?
Driver: Walk – the exercise will do you good.
Ray: Come on, we'd better get started. We'll have to be back home before it's dark or we'll get it!

Story-teller: As the boys walked along the street past the shops, there in a fishmonger's were some birds hanging upside down with a price sign on them.

Vic: Look at those birds, they're like the ones we gave to that man.

Ray: Yes they are. And look at how much they are: five shillings a brace.

John: Come on, we might catch that man who has them.

Story-teller: They turned back but there was no sign of the car. Wearily they started on the long walk back home, not fully realizing the lesson they had learnt.

The use of the story-teller to set the scene and move the story along offered the children the opportunity to write reflectively and descriptively in the third person, while the dramatic dialogue offered the opportunity for tension and conflict in direct speech. This technique provides a useful structure for children as it has much flexibility and encourages an imaginative, expressive response.

The appearance of the story-teller live at intervals gave more variety and life to the visual effect. The voice-over/still pictures technique worked well – to stage the whole thing would have been more difficult. Here the pupils were able to concentrate wholly on the vocal aspects of the characters – the reading and making the character come alive – rather than having to cope with acting as well.

This is probably a valuable initial structure. After working for a time with simple audio-visual structures of this kind, children do begin to demand more complex forms, at which stage it may be appropriate to offer dramatized inserts, live studio sequences, recording on location and documentary formats.

There is a clear need for a series of audio-visual formats starting with the simple and moving to the complex as the children develop an audio-visual vocabulary and control of the equipment.[2]

The Younger Teacher

The younger teacher in this school set his fourth-year class the task of making a television programme about the school. These children had not visited the television studio, but were told that they would be using a portable television camera and videotape-recorder to record their script. Their locations were to cover various aspects of school life.

Each pupil in the class wrote the sort of script they felt was most appropriate for each scene. The teacher discussed these with the class as a whole, and the class selected the ones they considered most suitable to convey what they wanted to say. The teacher typed all the selected pieces, put them together, and

[2]These are being developed in the packs mentioned in the Preface.

presented them to the class as a working script.

Because the treatment was different for each scene a very interesting, varied set of sequences resulted:

Scene 1 – The Playground: This used the background noise of the playground and a voice-over commentary introducing the programme.

Scene 2 – Assembly: This used the basic elements of assembly – the teacher's voice and pupils singing – with a scripted voice-over commentary.

Scene 3 – Registration: This used a dramatic scripted voice-over/dialogue sequence.

Scenes 4 and 5 – English and Maths: These used examples of the teacher teaching and pupils answering with a voice-over commentary as an introduction only.

Scene 6 – Modern Languages: A group of pupils interviewed the teacher and asked her about teaching modern languages. The camera panned from the group interviewing the teacher to a class using the language laboratory.

Scene 7 – Domestic Science: The camera panned round the room while a scripted voice-over described what was happening.

Scene 8 – Science: Pupils performed an experiment and described what they were doing throughout.

Scene 9 – Woodwork: This consisted of a dramatized sequence showing boys walking through the school grounds to the woodwork block chatting to each other, then pupils waiting to go into a woodwork class. All this was recorded live with synchronous sound.

Scene 10 – Art: The camera panned around the art room to show specific things which the scripted voice-over explained.

Scene 11 – Games: First the girls played a mock game of netball inside the gymnasium while a voice-over explained and introduced the gymnasium. Then a group of pupils went on to the sports field, and while one boy showed how to throw a discus, another improvised voice-over talked about the pupil, his sporting achievements and his technique.

Scene 12: The final scene showed pupils leaving the school and getting on to the school bus – with a scripted voice-over.

The pupils used the following techniques:

1. Scripted voice-over (Scenes 1–3, 7 and 10)
2. Improvised voice-over (Scene 11)
3. Interviewing (Scene 6)
4. Demonstration (Scene 8)
5. Live action with synchronous sound (Scenes 4 and 5)
6. Dramatization (Scene 9)

School

Form entry	7
Catchment area	Mainly council estate
Buildings	Post-war
Situation	Urban: on edge of private housing estate, surrounded by terraced housing
Size of sixth form	None (11–16 yr)

Class

Number	29
Boys/Girls	Mixed
Streaming	Mixed ability
Age	12–13 yr
Time per week	4 × 35 min
Subject	German
Examinations	CSE, GCE

Teacher

Training	B.A.
Subjects taught	German
Years teaching	12
Special responsibility	Head of German
Sex	Female

CHAPTER 6

Modern Languages: Tape-slide

The importance of the Project's involvement with modern-language teaching is greater than its importance for many other subjects in the curriculum. This is not because a modern language, in this case German, is of greater importance or of greater significance to the pupils, but because it is a subject for which there is least interference from outside factors; more than for any other subject, what the children learn here is the result of activity in the class-room. Unlike English, the children do not practise the language outside school. German is not used anywhere else in the curriculum, and children are not usually faced with problems in everyday life that require modern-language skills. Children do come in contact with maps showing urban and rural geography, can see the results of history around them, and do use ideas of mass, size and a whole host of concepts from physics and mathematics, but to most children Germany seems a long way off. This lack of a meaningful context for modern languages in the world of most schoolchildren perhaps makes it harder to teach German than to teach other subjects. The significant gains in learning and motivation achieved by the methods described here in the field of modern languages provide even stronger evidence of their effectiveness than their success with other subjects.

The teacher, Head of German in an inner urban comprehensive, had been integrating production by pupils of tape-slide material into her normal course. She had been working in this way for two years, initially with a second-year group, but gradually the work had spread to other groups. All her language groups were of mixed ability, and became option groups in the fourth and fifth years.

The following report by the teacher is the result of an evening we spent at her home during which she looked back over the two years' work. She started by explaining when she first introduced the Project's methods.

'I feel it is important to adopt a practical approach to learning a foreign language so that my pupils immediately understand that German is first and foremost a means of communication. My strategy has therefore been to involve the pupils actively in using the language to communicate with myself and with one another from the outset.

'They first learn to introduce themselves in German in response to the simple question "Wie heisst du?" (What are you called?) and then proceed to giving information about where they live, how old they are, what sort of school they attend and so on. The course we use is aimed at a wide range of ability and allows the pupils to progress gradually and systematically through basic language patterns, grammar and vocabulary. At each stage I make sure that the pupils use creatively what they have learnt, by employing visual aids and other resource material to provide relevant and varied situations that require them to speak or write German. As they gradually acquire basic language patterns they get closer to the stage where they can use the language more flexibly to talk about some of their own interests and to say things in German which interest others in the class.

'It was at this point that we first embarked on a tape-slide project. The project was largely conducted in one mixed-ability second-year class (in their first year of German). The obvious choice of subject seemed to be "Selbstporträt" (self-portrait), as we had practised most of the material orally over a number of months and the pupils had then been asked to write an account of themselves, organizing their facts as they wished. When the first rough draft had been completed and corrected the pupils were then asked to read out their accounts to the class. They were very much aware that this was not a pointless exercise but part of the preparation required to produce a good tape-slide sequence. So the reading aloud was taken very seriously indeed: pronunciation was corrected and I was not the only one listening out for faults – other pupils chimed in and corrected reading errors. Generally they were quite critical, commenting "You're going to have to speak up a bit!" or "I don't think you can say that – you've mentioned your pets before your family". Nobody seemed daunted by the steady flow of criticism – the whole thing was taken in good part! I left it largely up to them how they should organize their facts.

'Having covered the basics and practised a few reading techniques – how to project one's voice and speak with good intonation and unhurriedly – we then introduced the machinery. Nothing elaborate was used at this stage, just a small cassette recorder which one pupil would operate for the pupil who was speaking. Thus each pupil was now able to hear himself and in general they became quite self-critical: "Oh, I agree, I'll have to speak louder there" or "Oh, I don't like that at all, I'm doing it all again". After the initial writing stage we probably spent part of about two weeks' lessons (part of about six or seven periods) training the pupils to become so familiar with their accounts that they could speak them fluently and without much reference to the written sheet (although they preferred to keep this with them as it gave them more confidence).

'At the studio the pupils were first of all introduced to the machinery and were given advice on how to speak across the head of the microphone and not to look down (in later tape-slide work we used "idiot cards" to ensure that the pupil looked up as he spoke and yet did not have to know his text by heart). Then the pupils gave a voice sample and often had to have more than one try before this was satisfactory, after which we went straight into the final version.

'When we record now we usually make a videotape so that the pupils see themselves on TV as they speak, but the first time they made their recording without experiencing the full audio-visual effect immediately. When the slides did finally arrive we had to arrange them correctly to fit the contributions. Then in the final editing (which was done by six pupils and myself) we added bleeps between contributions and prefaced the whole thing with a marvellous burst of Mozart's Posthorn Serenade, fading it out at the appropriate moment. We then used the Finale as our own closing music. This exercise in itself involved careful listening. All our visits to the recording studio when making tape-slide pieces took place in my free periods.

'That was our very first tape-slide attempt. Since that time, making tape-slide programmes has become a regular part of our work. We have made one on clothing with the same pupils, and a later class of second years has written and produced a videotape-recording of café dialogues. At present we are working on five projects. Another version of "Selbstporträt" is being made by a mixed-ability third-year class and a series entitled "Mein Tagesablauf" (my daily routine) is being made by fourth-year pupils about to enter the fifth year. The latter will be a more complex programme, more complex from the point of view of time and language, that is. We shall have to find time to go out and photograph them getting out of bed, coming downstairs, making breakfast, and so on. We have decided to do this as a tape-slide sequence first (as opposed to video or film) because the time spent playing back any given slide can be controlled.

'When the pupils saw their finished product, the response was immense: the atmosphere was electric, everyone full of anticipation and then sheer delight. They were really very proud of what they had done, very impressed. The rest of the class was generous in its praise.

'I selected the pupils who were to record simply by asking for volunteers. I usually do this as they are pretty keen. About thirteen children actually recorded the first tape-slide sequence, but the whole class was involved in preparing, listening and criticizing.

'They were used to being asked to criticize, so they understood their role. During the initial trial tapings of the class you could hear a pin drop. I said, "We're going to simulate the recording studio." In the recording studio, to which the whole class went, I said, "You're all going to participate, because you're going to be the audience."

'Every aspect of the class-room was photographed, so everybody is present somewhere in the photographs. That was as much as some pupils wanted to contribute at that stage. In the first class about half the children wanted to be involved whereas in one later class everyone wanted to join in except one or two little boys, who wanted to be involved on the technical side only.

'It took us about four weeks to produce our first tape-slide, including the week when we went to the studio. We had to put all the material together, which we did orally, so that probably took a quarter of the time. Another quarter was spent writing and checking that the material was presentable, while the rest of the time was spent on learning and developing the recording techniques. Talking went on when, for example, the class had to decide which version of part of the sequence was best. It also occurred when they were using tape-recorders in the class-room and having to get used to speaking into a microphone, because some pupils froze in front of a tape-recorder. Finally, photography was going on all the time because it had to be done on days when the light was right in the class-room.

'One of my worries is whether we can speed up production of the slides. Because we had to wait weeks for them to come back, we had to concentrate on the oral side before the children knew how the whole thing was going to turn out. We could have taken the slides in advance and had them ready, but we had embarked on the two aspects of the project at the same time.

'I would advise anybody starting from scratch to go ahead with the visual side before beginning the written and oral work. Then, when the slides come back you can say, "Now let's put this together, let's see how it is going to look!", which is something we could not do until the very end. I think it pays to start by just taking the photographs, asking the pupils how they would like to be taken and what they want to wear but reminding them that they will have to talk and write about themselves.

'If they wanted to say something we had not prepared then we included it if they could say it. Sometimes I suggested a simpler way of saying something, but I was quite prepared to accept that they would be able to digest the particular construction. They knew why they were saying it, they knew what it was about, therefore it was not a problem.

'They did the written accounts individually in class, but of course a lot of what they wanted to say overlapped because pupils of that age have got similar interests. Answers to questions like "I want to say such and such! How do you say it?" were often put up on the blackboard as they were of interest to several pupils.

'In the very next lesson the class insisted on seeing the sequence a number of times, so we used it very very fully. What is more, when I reintroduced it six months later it was fresh and interesting to them and they saw the whole thing with different eyes.

'When I had shown a tape-slide sequence to a class I would ask questions in German on the information given. So not only did the children hear German being spoken, they spoke as well. This has been very successful, even with a fourth-year CSE class who needed a little bit of stimulation and who needed to revise some particular vocabulary. I ask questions like: "What did Michelle say her father did?", "What was Carol wearing in the picture?", and "Describe Carol". A tape-slide sequence can thus be used simply for listening or for oral practice.

'When the uses of the tape-slide from a language point of view had been exhausted, we looked at it from the technical point of view. I would ask the children how they thought a particular person had performed, and they would say whether they thought the diction was clear. They would also say whether the person had spoken at an audible level. Speed was one of the problems because the tape-slide programme was to be used as a teaching aid and therefore had to be slow enough for other classes to understand.

'On questions of content they simply made comments: "Maybe you should have mentioned all your family together" or "Do you think that friends should go together?" As a result of this sort of comment, I have decided that with the present second year it would be a good idea to introduce subheadings, such as themselves, their families, their hobbies, the school, to get more cohesion. From the start we realized that the content tended to skip from one subject to another, whereas from the point of view of good German style and also from the point of view of listening and asking questions, it would have been much easier if the content had been grouped systematically. After having seen the original tape-slide, the new second year decided to work in this way. I find now, listening to that first tape-slide, that although it is very good, a little more direction with respect to content and organization would probably have been a good thing. However, at the beginning, I didn't want to impose any restrictions.

'I was very pleased with the amount of collective encouragement and praise. For example, the second time we went to the recording studio there was a girl who could not get the right level of audibility, although time was running out. The rest were saying to her, "Come on, Carol, you can do it. Come on, just practise shouting." I sat at one side of the studio and said to her, "Come on, shout!" She did shout something, so I said, "There you are, speak like that." When she came on at the very end of the programme, what she had to say was beautifully audible and the whole class applauded. They had immense enjoyment from producing the thing themselves and they did not want Carol to go away without having had that success. On the recording side there is a lot of solidarity. Everyone gets slightly nervous but all the children are trying to make a programme which sounds very competent.

'We are hoping to branch out and do some filming. We have also done some play-writing and have recently recorded some plays. The children have written dialogues for a café scene. There again I had to give them the basic vocabulary, but having given it to them, I said, "Right, you write your plays."

'What they seem to enjoy more than anything else is seeing what they have produced being used as a teaching medium: when I'm saying, "Now, listen to Michelle. I'm going to ask you questions in German on what Michelle is saying." It certainly increases their confidence: there is absolutely no doubt about that. The children who have been involved in the various projects are very very keen to do that kind of work again. Every single one who worked on the first tape-slide has opted to do German in the fourth year, which is most significant. It has heightened their interest in the subject. They realize that they can produce something which is very worthwhile seeing and worthwhile showing, and they are extremely keen to go a little further and produce something for an outside audience.

'The second tape-slide sequence was on clothing, and this time we had a specific grammatical object in mind. We wanted to teach the use of the accusative case in German and the use of the irregular verb *tragen* (to wear). We were going to explain what people were wearing. The garments they were wearing were to be the object of the sentence, and therefore in the accusative case. I wanted them to put in as many adjectives as possible, all taking accusative endings. They decided well in advance what they were going to wear. "Now for that," they said, "we must have someone wearing something striped if possible because we want to use this adjective. We must have somebody wearing trousers and we must have somebody wearing something long." They then dressed to fit the part and we went ahead with the visuals first. However, we were not doing this in a vacuum because we knew what we would be saying. When the slides came back we were able to make the exact sentences and kept this specific grammatical objective in mind.

'The second tape-slide was produced much more quickly than the first, which took four weeks. The second one, bearing in mind that we took the slides first, was completed in about two weeks, because I was familiar with the techniques. Because it was more specifically aimed at grammar, it was much shorter and less creative, inasmuch as the pupils were working to a more structured theme, but it was very useful. They were as elated by the second tape-slide as the first. It has certainly been used more than the first one because pupils must get this particular construction right. Often when we need to practise the accusative case we use this particular tape-slide.

'The children had just entered the third year when they made the second tape-slide. However, the course then involved a lot of picture description so it seemed a little artificial to continue with tape-slide work. Now that we have reached a point in the course where we are talking about schools, we have been able to base a new tape-slide sequence on pupils' own accounts of a day at school.

'The whole project has expanded: other classes have seen the two original tape-slides and are becoming involved. The fourth year has embarked on producing a much more complex tape-slide showing a typical daily routine, which will involve using all sorts of complex separable verbs and complex constructions with "because" and "when".

'The present second year are doing a "Selbstporträt" and have also written some café dialogues. The question is which visual medium to use. We may stick to tape-slide or we may go on to video, which might be more interesting and more suitable for the dialogue.

'The pupils' motivation does not depend solely on whether or not they are involved in the tape-slide work. There are many other aspects of the language course to keep them interested, and I never allow these to become boring in contrast. Tape-slide work is only part of the course. The original class of third years was neither disturbed nor bored when filming was temporarily dropped after the second tape-slide, and they were doing different exercises. Tape-slide has simply become one facet of a multi-faceted course.

'As a modern-language teacher I'm interested in how the technology can help the whole course. It certainly wasn't difficult to move from tape-slide to using the language again in class, or producing another essay. Now, when we are writing essays I say, "We shall probably either make a little booklet of this or keep it in mind for a possible tape-slide." So, for example, the "daily routine" exercise which the fourth years are producing has been building up over the last few months, and in this way has become an integral part of their total work in German. The café dialogues are also the result of a great deal of earlier work.

'Making our own tape-slides has cost us slightly more than using conventional materials because we had to buy the films. But we do have as a result permanent teaching material, and such exciting teaching material. Part of the interest is the very fact that the pupils themselves have made it. They know that they have produced something which is being used in their own class and with other classes.

'I am very pleased with the results. For example, in the third-year exam the pupils had to write an essay on themselves. A lot of pupils who had taken part in the tape-slide wrote extremely good essays, because they had memorized phrases from their own performances. Their essays were much better than those of parallel groups. They had written complex phrases like "My family *consists* of my mother, my father and my brother", which is a very difficult phrase in German because it involves the dative case. The child who said that on the tape-slide wrote it in her German essay. They have watched the programme a number of times and remembered it. It has meant much more to them because they have actually spoken the words on to tape, much more than if they had said the words fleetingly in a lesson or written them in an essay.

'With this method we cover more ground because we are working towards a specific end. A lot of German is taught and developed over a number of months then drawn together and used very creatively. Because this is a cumulative process and they are speaking in German about themselves, the pupils tend to memorize the German much more readily.

'The time we spent recording and practising the recording techniques in class was very worthwhile in terms of the knowledge that the pupils gained, not to mention the confidence that it gave them and the ability to project their voices. These very important arts and skills are often almost completely neglected in schools.

'As a teacher of German, it is my concern that the pupils hear good German, that they are motivated by the visual image, that good German is spoken, that good German is put together and that the pupils see that German is basically a means of communication. This is why I use this particular teaching method — there is no doubt that it is both a reinforcer and a highly successful learning experience.'

School

Form entry	8
Catchment area	Council estate
Buildings	1964
Situation	Urban
Size of sixth form	20–30
	(some new sixth;
	school intake 14–18 yr)

Class

Number	22
Boys/Girls	Mixed
Streaming	7th set out of eight
Time per week	2 × 35 min on average
	(out of 6 × 35 min)
Subject	English
Examinations	CSE

Teacher

Training	B.A., Cert. Ed.
Subjects taught	English
Years teaching	11
Special responsibility	None
Sex	Male

CHAPTER 7

English : Film

In this case study we describe the work of a teacher who decided to remotivate fifteen-year-olds of very low ability to write, read and discuss in their English lessons. He chose the medium of cine-film because he had developed techniques for teaching film-making which made it easy to integrate film with English studies.

The first stage was to teach the children a simplified 'film vocabulary' so that they could talk in the technical language of film-making; he felt this to be necessary as it helped to suggest to them how they might record their subject-matter in a meaningful way. For example, he found that as soon as the pupils had been introduced to a classification of the types of shot possible and given a chance to experiment with these, they immediately began looking in a different way. They were more selective and discriminating. So early on he illustrated the terms with examples simply sketched on a blackboard, and showed the pupils a series of abbreviations referring to each.

Note that the diagrams show only one of several ways of classifying shots. A common alternative is to call the long shot a 'full-length shot' (F.L.S.) and the extreme long shot an 'establishing shot' (E.S.), since it establishes the overall scene.

The next stage was to introduce the pupils to making a story-board consisting of drawings of what would be seen on the final film each accompanied by an appropriate shot description. The pupils were then asked to apply this drafting technique to a series of short exercises. This served to reinforce what

Extreme long shot (E.L.S.)

Long shot (L.S.)

Medium shot (M.S.)

Close-up (C.U.)

Extreme close-up (E.C.U.)

they had been shown, as well as providing a first attempt to produce a logical sequence of visual images.

In the first exercise pupils were asked to draw a story-board illustrating a man having breakfast when the postman delivers a surprise parcel. The following is a typical result:

At this point the pupils had described the types of shot they had drawn in the way they had been told to, but many of the results produced suggested that they were already selecting the point of view or angle from which the pictures were to be taken. The teacher used this development to introduce the pupils to a further classification for identifying camera angles.

The teacher then explained and named the normal camera movements:

Pan: turning the camera in a horizontal plane to follow movement or to survey a scene.

Tilt: turning the camera in a vertical plane to move from a low angle to a high angle or vice versa.

Track: moving the camera to follow action.

Zoom: moving the camera lens to change from a close-up to a long shot or vice versa.

Camera angles:

Low angle (L.A.)

Straight (usually left as a drawing with no instruction)

High angle (H.A.)

Camera movement:

Pan

Tilt

Track

Zoom

The possibilities for changing from one scene to another were also introduced:

Cut: an immediate change.
Fade in/out: fade to/from a blank screen.
Mix: fade one picture in over another as the latter is fading out (this involves superimposing at the halfway stage).

After the pupils had written down these terms and drawn the teacher's illustrations in their notebooks, he asked them to draw a series of shots of their own to illustrate each of these terms.

Following a discussion of the results of this exercise, the teacher introduced the class to script-writing. This he did by first introducing the headings used when laying out a script:

Shot   Cam. angles   Speech and sound   Vision

He then applied this system to a short dramatic sequence in the following way.

He moved from behind his desk and walked slowly towards a pupil sitting in the third row beside the window. He placed himself as close to the desk as possible and, standing still, raised his arm in a threatening gesture and shouted, 'Stop that and pay attention.' He then returned to his desk and asked the whole class, 'What ought to be the first shot in that sequence?'

Having regained its composure, the class discussed the teacher's question and finally decided that the first shot should be a long shot of the teacher in front of the class. The teacher noted this on the blackboard, then asked what camera direction should be given. The class favoured a straight position. He then directed their attention to the third column and asked if there would be any speech or sound accompanying this shot. The class replied that although there would be no speech, as he had not spoken at that point, there would be general class-room noise. The teacher finally asked the class to describe the activity that would be seen in this first shot. They responded that the teacher should be standing behind the desk then move round the desk, towards the class, looking angry.

In this way the class gradually described a series of shots until they had completed the sequence. They then copied this into their notebooks.

At this point the teacher offered us a rationale for his work:

'Many of these children have failed to communicate very adequately through the written word but this form of expression, relying on other abilities, allows them access to levels of expression otherwise possibly denied them. I find that these children, who are often reluctant to learn in other, more traditional situations, are ready and able to think creatively and actively with this approach.'

He went on to cite the example of a similar class to which he had presented a list of topics from which they had to choose the subject of an essay. The following week he presented the

Shot	Cam. angles	Speech and sound	Vision
1. L.S.	Cam. angle straight	Background class-room noise	Teacher in front of class behind his desk. Moves out round desk towards class.
2. M.S.	Cam. low angle	'Stop that and pay attention.'	Teacher stops in front of one pupil, raises his hand and shouts.
3. C.U.	Cam. high angle	Background class-room noise	Boy cowers. Looks up at teacher.

list again and asked the pupils to construct story-boards based on the topics they had chosen for their essays. He found that the story-boards showed more careful logical structuring of their statements with many more original ideas and a spontaneity and freshness of approach which was missing in their essay-writing. He felt that the children were aware of this themselves and that their feelings of success did much to generate a new interest in the subject-matter under consideration.

After the early exercises concerned with a notational vocabulary for film-making, the teacher set the first film exercise. It was now approaching November so he split the class into three groups to consider three projects about Bonfire Night:

1. An animated documentary on Guy Fawkes
2. A still-picture sequence on the glamorous aspects of fireworks
3. A film illustrating the poem *Bonfire* by B. Holland Martin:

> The last time I saw Jimmy
> He was standing by the fire,
> Setting off his fireworks as the
> Flames rose even higher,
> I remember how he called me,
> The best friend that he knew,
> As from his open friendly hand
> A thunderflash he threw.
> The last time I saw Jimmy
> That's how it now must be
> For I have never seen him
> Since the night he blinded me.

The teacher commented as follows on the work on *Bonfire*:

'This is a short and very straightforward poem which requires little discussion other than on how to start and end the film. This was finally solved by setting the film in a park where boys are playing football, to show just how much blindness can affect the boy, by taking away from him something he loved to do.'

As in Case Study 1 (Chapter 2), the teacher encountered considerable managerial problems when the class was working in groups, and preferred to have the whole class working on one project since this led to greater cohesion and a more controlled end-product. For the Bonfire Day projects some of the groups ran into problems of weak leadership and a poor mixture so he did some rearranging, even though the children had initially been allowed to group themselves. This worked, but for the next project he selected the groups himself, ensuring that there were strong leaders (able, especially, to integrate all the activities and personalities) in each group, and that each group had somebody creative in it, to stimulate new ideas. For the film project 'Treasure Underground' (suggested by keen bottle-diggers in the class), the class worked as one group.

He had problems with being time-tabled mainly for single 35 min lessons with the film group – it was almost impossible to get anything worthwhile done in one lesson. What is more, he experienced a conflict of roles. Like the art teacher in Case Study 2 (Chapter 3), initially he felt insecure, not in control of everything all the time. It might have been better if this class had been a class on film, for then he would not have felt nagging doubts about how much English he had succeeded in teaching in each lesson.

The final exercise we shall look at in detail was devised by the teacher to encourage his pupils to look more carefully at the lyrics of a popular song – *Alone Again*. He had found that in interpreting a set of lyrics for filming pupils would readily engage in all aspects of comprehension and the techniques of literary criticism. Where, as in this song, the words explored a situation involving social stress, the pupils would in addition willingly discuss moral and social considerations.

He started with an analysis of the song lyrics using the same analytical tools as he would for examining a poem or piece of prose.

Alone Again

[Piano introduction]

In a little while from now
If I'm not feeling any less sour
I promise myself to treat myself
And visit a nearby tower
And climbing to the top
Will throw myself off
In an effort to make it clear to you
Just what it's like when you're shattered
Left standing, in the lurch, at the church

With people saying, My God it's rough she's
                                    stood him up
No point in us remaining
We may as well go home
As I did on my own. . . . Alone again,
                                    naturally.

It seems like only yesterday
I was cheerful bright and gay
Looking forward to the things I wouldn't do
The role I was about to play.
Then as if to knock me down, reality came
                                    around
And without as much as a mere touch
                    knocked me into little pieces.
Leaving me to doubt all about God in his
                                    mercy.
Who if he really does exist why did he desert
                                    me
In my hour of need I truly am indeed
Alone again . . . naturally.

It seems to me that there are more hearts
                    broken in the world
That can't be mended, left unattended.
What can we do, what can we do.

[Long guitar and piano instrumental. The
    pupils used photo montage.]

Now looking back over the years whatever
                    else that appears
I remember I cried when my father died
Never wishing to shed any tears
And at sixty-five years old, my mother God
                                    rest her soul
Couldn't understand why the only man she
                    had ever loved had been taken
Leaving her to start with a heart so badly
                                    broken
Despite encouragement from me no words
                    were ever spoken
And when she passed away I cried and cried
                                    all day
Alone again . . . naturally.

The teacher explained:
'The way that we approached this was first
of all to decide exactly what the song is about.
To do this I asked for an explanation of each
verse in simple terms. If he is going to commit
suicide, has he been jilted? Is he dwelling on
the deaths of his mother and father? I then
asked specific questions to draw out the meaning of difficult lines or sections, e.g. "Why was
he looking forward to things he wouldn't be
doing (Verse 2)? What would these be? What
was the role he was going to play?", or "How
could he encourage his mother without speaking (Verse 4)?"
'All the answers were used when we came to
the next stage: the script-writing. Although
script-writing with the whole class is rather
laborious it often produces the best results.
The way we did it here was to take the lyrics
line by line and translate the physical actions
inherent in the lines into camera shots and
angles.'
The teacher valued the opportunities presented for discussion and analysis of human
relationships, prejudice, and socially accepted
norms.
'Take the discussion in the lyrics prior to the
long instrumental piece in the middle. That
took an awful lot of working out. A tremendous amount of talking was involved. We
really dissected the lines that preceded it as a
clue to its meaning. Eventually they came to
the conclusion that the world is a very
unhappy place, so we set about looking for
pictures suggesting unhappiness. This took us
into famine, poverty, war, and all the
intricacies of human relationships. That
depth, that length and that intensity of discussion of the song would never have arisen had
they not known that they were going to film it,
or find images for film-making. I suppose their
statement through the medium of film was
permanent to them and they were committed
to getting it right.
'The final verse also produced some interesting discussion, particularly on the idea of
how best to get over the idea of two funerals.
In the end this was done by mixing the boy to
the boy and his mother (at his father's funeral)
and then superimposing a photograph of the
wedding day so that the husband became the
boy. I think this, particularly, showed how the
class had grasped the idea that in the cinema
one can move backwards and forwards in time
by means of cinematic devices such as mixing
and fading.
'In the film there are four different shifts in
time. Most of the film is set on a single day,
but there is a flashback to the night before,
then another to seven nights previously, then a

projection into the future (in which the boy, now married, is watching TV with his wife), and finally a flashback to the boy and his mother at his father's grave.

'Pupils of this age and ability do not play with time in this way in their essays. The reason why the boy in *Alone Again* felt the way he did was related to his earlier experiences and his projections into the future. This is of key importance if the pupils are to understand their own feelings – to understand that life concerns not just what happens to you but also how you recover from what happens to you and what you do about it.

'Having completed the script we moved on to filming, and here I liked the way in which the children proved their adaptability. For example, a basic close-up of feet climbing the tower was changed to three views because the steps were of wrought iron. Also when wanting to film the boy across a small lake they suggested doing it through the bars of the fencing to show that he was trapped by life (a slight cliché but at least they had thought it out).

'Another interesting point is that the children were quite surprised to find how much co-operation they got when arranging the location shots such as those in the church and the public house.

'More recently I have tried an integrated approach based on a theme. For example, the fifth years have been working on love, marriage, birth and death. At the moment they are on birth. Now with love I steered clear of using film because I thought we would get all the "schmaltzy pops", clichéd images leading to a superficial appraisal and limited expression, so here we worked through the medium of poetry, both reading and writing it. But with marriage we have gone into film, and some very sensitive creative work is developing.

'Overall, making films produced many problems which the children would not normally tackle. I think that they managed to deal with problems of continuity both in the class-room and on location. They planned the different sequences so that as each shift in time came they could end with a shot that would relate that sequence to the first shot of the next sequence. Thus at various locations they had not only to remember how the key character was dressed but also to make sure that they brought with them everything they needed.

'Timing the action to fit the dialogue or music was another problem they really had to work at. It is not easy to do this so that the overall pace of the film works but also each sequence fits its piece of dialogue or music. In some of our film-making the children wrote dialogue and chose music, which again involved them in thinking about the length and speed of different pieces.

'Pupils often try to introduce humour into a film, and although this is not easy they have some good ideas which often make them think very carefully about what sort of character they want to use. As in the analysis we did of "Alone Again", I often find this a good way to get them to consider what makes people the way they are. They are prepared to talk a lot about characterization and struggle to find the right words to express what they want to say, as well as thinking of pictures that will create the impression they want. Thinking about words and pictures together certainly helps these pupils to understand people and to develop their vocabulary and use of English.

'Studying characters in books or inventing characters of their own helps pupils to learn both about people and about themselves. They often put characters in their films in situations that build up tension. This leads them to think about what causes this tension or stress and how people resolve it. Also, they are more ready to discuss such feelings in relation to a character in a film than they are to expose their own feelings and experiences in front of the class. Their enthusiasm for filming makes these discussions much deeper than those in conventional English lessons, since they are keen to show their understanding on film. I am sure that such discussions will help them to cope better with life both inside and outside school.

'I think that these particular children (lowest ability, non-exam) also need to learn practical skills. For example, if I had a room for them I could teach them how to wallpaper it. At the same time they could make a film about how they were doing it. The film could be shown to the examination classes, who would not have time to do it themselves. All these children will in six to ten years be decorating their homes, so will really need this skill. They would both learn the practical skill and have the opportunity to develop communication skills through filming it. Such a project would require reading, writing and discussion, taking decisions and working co-operatively.

'I would like to see three or four teachers in one school who are interested in these particular kids, but whose subjects are different, teaching as a team.

'Making films with these low-ability pupils has definitely increased motivation. This has been indicated by an improvement in attendance at school, and I feel sure is related to the use of a new medium for expression. On the basis of my experience I believe this could be used for learning other subjects in the curriculum.

'The children are committed, and want to engage and use initiative. I have been using film with these sorts of children for several years and the motivation has never waned. I would love to have the opportunity of using film with my more-able classes because I am sure of its wider values, but I am restricted to the educationally accepted methods of preparing classes for examinations.'

Asked if the process the children went through in making a film was more important than the quality of the end-product, the teacher replied:

'Both the process and the product are important. As well as using film I also coach the football team. We practise five times a week and this is obviously beneficial in terms of physical fitness, team loyalty, etc., but if they lost on Saturday I'd go mad.'

School	(I)	(II)
Form entry	8	11
Catchment area	Former mining district	Rural, working class
Buildings	1911 onwards	Modern
Situation	Urban	Mining community
Size of sixth form	45	200 (approx.)

Class	(I)	(II)
Number	22	12/24
Boys/Girls	Mixed	Mixed
Streaming	None	None
Age	14–15 yr	16–18 yr/15 yr
Time per week	3–4 h	3 h/35 min
Examinations	CSE Mode 3	A-level/CEE/CSE

Teacher	(I)	(II)
Training	B.Ed.	B.A., Dip.Ed., M.Ed.
Subjects taught	English, drama	Classics, English
Years teaching	4	8
Special responsibility	Head of drama	Head of classics
Sex	Male	Male

CHAPTER 8

Drama / Media Studies : Television

This case study describes work in two schools with a CSE drama group and a sixth-form media-studies group respectively. In both cases the medium of recorded sound and vision was studied and used for its own sake, rather than to explore a traditional curriculum subject. Both teachers approached their work as a means of developing in their pupils an awareness of an audio-visual 'language'. Thus it represents a further aspect of the work we have been developing and monitoring.

In both cases the medium chosen was television. One school possessed its own three-camera studio, while the other was able to borrow a portable facility for short periods and could also travel to a central facility in a nearby college.

School I

This school is in an urban coastal area where coal-mining was until recently the dominant industry. The local community is now trying to develop and adjust to new, light industry and to cope with a fairly high level of unemployment. The school was attempting to create a lively and stimulating environment in the hope that this would challenge its pupils to be open and adaptable in their attitudes, because on leaving they would face an uncertain job market and might have to move away or continue with their education.

It was in this spirit that the drama teacher was trying to improve the communication abilities of his fourth-year CSE option pupils and to make them aware of their own potential, through their relationships with each other. He welcomed the opportunity of allowing the pupils to record their drama work, and in particular, to replay their work. With drama, the lack of a recorded end-product had always made it difficult for the pupils to assess their work objectively. He felt that many pupils were over influenced by television, mainly because they had little insight into its techniques and purposes, and he hoped that the television work might increase their critical awareness of this powerful medium.

For their first practical experience the pupils were taken to a studio in a college thirteen miles away. They were introduced to the machinery of a three-camera studio and to the various stages of production, from early discussion and planning to recording. They then worked together to record a prepared script. For the pupils' second practical lesson the Project team arranged for a small portable studio to be taken to the school. The equipment was transported by car to the school and set up in the school hall, which was the room allocated to the class in the time-table.

Before the class arrived, the teacher asked us not to insist on the use of a particular recording style or format but to allow an appropriate format to emerge as a result of the pupils' work. He also wanted to allow the pupils to work without writing a script unless they themselves saw a need for it. In the light of his overall social and intellectual objectives, he favoured giving free rein to the pupils' own initiative and allowing as much experimentation as possible, because he felt it to be important for the pupils to generate their own goals, to analyse their own failures and gradually to build up experience by trial and error. The Project team accepted this general strategy, but suggested that, if the pupils consistently failed to achieve anything during the afternoon, it might be destructive to morale, and they might need guidance at certain stages in order to experience success. As the teacher was familiar with the group and could gauge the pupils' progress, it was left to him to ask a member of the Project team to step in and offer guidance whenever he felt this might be useful.

The pupils entered the hall to find the equipment already set up. At one end of the hall were the videotape-recorder, vision-mixer, sound-mixer and two monitors on tables. The rest of the hall contained the two cameras and the class. The teacher started by gathering the class around him in a circular group on the floor. He then led the session by asking them what they had planned during the previous lesson. They replied that they had divided into two groups and had worked on improvisations which they wanted to televise. He asked the class whether they wanted to televise both improvisations, or whether they felt that there would be time to televise only one. The class decided that they would probably have time to record only one improvisation. At this point a spokesman for each group emerged spontaneously and described their group's ideas. The class then discussed these and selected the improvisation that they were going to concentrate on. (It was interesting to note that the improvisation changed when the whole class became involved. Some of the pupils questioned felt that it was improved by the reshaping and focus generated by the participation of the whole class.)

The teacher then asked the class what technical aspects they felt they needed to consider. They went through the various technical roles and allocated jobs to different members of the class. Although they decided among themselves who was to take on which role, the teacher's presence within the group (watching the activity and occasionally questioning decisions or encouraging participation by more retiring pupils) helped create an atmosphere of supportive co-operation which contributed to the productiveness of the session. At this stage they had had only two hours' television experience, but by the end of this second two-hour session they were sufficiently

familiar with the medium that the drama and the recording of the drama on television were becoming a single, continuous experimental activity. Perhaps this was aided by having the control area, cameras and action in the same room. If the studio and control room are separate, children in the studio tend not to know what is happening in the control room, while children in the control room see only the activity selected by the cameras rather than the overall activity within the studio.

Following the allocation of responsibilities the teacher asked the pupils to split up into smaller groups to prepare themselves for the practical session. The actors moved away to discuss the action, making a number of modifications to the original ideas. The camera crew went to the equipment and busied themselves in becoming familiar once more with the various controls and actions, framing pictures and focusing lenses in an effort to reinforce the knowledge of their first studio session. The control team reminded themselves of mixing and cutting, sound control and operation of the video-recorder, whilst the director re-established her control over the vision-mixer and cameras by giving instructions and monitoring the response on the three television screens in front of her. The scene engendered a feeling of self-directed professionalism with all pupils active and absorbed in preparation for a television production.

The teacher called for attention, and recording began. Seizing upon the opportunity the teacher had created, the pupil director took over. Action was called for from the actors and they began their scene in front of the cameras. The cameramen tried hard to follow the unfolding action, moving cameras from one position to the next, refocusing, zooming and panning, in an attempt to predict the actors' next moves, with increasing desperation. The director's position was even more hopeless since she ordered cuts from one camera to the other, to avoid recording an out-of-focus shot, only to find that the second camera was moving between one shot and the next. She had to halt the whole process, then gathered all the pupils together and complained bitterly that she did not know what was happening and therefore could not co-ordinate the recording of the work. The cameramen chimed in that they had no idea what was going to happen

next and that made it nearly impossible to follow the action. The whole group discussed the
problem. The teacher suggested that some sort
of script might be the answer. The pupils all
agreed, at least in principle, that it would have
been far better to have started with a script.
However time was moving on and, conscious
that the equipment was at the school for that
afternoon only, the pupils felt that they would
have to forego the security of a script and
attempt to capture at least a small piece of
their improvisation by scripting as they went
along.

So began a process, not previously observed
by the Project team, in which a recording of
drama was planned and organized without the
use of a story-board or script. The director and
camera team asked the performers to enact the
first few moments of the improvisation. When
they had watched this action they discussed
how they would record it. In the first sequence
a schoolgirl was being ostracized by the rest of
her class. The scene began with the girl sitting
on the school steps (some steps from the hall
floor to the stage) whilst the class, as a group,
passed unkind comments about her behind
her back. It was decided that one camera
should film the girl on the steps whilst the
other filmed the group of children in the
class-room. The pupils took up their positions
and the recording began again, but this time
the cameramen knew exactly what they had to
record, and the control team – the director,
vision-mixer and sound-mixer – knew exactly
what to expect. When the action began the
director selected the picture of the girl on her
own and slowly mixed through to the group,
holding a superimposition for a short while so
that the audience could see the class talking
about the girl and at the same time see her
reaction. The director then asked the vision-
mixer to lose the superimposition so that just
the class was shown on the screen. She
requested the cameraman responsible for this
shot to close in on individual faces and pan
from one to another as they took part in the
general talking. The scene ended with a slow
mix back to the girl on her own.

For this first run-through the pupils acted
their parts but did not speak, feeling that this
would lessen the complexity of the piece. The
pupils did speak the second time and the
cameraman responsible for the group shot
embellished his contribution with more careful
and intricate movement of his camera.

At the end of this second take the pupils
asked to see what they had recorded. The
video-recordist wound back the tape and the
group clustered around a monitor to watch.
They discussed the mixing and superimposition techniques used by the director and
vision-mixer and gave their approval. They
discussed the camera work and the acting, all
with little guidance from the teacher, and
then, expressing general satisfaction with the
recording, moved on to the next scene. The
whole group discussed the action, then the
technical recorders watched the performers
act out the agreed scene. There followed a discussion between the actors and the recorders
on what the cameras ought to film, then a
further recording session in which their decisions were put into practice. After this they
once more viewed their results, discussed their
strengths and weaknesses and moved on to the
next section.

The decisions they took could have been
written down, and indeed, if they had wished
to record their drama continuously from
beginning to end, would certainly have had to
have been written down. However, the series
of short recordings which they made displayed
an increasing mastery of the medium as well
as providing a recording of an interesting and
successful piece of drama. They had introduced their subject, developed the relationships of the characters, brought the drama to a
climax just before the end of the sequence, and
had finally resolved the conflict between the
class and individual at the close of their programme. The success of this dramatic shape,
intuitively developed by the pupils, did much
to aid the children's success in recording and
analysing their finished product.

It was noticeable that the variety and precision of the language exchange during the
preparation and organization of the work was
far superior to that of the recorded piece itself:
the pupils seemed fluent at informing, negotiating, arguing, suggesting and giving and taking
instructions. Whether this was because the
choice of subject-matter did not readily lend
itself to a more varied and complex oral
exchange or whether further guidance and
encouragement from the teacher would have
stimulated a richer language performance is

unclear. There was certainly added self-consciousness on the part of the pupils during recording. Some pupils felt that this was because the recorded words were not said and lost but said and recorded.

The class was pleased with the afternoon's work. There was a satisfied feeling in the room. Certainly as far as the process was concerned they had successfully unified all the various aspects of the work into a product that could be 'held' and analysed. Also, the lessons to be learned from it could be used as a starting-point for their next project.

After this session the teacher said that three main aspects of the work had impressed him.

1. THE VALUE OF THE MEDIUM

The use of a recording medium focused the pupils' thinking and expression. It made them structure their work in a disciplined way. It also enabled them to 'hold' their dramatic statement so that they could look at it and analyse what they had achieved. A new range of experiences was offered and the pupils became more conscious and critical of their own individual parts in the activity.

2. THE EMERGENCE OF AN UNTAPPED KNOWLEDGE OF MEDIA EXPRESSION

These pupils watch a lot of television and one would expect them to be influenced by the values expounded in what they see. One would also expect them to follow storylines and relate to particular characters, but perhaps what one would not expect is the amount they subconsciously pick up about the medium itself. The medium uses a 'vocabulary of sound and vision'. This may not as yet be fully apparent to the youngsters, but when they took a camera into their hands and made their first visual statement by putting a frame around a person or object, they composed pictures of surprising quality influenced at a subconscious level by this same 'vocabulary'. Their sensitivity in the use of the long shot to establish a person and his relationship to other people, or the close-up to get right into a character, occurred with hardly any formal instruction. The continuity between shots and camera movements and angles revealed an immense store of knowledge about the conventions of using sound and vision as a language. It was as though they had been reading books every night for several years then had been suddenly asked to write a story.

3. THE RELATIONSHIP BETWEEN MAKING AND LOOKING AT TELEVISION PROGRAMMES

In many ways this is the reverse of the previous point. Looking at television seems to have had an effect on the pupils' making of television programmes and similarly the making has affected their watching. It has been quite dramatic. Before their first visit to the studio their comments about what they had seen on television were fairly naive: 'I did like such and such a programme', or 'Oh, wasn't he nice'. However, after that visit this completely changed, and their comments were much more searching: 'Isn't that clever because . . .', or 'I wonder how that was done'. In fact it was not unlike the change experienced during a course of literary study.

Another point that was very evident was the children's growing understanding of bias in the making of television programmes. Many of these children had regarded what they saw on television as gospel truth and it would never have entered their heads that someone might be expressing a point of view or even telling a downright lie. But when they were making their own programme, on a number of occasions they were faced with a choice between alternative ways of presenting various points,

each of which gave a different version of the truth. They were very aware of these choices in their discussions, and this, combined with their more critical attitude in general towards television, was one of the most important aspects of this work.

After this first dramatic work the teacher felt that the pupils should move on to a more structured and extended project. His aim was to stimulate study of an English text by making the pupils organize their response to a novel into a television programme. He intended to use drama to deepen awareness of the text as well as to act as the mode of production.

The lesson began with the teacher explaining to the pupils that they were going to study the book *Walkabout* and use any ideas which it gave them to make a television programme. The teacher then read a short synopsis of part of the book which emphasized the differences between the worlds of two American children and an Aborigine featured in the book. The children became fascinated by the differing values assigned to everyday situations which they had normally taken for granted, and a lively discussion ensued which explored the way in which civilized and technological societies reduce the survival capability of an individual if he suddenly has to be self-sufficient.

Intent on building upon the initial interest shown by the pupils, the teacher decided to explore the idea of primitive living in more depth, and to do so employed techniques of improvised drama. He asked the pupils to consider the synopsis of the book and their own discussions and to think of some activity that was central to primitive culture and survival. Then he asked them to describe how they would act out this activity.

The pupils thought that death was a crucial factor for primitive people and that enacting the rituals that might surround it would give them a deeper insight into primitive life. They felt that a death in a primitive tribe or community would be met with a far more open expression of feeling than is the case in our society and that there would be rituals surrounding such an event which encouraged this free expression of feeling and at the same time united the tribe in its everyday struggle for survival. The teacher encouraged them to pursue this theme, and to visualize an activity that would symbolize this for them. The group decided to stand in a circle around a body representing the dead person. They felt that the circle would symbolize their togetherness and the body would provide a shared focus for their feelings, in both spatial and emotional terms. When the teacher prompted the group for ideas for further activities one pupil suggested humming. The teacher asked for clarification. 'Humming, all humming the same note,' replied the pupil.

'What about the act of burial?' the teacher went on to ask. In the corner of the hall lay a number of leafy twigs that he had brought in to be available for the television drama if the pupils wished. At this point, one pupil reacted to the teacher's cue (a cue, incidentally, that reflected the teacher's assessment that the developing ritual needed movement to deepen further the pupils' sense of involvement). Noticing the twigs, the pupil asked if they could each place one of these twigs on the body until it was completely covered.

The pupils sat in a circle and the teacher hummed a note then moved around the circle getting each pupil to hum the same note. Through this they had emotionally committed themselves (they were doing it in public) to the group ritual. Having passed completely around the closed circle of pupils, the teacher encouraged each one in turn to pick up a branch and to stand with it raised, pointing to the sky, until each pupil was standing, humming and contributing to the leafy cone above the dead Aborigine's body. Then, slowly, in turn, each pupil lowered his branch on to the dead Aborigine's body until he lay completely covered from the sun. The bell went and the first session ended.

The teacher had planned the whole activity to last for four weeks using one afternoon each week, but in deference to the Project's wish to film some of the activity with 16 mm equipment, he had agreed, after consultation with his headmaster, to concentrate the activity into two complete days. The first session, therefore, ended at the beginning of the lunch break and the second began after lunch.

At the beginning of the second session the teacher presented the pupils with a framework for structuring their television programme. He suggested that they should consider using a narrator, dramatic sequences and an interview sequence (where characters from the dramatic sequences would be interviewed). He reminded them about the production of still pictures and background music, and recapped on the roles of the narrator, actors and technical crews.

After a long discussion about the overall shape of their programme the class decided to break up into four groups. The first group would research and script the narrator's passages, produce any still-picture sequences that might be shown during the narrator's pieces, and finally look for the opening music.

The second group was going to concentrate on the dramatic inserts. They decided that the first should represent the children's reaction immediately after the plane crash in *Walkabout*. A second dramatic insert would deal with the meeting with the Aborigine boy, and a short final piece would show the children getting instructions from an Aborigine adult on how to get out of the bush and back to civilization.

The third group was to work on an interview sequence in which a group of pupils would interview the characters from the dramatic inserts.

The fourth group was to form the technical crew and move among the other groups advising on how to record each sequence.

Desks were grouped together to form working spaces. One space contained a tape-recorder and some tapes of music and sound effects. Another contained paper and pens for graphics and a slide projector to enable two of the girls to draw graphics from a projected slide image, while the third space contained a range of books and material the teacher thought might be useful, covering Australia, the Aborigines and related topics.

The pupils began researching and script-writing, producing still pictures, selecting music, and developing and rehearsing dramatic inserts. They continued this activity until the end of the session. The teacher concluded the session by asking the pupils to read any parts of the book that they were not familiar with that evening, and himself undertook to tidy up and duplicate their script for the next session.

In the next session the pupils made final modifications to their scripts and then began to visualize how they would organize the recording to film their intended programme. Once again the television equipment was brought to the school and the pupils helped to assemble the camera stands, control panel and all the necessary connections. When the three-camera studio was complete and the pupils had moved to their various positions to remind themselves of controls and scripts, the pupil director called for attention. Satisfying herself that everyone was ready and aware of their various responsibilities, she started the first studio rehearsal.

The first sequence was an introduction that consisted of a series of pictures of Aborigine people accompanied first by music and then by the narrator's voice introducing the programme as a study of the book *Walkabout*. Towards the end of the introduction, in which the audience was told about the first few chapters of the book, the cameras switched to the narrator herself. After she had prepared her audience for the dramatic scenes she was faded from the screen and the first dramatic scene began. Two cameras had swung round from the still pictures and had moved into position. As camera 3 became live, camera 1 (on the narrator) also swung into position to offer the director a further view of the first scene.

The first scene showed the two children in the book huddled under a bush (the branches of the earlier drama) with the younger complaining of hunger. Cameras 1 and 3 provided most of the shots, and as the narrator's voice was heard explaining the children's situation and preparing the audience for the arrival of an Aborigine boy, camera 2 moved back and away from the scene, swinging to its left in preparation for the entrance of the boy. Camera 2 followed the boy into the original scene and then, as cameras 1 and 3 took over, moved once again to position itself for the next scene.

As an old Aboriginal lady entered from the other side of the set the director cut from camera 1 to camera 2. Again camera 2 followed the old lady in, and then with camera 3 offered a sequence of shots to the director. Meanwhile camera 1 pulled away and repositioned itself on the narrator to cover her final statement at the end of the drama.

The final scene was set up on the opposite side of the hall from the narrator. While the narrator was on vision, cameras 2 and 3 swung away to their right to cover the final interview sequence, in which three pupils interviewed the actors and actresses, still in their roles. This step-by-step rehearsal completed the morning session and the pupils broke for lunch.

The last session consisted of a final rehearsal, a recording and a playback. The pupils were delighted with their work, which for the first time they could see as a whole. Their results reflected the professionalism of the day's activity.

Impressions of the Head of English
During the final session the Head of English spent a short time watching and afterwards made a short note of his first impressions.

'As I walked into S Block hall during a video-recording session I had a slightly uneasy sense of trespassing, aided by red lights glowing on top of cameras, and a carpet of wires. I had the impression of walking into a studio. Then I noticed that among all the equipment there were pupils doing things, quietly engrossed. There was a break to watch the take, and the kids seemed keen to show me what they had done, made me very welcome in fact. They watched critically. Then there was a run-through of two pages of script, for my benefit, I suppose. Once the idea was put forward, the kids were in position, taking covers off lenses, putting headphones on, pinning up captions, etc. No orders were given at this point, just some reminders. There was a strong sense of a lot of things going on at once, with pupils therefore very much on their own, with precise responsibilities. The videotape was then viewed, and the children were very conscious when their mistakes appeared on screen. Shirley (the director) received about six separate sets of data (three camera monitors, master monitor, headphones, eyes) and talked through the mouthpiece and through her hands – driving.

'Apart from Shirley's, very few words were used during the run-through, though the words which were used were new, the sentences brief, concrete, direct. There was some reversal of roles compared with normal school behaviour – leaders being led, etc.'

Talk of Girl Director in Studio

To elaborate on the activity of the director we include the following extract produced by placing a tape-recorder in the lines between the director and the studio crew.

Director: Hold it there [to camera 1]. Aye, that's it. Tell him to keep it like that. Right, Copey, keep it like that. Right, keep it like that for God's sake. Who's that camera? Go on. What's the matter now? What's the marra? What you done now? Eh, man [laughs]!
Is Mr G [the teacher] not coming up? Alan, ask Mr G to come up.
God, I'm dreading this [to vision-mixer]. Well tell her to keep 'em [reference captions] still [to camera 2].
Copey, tell Mr G he's got to come up [to camera 1, sounding worried]. I'll go mad if he doesn't. Ah man, Copey, what's happened to your camera?

Pupil [entering]: Mr G not coming up with you. You're on your own.

Director: I don't really want to be [worried]. Oh man. What's happened now?
[She's told to move on because the actors might get bored.]
What? Eh? Peter gonna pan across [to camera 2]. Peter, get that caption in

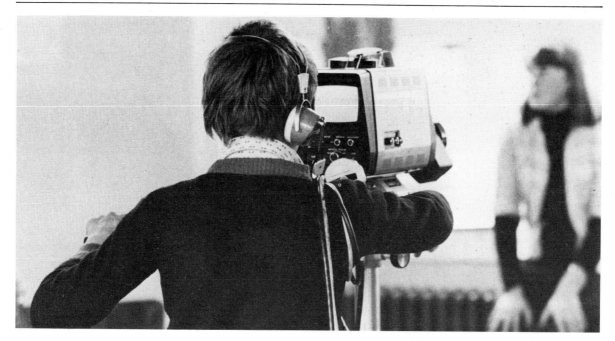

[whisper]. Get ready, then. Copey, will ye
. . . that's it. Hold it there. Right. Starting
now.

Videotape Operator: Sorry – tell us when it
starts.

Director: Right [to videotape operator].
Copey, tell them to stand by [to camera 2].
Starts in one minute. Right. Start from
'blank': 10, 9, 8, 7, 6, 5, 4, 3, 2, 1, action!
[Sign to fade up music].
Right, Peter, Paul, pan across to the next
one [from one caption to next]. Slowly,
that's it [to cameras 2 and 3].
Slowly, slowly. Camera 1 [signal to fade
music].
Cut to camera 2 [to vision-mixer].
Cut to camera 1 [to vision-mixer]. Paul,
Peter, are you getting Leslie looking over at
. . . [to cameras 2 and 3]? Follow her over
when she looks over right, now follow her
over. There, right.
Cut to camera 1, 3. That's it [to
vision-mixer]. Right, 3, follow him over
to Leslie [to camera 3]. Get the [grey] in.
Get the grey in. That's it.
Cut to camera 1 [to camera 3 then
vision-mixer].
Back to 3 [to vision-mixer]. Camera 1,
go round and get a . . . like . . . a side shot.
Oh! Really close up. Camera 1.
Camera 2 [cut to].

The Teacher's Viewpoint

'Because information and entertainment are packaged on television, one of the big advantages of allowing pupils to use this medium themselves is that a traditional body of information (the curriculum) can be presented in a manner which is more attractive, more manageable and more in line with the pupils' way of life.

'One of the difficulties with book-based learning is that it tends not to encourage group activity. Although the method of this Project provides scope for the child who wants to work by himself (do research, for example), there comes a point where he must work with other people. The pupils said over and over again that they feel that they are working to help the group. Thus a more-able pupil who is doing research and getting deeply involved with the subject has the satisfaction of knowing that he is not only benefiting personally but also doing his bit for his group. This feeling of mutual dependency gives them a tremendous lift.

'As a result of the social atmosphere the pupils do not just improve their reading vocabulary: they also improve orally as they have to explain their findings to the group and justify them if necessary. They use a vocabulary which every pupil knows but which is not often employed in more traditional lessons.

'Consider another example of the social aspect of this activity. If one cameraman decides that he has had enough and, for example, is going to sit around for half an hour, it affects the whole team. Then a particular vocabulary for negotiation arises from necessity. In this type of work the pupil director can see that one camera is not responding. This happened in one session. The girl director got very agitated because the cameraman became giggly for a few minutes, and as a result everybody suffered. The other cameramen were getting quite annoyed with him and he was put under a certain amount of pressure. However, it was not a destructive sort of pressure but perhaps the sort of pressure he will meet at work. He was told to stop messing about and to concentrate on the job that had to be completed. This peer-group sense of responsibility and the language the pupils developed to handle each other were interesting aspects of the activity.

'I found that my role as a teacher had to change considerably because the children were in a position of greater responsibility. I don't mean greater responsibility because they were using a £200 camera, but greater responsibility for their own learning. Thus what was needed was a watching eye rather than a directing hand. I have merely been going from group to group to advise and check, to point them in the direction that they were trying to go, to offer resources, or to deepen an area of inquiry. Instead of telling them exactly what to do, I had to listen to what they thought was important and guide rather than direct.

'Because of my new role and the social framework of the activity, I have gained some interesting insight into the pupils' personalities and capabilities. The most striking case is a girl who was rather a discipline problem in school. Her success with this type of work was due to a combination of things. One was the fact that she was placed in a position of responsibility and could use her energy and strength of character in a constructive manner. She had the ability to organize and control people – the ability to communicate with people in a positive way. The opportunity to demonstrate such skills does not usually arise in the class-room, and these qualities are neglected. An ability to control people, manage them and deal with them in a way which is not going to offend them should be developed by schools. Industry certainly recognizes its value. It was a major revelation to me that this girl, who had failed in the accepted sense in school, had these qualities and was able to put them to full use. She developed a knack of telling people what she wanted them to do in no uncertain terms, but at the same time the other pupils responded in a most positive and co-operative way. So she developed an interest in school, and thus in learning, which she did not have before. Admittedly, initially she was more concerned with organizing the activity and making the project work rather than learning about the subject. However, owing to her central role, during discussions or writing up she slowly managed to get involved in the academic side of the work.

'This type of work forced the pupils to know why they were doing things. One vital development of their drama work was that they became more visually perceptive when talking about what they were going to do.

'In a full afternoon session, which usually began with discussion of what they were going to do, concentration began to lapse by break time. I wondered whether to continue or offer a different kind of activity after break, which is what I normally had to do, but I was amazed to find that after break they were almost as fresh as they had been at the beginning of the session. They were ready to translate the earlier work of the afternoon into a recorded format with renewed zest and enthusiasm.

'The children were getting an end-product within minutes, which was bound to reinforce what they were doing. This also enabled them to be critical of what they had done but at the same time get a certain degree of satisfaction from their work.

'Also, many pupils turned out to have abilities which I did not expect. The old labels 'more able' or 'less able' no longer applied. Different expertise emerged because of the many different activities involved. This also changed the attitudes of many pupils to other pupils in their group. The need for interdependency heightened everyone's awareness of and respect for everyone else's skills.

'Finally, this way of working made the pupils widen their understanding and knowledge of specific subjects. They needed all-round accurate knowledge of a topic before they could explain and televise it. For example, during their study of the book *Walkabout* they requested numerous books on Australia and Aborigines in addition to the text they were exploring. This led to a lot of fruitful research and discovery. They were highly motivated because they wanted to know the answers to questions they themselves were asking. I doubt whether an ordinary lesson on Australia or the Aborigines would have encouraged such fervour.'

School II

The mass media and mass communications have become a recognized area of study in academic circles only recently. In a secondary school in a northern town a teacher of classics has developed a course of study to encourage the most-able pupils of the school to consider this important aspect of their environment. Alongside, he has developed a shorter course for a second group of sixth-form pupils which follows a pilot CEE (Certificate of Extended Education) programme. The more-able sixth-form group met as an option group for one afternoon a week over a period of a year and the CEE group for one hour ten minutes per week for a period of just six weeks. For the first group mass communications were studied alongside A-level subjects, while for the second the study of mass communications formed part of an integrated programme of further education. Both courses were centred around practical television production with emphasis on the development of a wide range of practical communication skills. The teacher provided the following syllabuses for the two courses of study.

COMMUNICATIONS SYLLABUS FOR A-LEVEL
PUPILS: TWO-YEAR COURSE
A. Theory
1. Historical development of mass communications
2. Need for large audiences
3. Pressures towards standardization
4. Effects on local culture
5. Impact on social and political attitudes

B. Practice
1. *Television techniques*

Techniques required for operation of a television installation:

(a) *Camera skills:* shots, tracking, crabbing, use of zoom lens
(b) *Production skills:* cutting, mixing, effects
(c) *Operation of videotape-recorders:* editing, videocassette-recorders
(d) *Operation of sound systems:* tape-recorders
(e) *Studio lighting:* arrangement of lights
(f) *Outside broadcasts:* portable camera

2. *Programme content*

Techniques required for the preparation of material for a television programme:

(a) *Script-writing:* use of television terms and abbreviations, organization and presentation of script
(b) *Making and using graphics for television:* design and presentation of captions
(c) *Incorporation of music and background sound*
(d) *Credits:* choices available

3. *Presentation skills*

Techniques required for appearance in a television programme:

(a) *Direct presentation to camera:* organization of material to be televised (personal and impersonal)
(b) *Interview techniques:* positions of interviews, 'camera' script effect
(c) *Dramatic presentation:* organization of actors, effective use of studio space
(d) *Voice-over techniques*

4. *Evaluation of television programmes*

Pupils will be required to evaluate current television programmes with special reference to:

(a) Suitability of subject
(b) Methods of presentation
(c) Programme content

Special productions will be chosen for study from all the main categories of television, e.g. *documentaries, natural history, popular serials, news-casting, comedy.*

5. *Special project: practical*

The creation of a television programme. Pupils should submit one of the following:
(a) A complete written script, including research notes
(b) Graphics to illustrate a script
(c) A videotaped programme produced by pupils not less than *ten* minutes or more than *twenty* minutes in length

CERTIFICATE OF EXTENDED EDUCATION:
TELEVISION AND COMMUNICATIONS SYLLABUS
The aims of this course are:

1. To increase awareness and understanding of the concepts of broadcasting
2. To encourage a critical approach to television programmes
3. To promote knowledge of the basic techniques required for the operation of a television installation
4. To work co-operatively to produce a short videotaped programme

It is hoped that during each six-week session the pupils will become conversant with the techniques and skills listed below and thereby produce their own videotaped programmes. It is envisaged that in so doing each pupil will not only develop a more critical attitude to television programmes but also realize the benefits of co-operation.

1. *Television techniques*

(a) Camera skills
(b) Production skills
(c) Operation of sound systems
(d) Studio lighting

2. *Programme content*

(a) Script-writing
(b) Making and using graphics for television
(c) Incorporation of music and background sound
(d) Credits

3. *Presentation skills*

(a) Direct presentation to camera
(b) Dramatic presentation
(c) Voice-over techniques

4. *Evaluation of television programmes*

(a) Suitability of subject
(b) Methods of presentation
(c) Programme content

The school was one of several in the area that had television studios of their own. In this case the studio consisted of three television cameras, controls and viewing facilities. It was housed in a converted class-room which had one end partitioned off as a control room. A large window allowed the pupils working in the control room to see what was taking place in the studio. The whole facility was maintained by a school technician with skills in electronics, who was also responsible for the recording and playback of broadcast programmes throughout the school. This was assisted by a system of cable links between the studio control room and a number of class-rooms equipped with playback monitors. These could also be used to play back programmes made by staff or pupils when required. A small library of videotapes and graphics had been built up and was often used in the making of programmes. The studio was entered through the control room, and there was a dramatic change of atmosphere as one moved from the business and gadgetry of the control room into the hushed professional atmosphere of the studio itself. It was in this environment that the pupils worked on their mass-communications course.

In both courses the emphasis was on practical work, with theory and class discussion introduced mainly when the teacher felt that it arose out of the practical activity or would feed further practical work.

In many ways the short course followed the same pattern as the longer one although at a more superficial level and with a number of the activities redesigned to ensure completion within the shorter teaching session. The pupils underwent a thorough introduction to the practical activity of programme designing and production, with the result that many felt that the mystique that often surrounds television production had significantly lessened. In their work, they went through a process of discussion, negotiation, research, etc., similar to those in many of the schools, and managed to master the medium to a level at which they could make coherent and meaningful statements. The pupils enjoyed their lessons although a number stated that they could be very hard work. Most agreed that it had been an enlightening experience and one very relevant to their own extensive contact with mass media in everyday life.

It was, however, in the course designed for the most-able pupils, the A-level option group, that the teacher was able to take the study to a depth which he found most satisfying. Here the study of the television medium was quite rigorous as well as including a number of complex production activities. The group explored the general role of the mass media in society and in particular concerned itself with the media's psychological and sociological implications, relating these to examples of actual programmes. They explored television genres, performed detailed critical appraisals of existing programmes and, perhaps most rewarding of all, used the knowledge thus gained in the creation of their own television programmes.

In order to give a more detailed picture of the pupils' activity, three aspects are illustrated here. The first is part of an early discussion in which a group of pupils were sorting out their ideas prior to script-writing. The second is an extract from their fourth and final draft of the script, while the third is an example of an early session in which the teacher was attempting to stimulate a critical approach to television and build a foundation for practical work.

The Planning Discussion

The pupils' idea was to produce a programme about war-gaming in the hope that it would generate an interest in the subject in those who viewed the final programme. First they discussed what was to be said:

Pupil A: O.K. then, so we are going to say. . . .
Pupil B: You can't have much.
A: Well, it's relative.
Pupil C: Here we have the ancients' period.
B: Yeah, the ancients – a period of highly disciplined armies.
C: Well a lot of them were.
A: You could show war-games between Romans and Ancient Britons.

Later they talked about the practical implications:

B: If you know how much noise it makes, O.K.
A: Camera 1 picks up the presenter most of the time, doesn't it? So if we have the presenter 1 on this side. Then presenter 2 over here. . . .
C: Chart.
A: Pardon.
C: Chart.
A: Chart what?
C: Chart. We'd decided before, haven't we, that presenter 1 was supposed to go over.
A: To the chart?
C: Yeah.
A: He's going to be trapped by the camera. We'll have to change the position of the presenters.
B: So camera 1 will follow him. . . .

Still later they went back to what was to be said:

C: I think we've got right up to date.
A: Fantasy war-gaming covers virtually anything.
Pupil D: Yes.
A: Examples of it are. . . .
B: Middle Earth based on. . . .
C: J. R. R. Tolkien.
A: Examples of it are based on Tolkien's books.

B: Lord of the Rings and *The Hobbit*.
C: There's only one battle in *The Hobbit*.
A: Lord of the Rings offers a lot of scope.
B: With fantasy, then, anything goes.
D: How long's this science-fiction war-gaming been going on?

The Final Script

This extract shows part of the pupils' fourth and final script. In this instance they produced a first script which listed the subjects to be covered and then a second that detailed what was to be seen at each stage. The third script took the information from the previous two and worked them into a story-board format. Finally this was translated into a shooting script giving details of sound and vision and all the relevant instructions for the recording session. The title of the programme was 'The World of War-gaming'.

Shot	Camera action	Video mix	Audio mix	Script
1	Cam. 3: figures Cam: 4: caption 'The World of War-gaming'	Cam. 3 super 4 on S/FX Thro. A and B bank F.U. A and B bank	F.U. phono./tape	
2	Pres. 1: L.S., M.C.U.	F.O. A and B bank F.U. L bank (Cam. 2) Set up Cam. 2 over 1 on mix	F.O. phono./tape F.U. Mic. 2	This programme is intended to give you an insight into the popular and growing hobby of war-gaming. We hope it will encourage you to find out more about this activity, and to participate in it for life.
3	Pres. 2: M.C.U.	Cut 1		An important misconception held by many people is that war-gaming is grown men playing with toys.
4	Table: M.S.	Cut 3		That is, a bit like this. . . .
5	Pres. 2: M.C.U.	Cut mix (Cam. 2)		Nothing could be further from the truth. War-gaming, in fact, is fighting campaigns (and battles) in such a way that everything will fit on the top of a table.
6	Napoleonic figures: C.U.	Mix 1		It is often fairly complex, and based on a strict set of rules which give quite reasonable historical accuracy.
7	Pres. 2: M.C.U.	Mix 2 Set up Cam. 4 over 1 on S/FX		The best way to start is to choose a period of history, a figure and ground scale to which your pocket and time will stretch. Then buy some rules, find an opponent – and start fighting.

Shot	Camera action	Video mix	Audio mix	Script
8	Pres. 1: C.U., M.S.	Cut 1	F.O. Mic. 2 F.U. Mic. 1	My friend referred to scales, rules and periods, but what are they? Quite simply they are the three pillars upon which all war-gaming rests. Well, let's run through each one in order before showing examples of a war-game.
9	Caption: 'Historical Periods'	Cut S/FX Cam. 3		
10	Pres. 1: M.S.	Wipe 1 Set up 2		In history there are many examples of one group of men attacking another. The earliest examples of this which can be represented in war-games are the many . . .
11	Ancient figures: C.U.	Wipe 2		. . . wars between the Greeks, Phoenicians and Persians, later followed by the Romans when they were building their empire.
12	Pres. 1: M.S., M.C.U.	Cut 1		An important requirement for many war-games is that the armies of the period they choose to represent should have some degree of organization. There is, therefore, little until medieval times, . . .
13	Medieval figures: C.U.	Cut 2		. . . when there is a chance of testing the English yew longbow against the knights of France.
14	Pres. 1: M.C.U.	Cut 1 Set up 3 Cam. 3 over 1 on S/FX		The struggle between the emergent nations of Europe provides many fascinating reconstructions, but the most popular war of independence is that of America.

Shot	Camera action	Video mix	Audio mix	Script
15	Caption Photograph	Cut 1 S/FX (Cam. 3)	F.O. Mic. 1 F.U. phono./tape	
16	Pres. 2: M.C.U.	Wipe 1 Change 3 to 2 on S/FX	F.O. phono./tape F.U. Mic. 2	The American War of Independence provides one of the few opportunities for the war-gamer . . .
17	American War, Indian figures: C.U.	Wipe 2		. . . to pit the brash American against the phlegmatic Briton, with added interest in the form of Red Indians, Germans and Frenchmen.
18	Pres. 2: C.U.	Wipe 1		By far the most popular period the world over is the Napoleonic era, with large numbers of brightly coloured . . .
19	Caption	Cut 3		. . . uniforms locked in mortal struggle. Men and horses of all nationalities . . .
20	Napoleonic figures: U.C.U., pan across	Cut 2		. . . swarming across the battle-fields of Europe and the world.
21	Pres. 1: C.U., M.C.U.	Cut mix (Cam. 1)	F.O. Mic. 2 F.O. Mic. 1	From the seventeenth century to the late 1950s there were many wars between the European colonial powers as they fought for control of areas of great natural wealth.
22	Pres. 1: M.C.U.	Mix 2		It is because of diversity in time and nations that this forms an important area of study.
23	Pres. 1: M.C.U.	Cut 1		For some people, however, this is not enough. They enjoy themselves by turning to a future of wars between worlds and galaxies.
24	Fantasy figures: C.U.	Cut mix (Cam. 2)		Still others turn to making their own worlds and people, endowing them with many strange and magical powers.

Shot	Camera action	Video mix	Audio mix	Script
25	Pres. 1: M.C.U., C.U.	Mix 1		It is in this branch of the hobby that the protagonists not only pray to the gods, but enlist their help!
26	Pres. 2: M.L.S.	Cut 3 Fade to black	 F.O. Mic. 1	Most non-historical war-games are based on books which are quite freely available: for example much fantasy war-gaming is based upon the writings of J.R.R. Tolkien. So as you can see, with a little imagination, anything goes.
27	Pres. 1: C.U. (Cam. 1)	F.O. Cam. 1 Set up 4 over 1 on mix	F.U. Mic. 1	Simply by looking at the figures available in any good model shop you can see one of the biggest problems facing any new war-gamer. What size of figures should he use?
28	Caption 1: 'Scales' (Cam. 4)	Cut mix (Cam. 4)		
29	Pres. 1: C.U., M.S. showing figures on table (Cam. 1)	Mix 1		Ever since military modelling and war-gaming became popular in the middle of the last century, an incredible number of scales have arisen. Fortunately only three or four of these scales have survived for table-top land battles. We have here examples of some of these scales.
30	Figures (men): C.U. (Cam. 2)	Cut 2		Two are used for war-gaming, the third for modelling.
31	Pres. 1: M.C.U. (Cam. 1)	Cut 1 Change 2 for 1 on mix		A more vivid example of the difference in size between each scale is shown in these four tanks.
32	Tanks (5 mm): C.U. (Cam. 2)	Cut 2 Set up 4 super 2		They all represent the German Tiger 1 tank. The 5 mm scale is most often . . .

Shot	Camera action	Video mix	Audio mix	Script
33	Tanks crabbing across (20, 25, 54 mm): C.U. (Cam. 2) Caption: 'Tiger 1 tank' (Cam. 4)	Cut mix (Cam. 4 super 2)		. . . used in modern warfare games in order to accommodate gun ranges of 10 miles or more without special rules. The 20 and 25 mm scale tanks would require an area like a tennis court. For a similar reason 54 mm tanks are simply too big for war-games and so are used for modelling.
34	Pres. 2: C.U. (Cam. 1)	Cut 1	F.O. Mic. 1 F.U. Mic. 2	Of course not all war-games are of land battles. Some people like getting their feet wet, so they use the very much smaller scale ships.

Early Development of Critical Abilities

The conversation below is from an early session in which the teacher was attempting to develop the pupils' critical awareness of television. The piece they were studying was a recording they had made a week earlier. It consisted of a number of interview sequences recorded when a careers adviser visited the school.

Pupil A [to the videotape operator]: Just that one. Play it back a bit. A bit more. Right, there, freeze. That other shot, that's it, keep that.

Teacher: Is that reasonable, do you think? This is camera 3.

A: It occurred to me it's a bit . . . it all seems the same at the moment.

T: That's right. It gets a bit monotonous. I was just thinking this when you were doing the programme. Can you continue please and freeze it on the paper [to the videotape operator]? That's where it gets stuck [to pupils]. Now. Now. What is important about that?

A: Well could we . . . he's looking at the paper.

Pupil B: So if he was . . . asking questions.

Pupil C: Perhaps writing on the paper.

A: So it was a bad decision to go back to that because we were repeating ourselves.

C: No movement in it neither.

T: So there is no relevance really. What do you think is the biggest problem in an interview situation like this?

A: Well, the camera is very static.

T: So all the movement comes from the technique – the expertise of the camera operators. What about the idea of showing this character interviewer who is not speaking but with the voice coming across from the other interviewer? Should we always have, do you think, the person who's speaking on shot?

B: No, you could see his reaction on his face.

C: We're too late on that shot. When he started to speak we should have anticipated it really.

A: Maybe.

C: I feel that we came out a little bit too late. Because we knew how he was going to finish – it was obvious from the first part of that last sentence – that would give us time to go to the next shot without arriving late.

The Teacher's Viewpoint

On the basis of his experience with the two sixth-form groups, the teacher extended his work to other groups in the school, including a much less able fifth-form group. This section records his reflections on his work with these various groups as well as a number of comments from pupils. First the teacher talked about the more-able sixth-form group:

'At present it is impossible to ignore the influence and effect of the mass media on society. If the next generation is to understand the implications of an electronic communications explosion then we need to prepare them in our schools today. Our present sixth form are already aware of the changing patterns of employment as computers and automation are incorporated in the industrial and commercial world. They realize that they may have to adapt and retrain to keep abreast of rapidly changing situations. Therefore they value the opportunity to learn about mass communications and appreciate the skills that they develop in the process.

'I found the usual situation, that once I get the group talking about something they can take over themselves. What I like about the course is that they start it, they get the ideas and they research the ideas. In other words, they have to do all the spade work themselves and the technician and I just fill in the gaps — give them information they need or tell them how to use the equipment or whether a thing is possible or not. The sixth-form groups can and do take the lead. They tend to select the documentary, semi-educational information, didactic, type of programme and are quite reticent about including any dramatic sequences or using the medium in an imaginative way. Perhaps this is a reflection of their academic training. I try to encourage them to take the occasional creative risk but they don't find it easy. They treat it as unnatural and I don't want to force them into this area until they feel secure. Throughout the school they have not had much opportunity to express themselves orally in class. This tends to happen with bright pupils as they are usually geared to getting ideas down on paper. I try and base the whole course on discussion and talk, and try to get them to explore their ideas orally. At the beginning they are very reluctant to do this, in fact find it almost impossible. As the course progresses they talk a lot more but still will not perform imaginative ideas in front of the camera.

'It is important to give sixth formers the opportunity to develop organizational and managerial skills. Many of them may well find themselves in positions of responsibility, and in addition the development of self-reliance could affect the degree to which they will benefit from higher education. When making a television programme they have to organize their own schedules to meet given deadlines, which requires analysing and justifying the use of manpower, resources and time. This is often a new experience for sixth formers who have had a traditional academic education.

'In contrast, my less-able groups are less aware of what they need to equip themselves for adult life. They are full of creative ideas, but they find the research difficult, particularly if they have to go away and write it all down and think about it. They prefer to discuss a programme, put it into shape, record it and view it within a single session. They are in fact very good at working in this way. However, the nature of this work does encourage them to research and to engage in fairly long periods of concentrated work. Thus I believe it is helping both my more-able and my less-able pupils to develop skills in areas where each are weak.'

This view was supported by what the pupils told us.

Interviewer: Who was in charge of your group? Did the teacher tell you what to do?

Pupil 1: Not really.

Pupil 2: He tried to keep in the background.

I: Did he succeed?

P1: A little bit.

Pupil 3: He took more notice of our ideas.

Pupil 4: Yeah.

Pupil 5: He didn't help us. He didn't get involved in writing. He just told us how to work the equipment and started us off. That was it.

I: What about at the beginning of the process when you were planning your programmes?

P4: He just gave us the basic idea. You've got, like, a television programme and that was it. He left it up to us to start a few ideas. Either a commercial or documentary sort of programme. And then we planned it from there.

I: And how did this affect the type of conversation you engaged in?

P4: Well, if the teacher was there all the time, you've got to watch the kind of things you say when the teacher's around.

Pupil 6: More easy feeling, more . . . without any sort of worry that the teacher might come down on you.

I: Don't you waste time without close supervision?

P3: Oh, yeah, you waste some time, but the work always gets done.

P5: It doesn't go down, degenerate too far. But you can be sure everybody understands what you mean if you try to do something that the group doesn't like.

I: And you use language that is much more readily understandable by everybody?

P3: Yes.

P5: It moves things along much faster.

Next the teacher commented on the pupils' criticism of their work:

'Generally, they know themselves how they are doing, and obviously with recorded material they can see for themselves what they have done and what sort of mistakes they have made. When they have seen something that they have produced, both the fifth- and the sixth-form group become self-critical, whether they have been working in front of or behind the cameras, and this critical analysis seems to increase all the time. They are often surprised at how inadequately they have expressed themselves and this gives them a self-awareness which encourages them to progress.

'Group awareness and criticism vary from group to group and from person to person. In the early stages they tend to regard their own contribution as distinct from everybody else's. So, for example, the presenter concentrates on his own performance, while the cameraman thinks, "Oh, that's my shot, what I did." I hope that later the group members will criticize not only themselves, individually, but also the whole production, and make a comprehensive judgement on it.

'I ought here to make a distinction between the lower-ability fifth-year group and the sixth-form group. The sixth-form group tends to criticize what each person says; the fifth-form group tends to be less critical of each other's ideas, each member concentrating on his own performance of various roles and tasks. I would like to think that in both cases they are gaining more confidence in their own ability to criticize and form judgements, to

express opinions and to assess things objectively as well as subjectively.

'One thing that is striking in both cases is that getting these groups out of the class-room, out of an institutionalized setting, and into the professional work environment of the studio is like moving into a new world.'

The pupils were asked whether they thought the work worthwhile:

I: Do you think that this work has a value in terms of your education? If someone said, 'Look, you ought to be sitting at a desk writing, listening to a teacher and learning what's important', would you want to defend what you've been doing as educational?

P1: Yeah. Why, if you're shy you obviously get over your shyness and things like that and it all goes towards life. I mean if you are shy you cannot get on in life.

P2: Develops your own thoughts. If you've got any ideas if Teacher's just dictating to you you don't get a chance to put them in. With an activity like this it's your own ideas that come out.

P3: It's like, it's a sense of achievement. You've done it by yourself without a teacher or an adult.

I: Are you implying that this doesn't happen very often in school life?

P3: Why, not really. Not as much. If you pass an exam that's a sense of achievement, but not as much as this.

P5: And another point. If you're just in a dictating class once you get outside there's no one to dictate to you so you don't want to do it. If you are in this situation you are on your own and when you leave school you are on your own out there. So it helps you.

The teacher also felt that his relationship with the class had changed:

'I get the impression that when I'm in the class-room the pupils view me very much as an authority figure. When I'm in the studio with them this authority figure seems to disappear. I'm a sort of guide perhaps rather than someone who says, "Do this, do that." When I go back into the class-room with a group I've had in the studio, the change of relationship continues. A more relaxed interchange occurs, although the discipline is still there.'

One pupil agreed:

'I think it helps to break down the barrier between pupil and teacher. A lot of people say it doesn't but it does. In this sort of situation the teacher is more or less a friend rather than a fellow that walks around with a cane.'

The teacher continued:

'Regarding still pictures, we're fortunate because our technician is very interested in photography. We have a school camera. There is also a camera club. The sixth formers can go out with the camera, get what pictures they need or they can photograph pictures from books and enlarge them to fit the television format. We do not have our own portable camera and videotape-recorder, but the local college is very good and we can usually borrow one from there when we need it for outside location work.

'Modes of speech – restricted and elaborated codes – are emphasized in this type of work. In this area, which is predominantly working class, the brightest pupils become victims to some extent when they come to school because they are exposed to a set of middle-class values. Outside school their environment governs the way they speak, but when they are in the class-room with me or in the studio, the sixth form particularly, they conform to my values and my way of speech.'

The pupils commented on this as follows:

I: And language. Does the way you speak change?

P1: The words we say are more kind of technical.

P2: And what we say. We try to make it clear about what we are saying.

P3: In the playground and in the class-rooms there's sort of the same kind of language, the accent and that. But when we are in this situation, in front of the telly and that, the way you speak, and that, changes. I find that.

CHAPTER 9

Students Aged 16-19: Sound / Tape-slide / Television

Although this report has been predominantly concerned with pupils aged 11–17, similar work has been done with much younger children and with older students. There seems no reason why such work should not be successful over a very wide age range. At one end of the age spectrum, the authors of the Bullock Report observed tape-slide work with primary children and commented on its richness in terms of oral-language work. At the other, the Project stimulated work with adult illiterates, students of higher education and technical-college students. This final case study takes a brief look at work in the 16–19 age range in one technical college.

The lecturer concerned worked with apprentices who attended college for one day per week. He met them for one hour during the day for general education. The students' qualifications ranged from one CSE to four or five O-levels. At one end of the academic scale were craft apprentices, bricklayers, joiners and semi-skilled engineers, and at the other, ONC students training as engineers. Many of the students resented the general-education component of their course, seeing it as an extra hour in a long day (often from 9 a.m. until 7 or 8 p.m.) and of little relevance to their career aspirations.

The first task was to increase these students' motivation towards general education, and in particular to develop their self-confidence, communication skills and social adaptability. Whereas the teachers in the previous case studies were concerned with the use of tape-slide, film and television, with these students it was decided to start with sound recording.

Using their specific vocational talents, the students built in the corner of their class-room a simple sound-recording booth which was lined with egg boxes and a layer of carpet underfelt to deaden the extraneous sound. A shelf was built inside to carry the microphone and scripts. The tape-recorder and record-player were outside, so a window was put in one side to enable the speaker to see hand signals (as cues for action) from the recording operators.

Starting from their experience of radio, the students were first asked to produce a news programme. In accordance with the aims of these sessions, they worked in small groups. They discussed the format of a news programme and listed the various items they decided to include in their scripts. It was suggested that a summary of the main points of the news at the beginning and end of the programme might be appropriate. Their attention was also drawn to the type of language used by newscasters (past impersonal) and a number of appropriate phrases were suggested: 'earlier today it was announced', 'news is coming in of', and so on. Some students incorporated an outside reporter in their programme.

Next the students were introduced to the controls of the tape-recorder and recorded their work in groups, each student speaking at least one part. The students were fascinated by what their colleagues had achieved and insisted on an immediate replay at the end of each recording. On hearing the replay they expressed surprise at the degree to which their own voices sounded like those of professional news-readers. This stimulated some discussion among them: they questioned whether this professional sound was a direct result of the phrases they used, or whether the phrases they used made them think of the news items in a particular way which forced them into a particular attitude that was reflected in their voices. These questions were never resolved but all agreed that in some way the nature of the activity dictated the way they sounded, and that they were not simply copying the sound of professionals.

The second exercise was to use a mixture of speaking and music. This involved recording the voice of the speaker and mixing this with music from the record-player. Again the students were asked to present a programme of a type with which they were familiar: a disc jockey introducing popular music. The results were once more surprisingly professional with many students pleased by their obvious success.

After this the students were introduced to sound effects. Rain, thunder and galloping horses were created by dried peas in a plastic container, a sheet of metal and two halves of a coconut. Alarm clocks and sound-effects records were tried out. The students then wrote all sorts of programmes: short stories, documentaries and sound experiments with poetry and music.

The students discussed and argued, wrote and performed their various pieces. Social interaction was certainly taking place, with a wide range of types of verbal exchange, but perhaps one of the most satisfying effects of using radio techniques was the motivation which developed and the opportunity for self-expression.

This conscious expression of their reactions to situations and events is very important and is something they would not normally do a great deal. It is one of the means by which they can be led towards a deeper understanding of themselves in their environment, which in turn may help create a basis for fuller, more active participation in society.

Perhaps this is best appreciated by looking at some of the results produced. Each poem was accompanied by music. The first piece was written by an apprentice bricklayer:

I opened the door –
And there was darkness
Running out of the gate –
Along the street
Late for the bus.

Up to the bus-stop
And on to the bus.
Going down the road.
On the bus.
Tired
Hungry
And cold.

Off the bus –
And over the road.
Waiting for the van to arrive
Dark –
Cold –
And alone.

Van arrives –
And brakes with a screech.
And door opens –
Step inside –
And everyone's there.

Sit down on the hard
Wooden seats.
The bumpy
Dark
Cold ride.
Just like taking cows
To the slaughter.

Once you're in you can't get out –
Till it's too late.
Travelling like cows
In filthy
Dark
Pigsties.
Smelling of diesel and smoke.
With closed eyes and
Dark faces,
Just there, sleeping their lives away.
The noise inside
Is driving me mad.

We've arrived
At work.
By God.
I'm glad.

This piece was written by an engineering student:

I have been running for many vales
Trying to escape the dreaded noise of the
hounds
And the familiar horn which brings death
nearer
With the savage dogs
Which speed up the bloody wasteful death.
My life for a single trophy
And an afternoon's so-called sport.

Is it really a sport
Or just something to do which is different
from the everyday routine,
Something with a bit of excitement
Watching a pack of hounds tear and chase
till death
A so-called pest?
Do I cause so much damage,
Or is there more damage in hunting me
down?
Damage in property, crops, fences,
Maybe lame a horse and lose a couple of
dogs,
Frighten a few sheep so that they run into a
barbed-wire fence
And come out the other side a mass of
bloodstained wool
And a pile of guts and skin.

I stop for a breather in some bushes
But not for long
The hounds approach, a horn blows only a
few fields away
How I wish it were dark
They might call in the pack and return to
the lodge.

But no, it's not to be
I must take to the water, make for the
stream
And head for the river,
Try to lose the scent which attracts death
like a magnet
The dogs never seem to tire
The horn and horses never far away
As I make for the river, other animals and
so-called pests take cover
To clear a way or be trodden on by the
careless,
Bloodthirsty people.

Cockfighting was abolished along with fist
fighting

Is this so-called sport not very similar
If not worse?
The horn blows again
I am saved
They call the hounds back
And head back for the lodge
They are disappointed
No trophy
No skin
Or satisfaction — the fox.

The final piece was written by an ONC (construction) student:

I am not a poet
But yet he says to me
Put it down in terms of thought
Thought — I don't think he'd appreciate
what's going on in my mind.

He tells me — put your experiences into
words
But have I ever had an experience worth
writing about?

Meter and rhyme that's what poetry is
about
At least that's what they taught me at
school.
But he says — don't worry about those
Worry — it's not a case of worrying
Just trying to formulate an idea
Twenty-three years of living
And when I look back
What's worth writing about?

Several groups worked through the medium of tape-slide. These included trainee electricians, craft and technician engineers, painters and decorators and nursery nurses. The aims were similar to those of previous work: to generate oral and social competence and general communication skills. The process was also similar, following a pattern of discussion and research, explanation, organization and justification with a group, then scripting, recording, presentation and criticism. This part of the students' work formed the general or communications element of an otherwise mainly vocationally oriented course and represented an attempt to integrate vocational study with the development of communication and social skills.

As an example we shall describe the work of a group of trainee nursery nurses. The lecturer concerned explained the process and set out the objectives of the work. She then asked the students to work in groups to produce tape-slides about aspects of their vocational training that might be used as teaching material for other groups of students on similar courses. The students used a simple tape-recorder and an Instamatic camera (to photograph a series of demonstrations and photographs taken from books and magazines). They produced programmes on 'The bathing of a baby', 'Finger painting', 'Early social education', and so on.

After choosing a topic they broke it down into its important elements, visualized how they could show each stage, prepared the spoken commentary and selected music. They noted their decisions in story-board form and then produced their tape-slides.

When the story-boards were complete they were presented to the staff responsible for the vocational subjects concerned, and their comments on the accuracy of the content were invited. They thought the work 'a useful re-inforcement of [the nurses'] studies'. Also, one staff member said:

'It was particularly noticeable that many of the students demonstrated an increased ability to organize their information compared with their written work. There was a greater accuracy, a greater attention to detail and a much better logical progression. If the students could present tape-slides on certain topics as part of their examinations, I'm sure they would do much better. Some of these students will fail, although they have the practical aptitude and abilities, because they cannot accurately express what they know in written form for examinations.'

Groups of students also made television programmes based on their vocational studies. Again the aim was to integrate the development of communication and social skills with the mainstream vocational course.

The students used a simple three-camera television studio. They were introduced to the technical aspects of the equipment and shown how to put an elementary programme together. The first exercise used a simple still-picture sequence with a commentary. The next exercise combined the components of the first exercise with a presenter. The final exercise for these groups was to televise a demonstration

of a process or of how a piece of equipment works.

The students (in groups) now set about writing their own programmes using the audio-visual structures introduced in the exercises. A typical programme would start with the titles and some music, then the presenter would introduce the topic. To illustrate the explanation given by the presenter, sequences of relevant still pictures would be used. These were a combination of pictures cut out of magazines, pictures drawn by the students and photographs of pictures taken from text-books. Where greater detail was required (for example, one group wanted to explain an electrical circuit) a model was brought into the studio and a demonstrator was able to show clearly the points he was trying to cover.

The following extract is part of an interview with a group of trainee craft apprentices held after they had completed a television programme explaining the principles of domestic electrical installation:

Teacher: What happened in that first discussion?

Student A: Well, you know B wrote it out and they all got reading through it.

Student C: We all took it to pieces.

A: We all pulled it to bits but, I mean, that's the way to do it.

Student D: Yes. We all read it through as we put each point. When we all felt agreed on one part of it we put that in and went on to another part, agreed on it and then wrote the script.

When the script was rehearsed, another problem emerged. The presenter said he could not read the script. When asked why, he pointed out that as there was no punctuation he could not make sense of it. Punctuation took on a purpose, as did summary when the programme was considered to be too long and was shortened by a third. One reluctant student, on discovering he had been summarizing, declared that he would never have done it had he known.

After the script had been recorded in the television studio, Student B said:

'Well, when we were doing it, I was amazed how it was all falling into position: the presenter, the still pictures, the demonstration, cos before it was just on paper, you know.

When we were doing it, it was great. Everyone else was, like, coming together. It was fantastic.'

Apart from the obvious enjoyment these students felt at expressing what they knew about their trade through a medium like television, which often plays an important part in their lives, a great deal of useful learning was taking place. The vocational staff said that the students valued the end-product, and were prepared to be very critical and to put in the extra effort required to attain a quality item. This aided their understanding of what was required of them at work, where the quality of the product was crucial. Often those students who had been relatively unsuccessful at school lacked confidence in their ability to create an acceptable product. To succeed in the world of work they had to get over this lack of confidence. Working as a team made them more aware that others depended on them. Timekeeping, personal responsibility, versatility and adaptability to change became crucial and the students learned to take these areas in their stride.

In giving and taking instructions from each other they were discovering the importance of instructions: they were learning to interpret instructions, ask questions and listen to the whole instruction – a quality essential for success at work.

Today, more than ever, we need to look at the demands made on young people as they leave school and college. Any curriculum for the 16–19 age group must include opportunities for learning the practical life skills used at work. The ability to communicate effectively is fundamental. However, many young people have had little training or opportunity to develop their oral competence. Although the industrial and commercial world is full of visual signs and symbols, not much training is given in visual literacy. Complex organization demands social cohesion, yet many young people have rarely had the opportunity to operate effectively within a team. The methods described here offer some solutions to schools and colleges who want to prepare their youngsters for the transition from school to work.

Evaluation

CHAPTER 10

General Evaluation

Two years of systematic team work are not a sufficient basis for any categorical judgement. After all, these were two years in which the teachers set highly individual objectives in very different schools. Yet this investigation is possibly the most systematic ever made into the use of recorded sound and vision as a language for educational purposes. So it is with some caution but also some excitement that the following, very tentative, observations are made.

When first told about the Project the evaluator thought that high claims were being put forward for the use of audio-visual media by learners in schools and colleges. Clearly these media are very exciting to work with, but it seemed to him questionable that they could have quite the effect on the development of learning, and of language and social skills that the Project organizers were suggesting. However, having sampled much of the work of the Project over the last two years, he has now begun to lose many of his original doubts, and made the following comment:

'I have observed groups of children labelled of low ability, from manual-working backgrounds, speaking with confidence and ease in what can only be called, if one accepts Bernstein's jargon, an elaborated code. I have seen sixteen-year-olds who confess that their film-making classes are the only ones from which they do not regularly play truant, and I have seen the same children working responsibly and collaboratively in groups, making decisions, accepting arguments and moving from leadership to the acceptance of leadership, and much more. Clearly this kind of education can dramatically change the way youngsters see themselves, and from this can develop levels of ability otherwise untapped and unsuspected.'

Motivation

All the Project's teachers reported increased motivation among their pupils at some stage of the work. In most cases it was reported to be both significant and sustained. These reports were reinforced by many of the pupils' own statements and in some cases by improved school attendance.

Since motivation is such a crucial factor in learning it is clearly important to understand how this kind of work can be used to enhance it. The school-child lives in a world of competing interests: there is all the excitement of a consumer society and the pull of the peer group on one side and the difficulty and sheer routine of school learning on the other. School learning can be most stimulating and rewarding but it requires considerable self-discipline, in particular a capacity to put up with long periods of gestation (even relative frustration) so that sufficient experience of a subject can be gained for the proper development of new patterns of thinking.[1] The 'fun syllabus' is a non-runner for the most part.[2] In the face of this, and under the pressure of the examination system and frequently the demands of the pupils, teachers often have to resort to ready-made examination formulae, sets of notes, examination 'tricks' and an inefficient apparatus of rewards and punishments. The result is that the learning drive rarely comes from within the child (much the most powerful motivator), but has to be imposed from outside, often against the child's real inclinations.

The behaviourist Skinner accepts the need for externally imposed motivation but attacks traditional teaching methods for two reasons. First, he considers that they lay too much stress on punishments (such as fear of failure) which raise high and distracting levels of anxiety in the child and are not related closely enough to the detailed steps of a piece of learning to be of any use to reinforce that learning. Second, he attacks the way traditional teaching fails to control the exact structure of a piece of learning, using rewards as the mechanism of control. For maximum learning to take place, Skinner argues, each tiny step has to be properly mastered in turn. If the steps are small enough, then the mental jump that has to take place each time is not too great. The child is rewarded by the knowledge that he has the right answer, and so is drawn on to the next step. In this way the frustration of long periods of slow progress is overcome.

One of the practical outcomes of Skinner's theory has been the development of teaching-machines, which have proved ineffectual in many areas. One of the basic reasons for this is probably the different minds and personalities of different people. Machines must be programmed on the basis of a few people's analysis of the stages and relationships of a piece of learning, and this is unlikely to be just right for more than a small percentage of pupils.

Ideally, to conform to Skinner's findings (accepting their reality whilst rejecting totally the theoretical framework he uses), one needs a learning system tailored to fit each individual pupil, with a consistent pattern of rewards built in and precisely adapted to each step of the individualized learning process. While this involves rejecting teaching-machines for the reasons already given, the same principles can be applied with astonishingly high rates of success as in mastery learning systems.[3] It will be suggested below that the same principles were at work in the learning in the Project.

One does not have to accept that motivation has to be imposed from

---

[1]This is the general drift of Piaget's argument: since intellectual abilities unfold naturally through the developmental stages of growth, a minimum requirement would appear to be prolonged exposure to the right conditions for particular levels and kinds of ability. See particularly Jean Piaget, *The Psychology of Intelligence* (ed. C. K. Ogden; Routledge & Kegan-Paul, 1971).

[2]There are now innumerable critiques of the kinds of curriculum that rely on stimulating children – for example, the recent attacks on the creative-writing movement by people trained in linguistics. We do not wish to attack open class-rooms or open learning in any way, we wish to say only that learning to think mathematically or sociologically or to write well, for example, involves long periods of exposure to subject-matter, periods of frustration and struggle while the abilities are forming, and that these processes become much more difficult to put up with when consumerism is the prevailing ethos. To see teaching as a business of arranging appropriate stimuli is to fall into a kind of consumerism.

[3]James H. Block (ed.), *Mastery Learning: Theory and Practices* (Holt, Rhinehart & Winston, 1971).

outside in order to make a human being learn. Psychologists such as Bruner and Piaget stress that the desire to learn is inborn in human beings. Bruner[4] claims that the will to learn is the most basic human drive; what is more, he says, people have an inborn drive to control the world around them through developing manual, social and intellectual skills. If Bruner is right (and there is considerable research to support his view) then it seems amazing that many schoolchildren are as lacking in motivation as they appear to be. Hunt,[5] describing what he calls the 'problem of the match', explains that new learning has to be just far enough beyond the grasp of the child to stimulate curiosity yet not so far that it is too difficult to grasp. As Piaget[6] has described, new learning occurs not in separate small pieces that are simply added on to old learning but in the form of patterns of inter-related skills and ideas, and the key to effective learning lies in the formation of the pattern itself (in other words the mind is a pattern-forming instrument). Thus new learning is most effective when it can be assimilated within a pattern already existing in the mind, or when it can be hooked on to such a pattern.

Since each child is highly individual, the mental patterns he has already formed will be different from everyone else's. Therefore what is meaningful or relevant to each child is unique, and the 'problem of the match' is different for each child in each situation. What is more, Bruner has found that children tend to accept the goals and activities of the social group in which they find themselves (group reciprocity).

It is not surprising, then, that the natural will to learn is frustrated so generally in lessons which are dominated by the teacher's view of what a piece of learning consists of, which may be very different from the unique learning patterns already developed in most of the children. The presentation of the learning tasks may in itself cause the breakdown of learning through sheer frustration. Here the pull of the social group may take over, and the classroom situation itself may become more antagonistic to learning.

The evidence of the Project shows that this kind of audio-visual work, when handled well, reverses this situation and releases the inborn desire to learn and to develop skilled control over the environment. The following quotation from a long transcript of some sixth formers making a film on war-games illustrates how this happens.

Pupil A: Next come Medievals.
Pupil B: Yes. 'Next . . . come . . . the . . . Medievals.'
Pupil C: Come on.
B: Get down.
A: Kindly do not criticize my family name.
C: Person. Tribe.
B: Work this way . . . three at once.
A: Ah, but he didn't film from the shoulder, did he? Next comes the Medieval.
Pupil D: Was that the one we did of the moon?
C: Yeah.
B: Yeah.

[4]J. S. Bruner, *Toward a Theory of Instruction* (Harvard University Press, 1966).
[5]In the Open University unit *Motivation and Learning (Educational Studies: a Second Level Course, Personality and Learning Block 3)* (Open University Press, 1976).
[6]For a very lucid account of this aspect of learning and its implications, see Richard R. Skemp, *The Psychology of Learning Mathematics* (Penguin, 1971).

A: What are we going to say, then? 'Next comes the Medieval . . . ?'
C: . . . period, with all its er . . .
A: . . . which dates from . . .
C: Let's first have colours, have it written out with all its colours and explain
    that they symbolize the Medieval. You think of all these knights and . . .
A: Dates from 1066, from Arthur to . . .
B and C: Arthur!
C: He was A.D. 600, him, you know.
D: Yes.
A: In 1485.
C: Thought he was a bastard.
D: He is a bastard.
A: We're still on Roman Britain.
B: '. . . Medieval period with all its splendour . . .'

There is so much interruption of the main area of concern – getting the
historical development of war into some perspective – that one feels as if the
group will quickly lose interest through the distractions, and certainly lose
sight of what they are doing. Yet, in fact, when the transcript as a whole is
read alongside the videotape of which it is a memory, one sees a feverish
activity, very economical in comparison with tapes of more traditional learning, and an urgent sharpening and deepening of the ideas in order to get the
visual statement right. Many of the interruptions are occasioned by uncer-
tainties of individual pupils about the material, and about how to proceed.
But the group atmosphere is such that, whenever a pupil tries something out
and it is corrected, the group as a whole spends a few seconds re-establishing
cohesiveness before going on. An example is Pupil A's mistake about Arthur,
and the ensuing jokes about the bastard. There is a continuous and very
complex process of reinforcement and reward going on – a pupil tries out an
idea and the assent of the group, either tacit or verbal, is given before moving
on. If there is disagreement, then the group relations are usually such as to
turn a criticism into a positive reinforcer. This target meets Skinner's criteria:
that good learning situations should incorporate clearly defined points at
which the participants receive feedback on their efforts.

In the Project lessons information was usually integrated and tested (the
best form of feedback) at clearly marked stages corresponding to transitions to
a new type of activity. Most often these transitions were from discussion to
scenario, from scenario and research to script, from script and preparation
to recording, from recording to programme, or from programme (via the
audience) to communication. This system thus also fits well into the other
model of motivation – that of Bruner and Piaget. Instead of some pre-
programmed machine determining the learning, the individual pupil (operat-
ing inside the group) sees what is for him the next important step and tackles
it using his own learning strategies, which are then checked within the group.
So the group's reciprocity is harnessed to encourage the pupil's curiosity and
to help him to test his own patterns of learning. Thus patterns of specific
competence (linguistic, conceptual, psycho-motor) can be built up safely.
There is, moreover, always the urgent and compelling goal of the finished
performance (to be communicated to others with less specialist knowledge),
as well as the technical requirements of the camera work, etc., which provide
a familiar field of operations in which the new piece of learning is to be set.
Many pupils preferred recorded sound and vision as a medium for communication to other media used in schools. Many expressed this in some variation

of 'It's more real', or 'It means more to us'. This must be related to the degree to which film, and particularly television, has become the most widely accepted form of recorded communication with most of these young people.

Motivation has not in general been intrinsic motivation towards the subject-matter being filmed or taped – biology, history and so on. Rather, motivation has been concerned with the medium itself: the excitement of beginning to understand the techniques and technology that have so powerfully changed our world and, much more important, the excitement of being able to use this technology to make meaningful statements of understanding or opinion to others. Finally, the excitement has been that of being able to use a dramatic and powerful technology to discover meanings not known previously to exist (for example, when a painfully shy, illiterate sixteen-year-old girl found she could take vivid and beautiful video-pictures of people's faces and interactions and could make complex statements about these without uttering a word, confidence suddenly rose up in her and out poured words that were a mirror of the visual statement). This ties in very well with motivation theory for a number of reasons. There is a clear goal (the finished product), and the steps to reach this goal are complex but basically fairly definite. There is almost continuous activity rather than passivity. There is continual reinforcement at each stage of the process in the form of an image or a sound pattern (even poor visual and aural images made by pupils themselves are more reinforcing than half-understood facts and principles learned from books). There is relevance (the world is so permeated by these media that even really abstract creative explorations in them are relevant – think of Walt Disney's *Fantasia* or some of the dream-sequences in television advertisements) thus there is a meaningful context in which to be able to understand. Finally, there is creativity: if the learner makes his own statement, even about well-known facts and principles, then the learning is much more powerful. This is exactly what we would expect from the research and theories of Bruner and Piaget.

It is a platitude among teachers that the best way to learn something is to have to teach it, but in a way this is just what teachers were asking pupils to do in the Project. Thus, although the real motivation is the technical, creative task, the pupils must thoroughly master the subject-matter that they are communicating or they will not be able to fulfil the task adequately. This in turn should lead them on to intrinsic interest in the subject simply through having grasped it. In his book on mastery learning, James Block suggests that intrinsic motivation and thus persistence grow simply out of successful understanding.

Individual Differences

The critical importance of individual differences as a source of frustration in learning has already been mentioned. Many teachers seem to assume that intelligence is basically a single entity and that each child is born with a certain amount of intelligence. This implies that the chief source of individual differences is this amount of intelligence, so we hear teachers talk about bright children and dull children. In view of recent work in psychology and genetics[7] this is a bizarre idea. What must be acknowledged is the great complexity of

[7]Gerald Dworkin and Ned Block (eds), *The I.Q. Controversy, Critical Readings* (Quartet Books, 1977).

the phenomenon called intelligence. Elliot Eisner,[8] for example, responds to this by redefining cognition. He argues that the non-verbal forms of knowing are as valid as the verbal ones, and one has only to think of the way great dancers like Merce Cunningham interpret the world kinaesthetically or to consider the intelligence of Henry Moore as a sculptor to understand his point.[9]

It may be necessary for priority to be given to verbal and numerical intelligence by schools who are training future generations of scientists and professional and technical personnel, on whom our survival depends. (Though the current profound structural changes that western society is undergoing begin to cast doubts even on this.) But the crucial task of schools is to take each child as he is, to develop what is best in him, and to remedy his weaknesses. If schools recognize only certain kinds of verbal and mathematical ability and are not equipped to recognize other sorts of potential, then what happens to the child who has developed himself kinaesthetically, visually and so on? His ability may (or may not) show on the football field, in the craft workshops or the art rooms, but it is unlikely that the school will recognize this ability as the key to intellectual growth in the prized verbal and mathematical areas. Yet the one thing this study has shown overwhelmingly is that these other, disregarded abilities are the key to verbal and intellectual development (see the section of this chapter on 'Language and Communication').

Precisely because recorded sound and vision generate a wide range of forms of expression, pupils were able to contribute to the group learning and communication from a diverse range of individual abilities. Thus, while one pupil might produce good art work, another might contribute technical drawings, another poetry, another the handling of some part of the equipment, and so on. By thus helping pupils to develop and contribute their individual strengths, teachers were able to build up everyone's involvement in achieving the overall learning objectives. This also developed confidence in the children. As Rosenthal and Jacobson show in their research,[10] if children are expected to become more intelligent then their teachers will perceive and treat them as such, aiding this kind of growth. In the transcripts of learning sessions it is very marked that the children were deeply emotionally involved in the learning. There is little question that such emotional involvement (ranging from expressing feelings about people in history to communicating pride in the group achievement) is a great generator of intelligence.

[8]Elliott W. Eisner, *The Role of the Arts in the Invention of Man* (paper delivered to the 23rd World Congress of I.N.S.E.A., August 1978).

[9]A further and striking example of the need to redefine cognition is presented in a published correspondence between Albert Einstein and Jacques Hadamard. Einstein writes: 'The words or the language, as they are written or spoken, do not seem to play any role in my mechanism of thought. The psychical entities which seem to serve as elements in thought are certain signs and more or less clear images which can be "voluntarily" reproduced and combined. . . . The above-mentioned elements are, in my case, of visual and some of muscular type. Conventional words and other signs have to be sought for laboriously only in a second stage. . . .' Quoted in Brewster, Ghiselin, *The Creative Process* (Mentor Books, 1964, p. 43).

[10]R. Rosenthal and L. Jacobson, *Pygmalion in the Classroom: Teacher Expectations and Pupils' Intellectual Development* (Holt, Rhinehart & Winston, 1968). There was some methodological and statistical criticism of this work – see, for example, R. Snow, 'Unfinished Pygmalion', *Contemporary Psychology*, vol. 14 (1969), pp. 197–9; C. Taylor, 'The expectations of Pygmalion's creators', *Educational Leadership*, vol. 28 (1970), pp. 161–4; W. L. Claiborn, 'Expectancy effect in the classroom: a failure to replicate', *Journal of Educational Psychology*, vol. 60 (1969), pp. 377–83. Nevertheless a great deal of work by other investigators supports the general claim: see David H. Hargreaves, *Interpersonal Relations and Education* (Routledge & Kegan-Paul, 1975), pp. 34–43.

The Slow Learner, the Academic Child and Remedial Work

One of the startling things that was observed in these investigations was the high level of intellectual ability shown by children designated as of low ability. These children seemed, when working on the Project, to be capable of very complex ideas and creative solutions to problems they were faced with. There was, in fact, almost unanimous agreement among the teachers of the lowest-ability groups that the work was invaluable. To summarize what these teachers said, it seemed that when their pupils used recorded sound and vision in this way they were able to bypass difficulties caused by poor literacy. Many said that their pupils were far more able speakers than writers and that the planning of visual sequences helped them to organize their thinking. A number of the teachers pointed to the pupils' programmes as evidence of underlying intellectual ability masked by poor literacy and numeracy.[11] Several teachers suggested that this work allowed low-ability pupils new access to school subjects.

These findings are in harmony with the remarks made above on 'Individual Differences', and perhaps are not so surprising now that use of an I.Q. to measure intellectual potential has been largely discredited. Certainly they are just what would be expected from models of intelligence such as Guilford's structure-of-intellect theory, where, in a far more complex model than that of Burt or Vernon, he shows that there are probably at least one hundred and twenty separate kinds of intellectual ability, of which everyone is likely to have at least one developed to a fairly high level. At the moment, educational establishments tend to give preference to high levels of verbal ability and numerical ability, whereas many low-ability children are likely to be more highly developed in figural (or concrete) reasoning and behavioural intelligence. Work of the kind undertaken in the Project clearly incorporates these latter two forms of intelligence much more than does the formal curriculum. (For example, one young girl explaining her enjoyment of the work said, 'I learn best through me hands.') One of the consequences of Guilford's model (and of the unitariness of knowledge) is the idea that by basing new learning on an individual's special abilities, completely new ranges and types of ability can be developed from those he already has. This may be one reason why so many of the youngsters regularly attending Sevenoaks School Project Technology Centre improved their form placings in physics, and it suggests wonderful possibilities stemming from creative audio-visual work in schools.

Bruner's theory of instruction (based on a great deal of empirical work, particularly with slow learners) postulates three kinds of thinking: enactive (thinking by doing), iconic (understanding through some visual representation of the idea) and symbolic (thinking through abstractions). Clearly the last of these is ultimately the most powerful and the one that schools must develop in children, but it seems that schools arrive at this stage far too quickly for most children, so that their symbolic reasoning is superficial and uncertain. Audio-visual work gives children a chance to explore difficult concepts thoroughly through the enactive and iconic dimensions of thought, and

[11]Numeracy and literacy involve very complex and highly specific skills, and are among the tools whereby we understand the world around us and communicate our perceptions of that world. Clearly schools are dominated by these tools more than by any others. Where children are alienated from these two areas they obviously find it enormously difficult to display their intelligence and creativity as curricula are currently administered. See, for example, Neil Postman, 'The politics of reading', *Tinker Tailor* (ed. Nell Keddie; Penguin, 1975).

thus their mastery of them is likely to be very sound. Of course, this process is initially slow, and they do not cover as much conceptual ground, but it is a far surer foundation on which to build abstract thought than the more academic curriculum. Also, the slowness of covering the conceptual ground does not lower the children's motivation for, as we have shown, this is continually stimulated by the technical task and the reciprocity of the group. Piaget suggests that learning is patterned or schematic: we learn a concept well only when we have grasped the pattern of ideas and experiences of which it is a summary. New schemata develop during a slow, thorough build-up. Audio-visual work can allow this to happen without killing motivation.

Bruner spent some years at the Judge Baker Guidance Center working on the nature of learning blocks in children. He says:[12]

'There is a sharp distinction that must be made between . . . behaviour that *copes* with the requirements of a problem and behaviour that is designed to *defend* against entry into the problem. . . . Once our blocked children were able to bear the problems as set . . . their performance was quite like that of other children, although often less skilled since they had not quite learned to handle the technical instruments of the subjects they were supposed to be learning.'

This research of Bruner's is very encouraging if we can devise ways of getting the slow learner to face up to the requirements of new learning. The slow learner is usually avoiding this confrontation, increasingly to the extent of truancy. A fifth-form class whose attitude impressed us very much had the worst truancy record in their area yet never missed their health and hygiene classes, which used the methods of the Project. They were non-exam, bottom-band children, with a very low academic expectation of themselves and low levels of literacy, and clearly came from disadvantaged backgrounds. Yet their enthusiasm for this class was evident, and arose partly because of the humanitarian attitude of their teacher and partly because, instead of studying health and hygiene as an academic subject, they were busy making animated films to illustrate and explore the concepts. To do this they used communication patterns familiar and thus meaningful to them: images from the popular media, advertising slogans, etc. However, in the process of illustrating, for example, the dangers of smoking, they had to grasp basic biological and physiological principles in order to communicate their message and their explanations. If our summary of Piaget is right then meaning for the learner consists of patterns of concepts that are rooted in concrete, active experience. In other words, numerical and verbal concepts have little meaning until there is a good solid basis of physical experiences to support them. The Project's method of working enables pupils to grasp new ideas by linking them to known images and experiences. Further, because the pupils have to translate these ideas into a form of oral and/or visual communication, they also struggle to create concrete realizations of the ideas, which in turn clarifies and gives a basis for the ideas. The whole process is achieved through the sort of exploratory talk examined in the next section, and there are very surprising differences between the talk of this particular group and that of the normal or quick learner.

This group's digressions from the subject were very lengthy and sometimes rambling. They took a very long time to find their way back to the business in hand, yet all the time were busy working at the routine tasks. What was observed was evidence that their learning patterns were simply a long way

[12]J. S. Bruner, op. cit., pp. 3–5.

away from the school situation. They needed much longer to work through their own ideas, then make the bridge to the subject through concentrating on the interesting and simple techniques of film-making. The subject proper was explored in very small doses only. This was ample evidence of Bruner's description of 'learning blockage', since many of their conversations (even the occasional 'I'm bored') were avoidance activities designed to ease the pressure of facing up to new learning. Yet the method can accommodate all that, and gives these youngsters the chance to face up in their own time to difficult learning, which they then do very effectively.

So far in this chapter it has been implied that the symbolic mode of reasoning is superior to the enactive and iconic modes. In terms of the requirement that education should develop higher levels of scientific and managerial skill in all young people, there is something in this notion. But it does not take account of our other objectives – the development of important social skills and the generation of kinaesthetic and intuitive abilities. In fact, the training of academic children has been overconcerned with purely numerical and verbal ability. Their training is thus often ill balanced, and they are left without the respect for and experience in areas of concrete and social intelligence gained by those involved in craft work, drama, dance, etc. The result is a separation of mind and body, and a separation of thinking from activity. This process is legitimated and reinforced by I.Q. tests, by most forms of examining, by the elite status of pure as opposed to applied science, and so on. Talk of remedial work should therefore include the regeneration in many academic children of important areas of kinaesthetic, visual, social and auditory intelligence that may well be fairly highly developed in many non-academic children.

Language and Communication

The major evaluation task during the pilot survey was to explore the grounds for evaluating the development of language abilities. As Harold Rosen has pointed out, perhaps the most important job of a teaching institution is to give its pupils meaningful and confident access to those universal systems of thought (science, history and so on) by which understanding of and power over the real world is possible. To anyone in education there can be little doubt about the significance of language in learning. Whole patterns of language structure and subject-matter are interlocked in the most intricate way. One has only to pick up a physics textbook, for example, to be aware of the impenetrability of the subject because of its language. The reasons for each subject having its own special language or style are partly cultural and partly historical, but once a tradition of this type exists, understanding a particular subject requires facility with its special language patterns. It also clearly requires more than that: Piaget[13] has shown that conceptual development can occur independently of language development, and he feels it to be more dependent on appropriate concrete patterns of experience. Nevertheless, work by Miller and Luria, among others, has shown that the processes of organizing, recalling and developing thought are powerfully facilitated by the appropriate patterns of language. On the other hand, there is evidence to show that knowledge of particular patterns of language which is not supported by appropriate experience can distort a child's thinking very easily. One has only to think of the waffle present in so many examination essays to

---

[13] Jean Piaget, *Six Psychological Studies* (University of London Press, 1968), pp. 94–8, and *The Language and Thought of the Child* (Routledge & Kegan-Paul, 1959).

see this. A good learning situation is therefore one where experience goes hand in hand with appropriate language development.

Achieving this is more complicated than it sounds, mainly because the existence of language varieties is itself a complicated phenomenon. For example, in a Welsh-speaking part of Wales, Welsh may be suitable for intimate social relationships, at home or in the street among friends, whereas English would *perhaps* be used in certain formal situations. Choosing between Welsh and English in some situations involves very fine discrimination. As the competent speaker grows up he will know exactly when to use either language. The switch from one to the other is a complete switch from one system of language rules to another. The speaker's performance is dependent on the range of resources he has in the language chosen and his ability to match these as exactly as possible to the requirements of the situation. Even if the speaker speaks only English the situation is essentially the same, except that he has to switch from one variety of English to another: for example, from non-standard South Yorkshire working-class dialect to the class-room English appropriate for a particular physics lesson. As Douglas Barnes has shown,[14] the language used in a physics lesson would differ from dialect not only because of the subject-matter but also because children play a different role in the class-room. Though not as dramatic as that from English to Welsh, this switch also usually involves a change of rules. Similarly, it would obviously be inappropriate to speak like a lecturer conducting a sociology seminar when involved in intimate personal relations, even if one were a sociology lecturer.

William Labov[15] has researched the language of Negroes in inner areas of New York and shown that they speak a variety of English which uses special grammatical rules, special pronunciation and a special vocabulary. It overlaps standard English at many points but to the speakers it is clearly a separate dialect and marks their corporate identity very sharply. While the vernacular of many British youngsters is not as dramatically different from standard English as this black English vernacular, there seem to be considerable differences between the rules governing neighbourhood speech and the rules underlying school English and textbook English. It is highly problematic whether these rules are linguistic or social in nature, but the general effect is clear.

A number of researchers, including Labov[16] and Tanner,[17] have shown that almost any language can adapt itself, with time, to almost any kind of conceptual or social requirement. Labov[18] further shows that the black English vernacular is capable of the most powerful, condensed logical argument, but says that the linguistic form this logic takes is so different from standard English that speakers of standard English have to learn how it operates before they can understand just what speakers of the black English vernacular are getting at. The Project evaluator found from his own research into South Yorkshire working-class speech and South Wales working-class speech that what Labov says of the black English vernacular is also true of these two varieties of English. One of the important steps teachers need to take is to

[14]D. Barnes, J. Britton, H. Rosen and the L.A.T.E., *Language, the Learner and the School* (Penguin, 1971), pp. 53–62.

[15]W. Labov, *Language in the Inner City: Studies in the Black English Vernacular* (Blackwell, 1972).

[16]W. Labov, ibid., pp. 5–6.

[17]N. Tanner, *Speech and Society Among the Indonesian Elite* (1967), reprinted in *Sociolinguistics* (ed. I. B. Pride and J. Holmes; Penguin, 1972).

[18]W. Labov, *The Logic of Nonstandard English* (1969), reprinted in *Tinker Tailor* (ed. Nell Keddie; Penguin, 1975), pp. 21–66.

acquire sensitivity in this area. It is still true that, because of our social structure and for reasons of time, speakers of non-standard English have to acquire a very considerable facility with standard English and its variants if they are to get anywhere in the educational system. Even fluent speakers of standard English have to learn the rules for specialized styles such as the language of physics or how to talk to the Youth Employment Officer. Despite his advocacy of the black English vernacular, Labov understands this requirement.[19]

Failure to grasp some of the underlying concepts of a subject or a feeling of alienation in a particular situation probably involves rejection of the language of that subject or situation, or a tendency to memorize great chunks of the language without understanding. It is then that many youngsters turn back towards their neighbourhood or peer group for solidarity, further reinforcing the linguistic boundaries between themselves and the school. Much of the time teachers are deeply concerned (even if unconsciously) with the problem of getting their pupils to take up new learning roles. As teachers, we recognize our success in this field by the ease with which pupils who took part in the Project can handle the language varieties appropriate to these roles: we judge them on their ability to understand instructions, to read and grasp textbooks, to write essays and to formulate spoken explanations. For many of these pupils the difficulties of these tasks were very great; for them solidarity with their peer group was all important. This is especially true of children from the tightly knit communities of the North-East, where this phase of the Project has been centred. Thus it was all the more surprising that over and over again, in working with audio-visual media, they chose *by themselves* to use technical and social varieties of English that are very much more formal than their normal speech.

The following quotation is from the opening of the videotape 'British Breakfast', which was made by a non-exam fifth form:

'Almost every day British people eat bacon and eggs for breakfast but they do not know how it comes to be there or think where it comes from. In this programme we intend to show this to the people.

'When piglets are born they are put into the farrowing-pen. They are kept there until weaning. They are then put into their fattening-pen, when they are fattened to be ready for butchering along with other pigs of the same age. . . .'

This quotation is in what Barnes[20] calls final-draft English. The speaker is basing his words on a script written collectively by the group. This was largely a non-exam form, in part because of their failure to grasp the proper form and function of written English, which, if Labov is right, was at least partially due to the linguistic and social gulf between their own preferred speech style and the formality of writing. Yet here they have worked hard to produce sentences that are very close indeed to the written mode. This is presumably because they know how television announcers are expected to talk. Normally they might well reject such talk from their own speech as 'snobby' or 'cissy'. The choice of a statement like 'In this programme we intend to . . .' suggests a willingness to use a form of grammar and vocabulary that is hostile to the roles in which many working-class youngsters see themselves. Nor was this style limited to the final draft. Throughout their discussions the pupils continually made more formal statements when the situation

[19]W. Labov, *Language in the Inner City: Studies in the Black English Vernacular* (Blackwell, 1972), pp. 237–40.
[20]Douglas Barnes, *From Communication to Curriculum* (Penguin, 1976), pp. 108–115.

demanded them: for example, 'That would be the main title, then, with some subtitles such as how the egg comes about, or how the bacon comes . . .', or 'Ah, we need the radio don't we – the taping of the radio. Really we should have done that when we were at the cookery room.'

It is interesting that in the finished programme and at moments like this the children's accents seemed to change too. A completely new variety of language was brought effortlessly into play as the requirements of the situation changed. We can call such different varieties of language 'codes' (which need to be deciphered before their meanings are accessible). Tanner[21] argues that 'Within a community, the position of an individual with an extensive repertoire [of speech codes] will differ substantially from that of an individual with a limited one.'[22] He is of the opinion that 'Patterns of code specialisation vary with circumstances and must be viewed as an ongoing adaptive process. For these informants it is the principle of code specialisation that is the important characteristic of childhood linguistic experience, not the pattern of code specialisation itself.' In other words, those who are restricted to a handful of language codes are likely to be more socially and intellectually limited than those with a wide range at their disposal. If this is generally true, and we must remember that Tanner is talking about a multilingual community, then it is very important that schools should aim very deliberately to develop skill and confidence in a wide spectrum of language codes. (It is, of course, problematic whether 'code' is the right word to describe a variety of language within a single-language community. It is being used in the most general sense.)

The preferred speech style of these youngsters from the North-East is not inferior to standard English in terms of economy, vividness or logic, as shown by the following exchange between two non-exam fifth formers:

John: How do you hold a ferret?
Dave: By the back of the neck as soon as it comes out. Hold it at the back of the neck so it doesn't bite yer, cos it will, cos it doesn't know what yer fingers are.

This speech is in some ways a good deal more flexible and rich than the language of 'British Breakfast', but it does not in itself establish for the speakers the confidence with more formal varieties of English that 'British Breakfast' does.

A particularly vivid example of effortless code-switching was given by the headmistress of a middle school some of whose pupils had made a television programme about old people in their area. Before they recorded the interviews, the children explained to the interviewees in the local dialect what was expected of them. Then, when the taping began, they asked the old people the same questions as before and gave the same explanations but this time in BBC English.

The following extract is from the conversation of a group of twelve-year-old girls of mixed ability who were making an animated film on pollination.

Teacher: And are you going to put in letters explaining what is happening?
Pupil A: It should go on to these letters.
T: And some of the letters . . . would you be doing this on a coloured background, so the letters will stand out?
A: I think so.

[21]N. Tanner, op. cit.
[22]N. Tanner, op. cit., pp. 126–8.

T: Oh fine, good, so that's the anther that's going to die down there.

Pupil B: Yes.

T: Great, so you can write that the anther dies, and then goes on, and then you go on. What's the next stage?

A: Then pollen gets into the flower and grows down into the great big long style to fertilize the ovules. We've had to sellotape ovules, and we've had to do seeds like eggs.

T: Great.

A: Inside the ovary, we've had two doors opening. You'll like this . . . er . . . [Now there is a gap in the recording.]

A: Oh yes, with pollination.

T: With pollination, and what is that? I mean, what is it really?

B: It's more or less the same except that flowers, you know, that when we were little like, we were fertilized by male and female organs, just like flowers with their pollen and stigma and everything. You've got the ovary, right. But the male has got like big long tails or anthers on little filaments. The pollen gets out of these, and the wind carries it off, until it lands on the stigma of another flower, and then he fertilizes that, and that's the only bit we have got to do.

T: Great. Whereas in this one, wind isn't involved is it? What's involved in this one? How does it . . . ?

A: Insects.

B: Bees.

T: So all in all you've covered everything. I mean, where did you start the first one?

A: Self-pollination. We've done it with just bees. Then we tried cross-pollination, then we did self-pollination with things like geraniums. . . .

The language of biology consists of a general biology code, or register, and a series of overlapping specialized registers. The first stage of coming to terms with a register like this is probably willingness to learn the technical vocabulary and assimilate it into normal speech. It is evident here that the children felt slightly awkward about using this sort of jargon: 'But the male has got like big long tails or anthers on little filaments.' The familiar 'like' tacked on to the informal 'has got' loads the sentence with enough familiar language to allow the new terms 'anthers' and 'filaments' to be accommodated readily. It is the children themselves who choose to use this jargon, though their sentence structures are not yet really part of the formal biology register. Presumably this will come in time. The context is also supported by the concrete experience of cutting out and making the subjects for the film, then making the film itself, so that the biological concepts and the new language register are slowly assimilated within a rich, supportive context where the children are the experts and the teacher the learner.

The Project teachers testified to their pupils' improved levels of communication. It has been suggested by a previous Schools Council study[23] that the writing of most pupils addresses the teacher as its audience and that over half of that is to 'teacher as examiner'. In that study it was suggested that, though it was desirable to widen the pupils' audience considerably, this was very difficult. In the work of the present study the audience is very considerably widened. Pupils address their communication first and foremost to their

---

[23]The Schools Council and London University Institute of Education Joint Project: Writing across the Curriculum 11–13 years, *Why Write?*, The Project Team (1973).

peers, initially to the members of the group producing a particular film, then to the rest of the class, then to other classes as teaching material, and sometimes to groups outside the school – a parents' meeting, another school, a hospital radio service or local television. This need to make clear statements to a real and critical audience qualitatively alters the language context, considerably sharpens the learners' perception of their tasks and thus changes the quality of their language performance.

D. H. Hymes (1971)[24] has stressed the need for a socio-linguistic theory of communicative competence, i.e. an explanation of the ability to use exactly the right language for a specific situation. All of us have met people who know just what to say to meet a specific need (or when to stay silent). There are times when it is appropriate to lace one's speech with metaphor or references to poetry; equally, there are times when this would be totally inappropriate. Hymes stresses the need for people to have wide verbal repertoires. Such a repertoire would include styles or codes ranging, for example, from the local-dialect peer-group variety (formal or informal) to the variety used in abstract academic textbooks; it would also include the ability to switch codes sensitively, which involves having very considerable linguistic resources within each variety of the verbal repertoire. Presumably, the more poetry a person knows, and especially the more he is able to incorporate this poetry in his speech or writing, the richer are the resources within that area of his verbal repertoire. For example, it is most valuable for an O-level literature candidate to be able to write as in the following extract from a 1978 O-level script:

'Henchard appears and insults stupidly the machine. This is characteristic of the man, quick to give his own hurtful opinion, regretting it after. This overzealous and impetuous attitude recurs throughout the novel many times: he is quick to propose to Susan, and to Lucetta, quick to lose his temper with Donald, and quick to dismiss Jopp. He is also inconsiderate of another's feelings; although the machine is not human (but he can imagine it as Farfrae), he condemns it because it represents a challenge to him. He is inconsiderate to Lucetta when he "blackmails" her into marrying him, inconsiderate to Elizabeth's sentiments over Donald, and inconsiderate to Jopp when he refuses (the first time) to see him after promising employment.

'Hardy writes – "(Henchard's) greeting had been dry and thunderous", like the man himself – "dry" (inconsiderate, virtually empty of emotion) and "thunderous" (looming dangerously, quick-tempered). . . .'

Here the language of Hardy is richly and effortlessly woven into a complex, rhetorical style (full of embedded sentences) which seems to mirror both the book and the effect it is having on the mind and feelings of the child writing the essay.

While the building up of such a rich and sensitive area of the verbal repertoire cannot be taught directly, there are nevertheless modes of teaching and examining that can encourage it. The evaluation of the Project suggested that the kind of work done does encourage the development of a rich, responsive verbal repertoire and also the fundamental principle of code- or style-switching. For example, here once more are the non-exam fifth-form boys making 'British Breakfast':

Pupil A: We've got to plan out where it . . . where we are gonna put the still picture into. We've got to. . . .

[24]D. H. Hymes, *On Communicative Competence* (1971), reprinted in *Sociolinguistics* (ed. J. B. Pride and J. Holmes; Penguin, 1972).

Pupil D: That's like the end without the pigs, isn't it? That's like when we
    went down the road for the pigs. Put the still picture right at the end of the
    like . . . when we've been filming; 'n *that*, stick it on the wall, on something.
A: What are we gonna do for the title then, like put a title on them, with some
    pigs running about, or put the pigs on, then the title?
Pupil C: Put the title first.
A: Ah, you haven't done it wrong? What are you doing?
D: You'll have to rub that out.
C: Go over it in black felt-tip.
A: I've got to know what shots I'm gonna be taking, don't I? You've got to
    know . . . you've got to tell us all, John, cos you're the director.

In this brief extract there is evidence of a very systematic, economic shaping of the visual material by discussion and a very sensitive interplay of group
relationships, even to the extent of one of the group suggesting to the director
that he should direct more forcefully. This is reflected in the language. The
pupils seem continually to be on the point of breaking through into the highly
technical formal statements associated with film-making. For example, consider the sentence 'Put the still picture right at the end of the . . . when we've
been filming'. Something like 'the final moving sequence' was required to
finish this sentence adequately but the phrase would not come, either because
it was outside their repertoire, or because this peer group had, for social
reasons, to keep partially within the boundaries of traditional peer-group
language when working together. Nevertheless, this incomplete sentence is
evidence of the beginnings of what Hymes calls a 'performative routine': in
other words, a set of specialized utterances that are absolutely essential to a
particular task. A particularly clear example of this process is provided by the
extract quoted in Chapter 8, pages 98–99, in which a fourth-year girl taking
optional drama is directing the video-filming of a sequence for the first time.
The failure of the teacher to appear, the need to get on with the job in case the
rest of the class gets bored, and the presence of the technical task bring about
an extraordinary shift of role from the uncertain 'I'm dreading this' to 'Follow
her over . . . get the grey in'. Also, there is a linguistic precision, a clipped
economy of utterance, that is an absolutely essential linguistic routine for this
particular task – how else could it be done? These language routines appear
throughout the tapes: the pupils are effortlessly becoming used to learning
very specific technical linguistic short cuts that enormously facilitate the
understanding of large quantities of subject-matter.

The Project clearly holds great promise in this area: if the teacher can
analyse the language routines that best aid learning in the class-room, then it
should not be too difficult to set up audio-visual work which will bring about
the rapid development of these routines. Such a necessary language routine
might be the ability to mingle the technical language of a particular subject
with the role language of class-room and school relationships (as Barnes
describes[25]). The children making a videotape of the novel *Walkabout* had also
embarked on a linguistic exploration of the plot and the characters. Not only
had they come to terms with the novel as a literary experience, they had also
developed a series of language routines that could be used to form the basis of
an advanced course in literature – ways of thinking and expressing themselves
that would enable them to come to terms rapidly with complex novels such as
Great Expectations. So often the lack of facility in these modes of thought and

[25]D. Barnes *et al.*, op. cit. pp. 53–62.

expression is the real barrier to youngsters studying an academic subject. The last chapter of this book deals with the relation between audio-visual logic, language and thinking and tries to suggest why the audio-visual work so readily breaks down the language and thought barriers.

Although the initial motivation was provided by the technology, it became clear that this impetus soon died away and the motivation was sustained by something else which was a necessary linking stage before the intrinsic motivation of learning itself could take over. The factor that replaced the novelty and excitement of the technology was identified by teachers as successful communication. The overall theoretical background to this has just been outlined; it now remains to look at how each stage of the work generates specific language abilities. These are the following oral-language abilities, taken mainly from the Bullock Report:

1. Shaped narrative, aided by voice qualities, timing and emphasis; language development from 'simple anecdote, strung together mainly by co-ordinate syntax' to more complex and meaningful speech.
2. Extension of span of utterance; lengthening and increasing the complexity of speech.
3. Total discursive awareness; 'ability to range backwards and forwards over the discussion with an awareness of the relationship between its parts as it develops'.
4. Openness to complex dialogue; 'ability to modify . . . own viewpoint to accommodate the contributions of others'.
5. Positive contributive attitude; to 'encourage and interpret other opinions as part of a co-operative activity'.
6. Objective language; precision in communicating facts.
7. Ability to give and receive instructions.
8. Confidence in public utterance; development of the ability to speak clearly and effectively in front of people, especially strangers.
9. Confidence in social intercourse; the ability to speak clearly, effectively and with purpose in a small group.

After being introduced to a topic the pupils break up into groups and then work through the following processes: discussion, research, improvised drama, script-writing, translating the script into audio-visual form, and recording sound and vision.

DISCUSSION

The pupils discuss how to approach the topic. This is not a discussion in isolation, but one that is leading to group activity – it has an end result.

This develops:

> A total discursive awareness
> Openness to complex dialogue
> Confidence in social intercourse
> A positive contributive attitude
> The ability to accept and encourage the modification of one's ideas
> The ability to cope with rejection of one's ideas

RESEARCH

The pupils research the area they have chosen. This research may involve any or all of the following:

1. Reading and selecting prose, poetry and information related to the theme, in light of it being spoken

This develops:

> Awareness of shaping narrative
> Interest in prose and poetry
> Reading ability

2. Formulating questions to put to teachers, librarians and specialists (inside and outside school)

3. Conducting interviews, which may be taped and used as part of the programme

This develops:

> Confidence in social intercourse
> Confidence in public utterance
> Total discursive awareness

4. Conducting a survey (for a documentary)

This develops:

> The use of objective language
> Self-confidence

IMPROVISED DRAMA

The pupils are led in drama for two purposes:

1. To explore further the theme or area of concern

This develops:

> Shaped narrative, aided by voice qualities, timing and emphasis
> The use of abstract language
> Confidence in social intercourse
> Self-confidence

2. To produce dramatic inserts

This develops:

> Shaped narrative, etc.
> Confidence in public utterance
> Self-confidence

SCRIPT-WRITING

The discussion, research and drama are brought together in a script: a written plan of the intended sound and vision. This involves working with the written word, sounds, music and visual images. Also, the details of what is to be heard and seen must be written down. Discussion and argument will be prevalent during the finalizing of the group script.

This develops:

Openness to complex dialogue
A positive contributive attitude
Total discursive awareness
Objective language
Writing skills
The ability to accept and encourage modification of one's ideas
The ability to cope with rejection of one's ideas
The ability to abide by a majority decision
Awareness of the interdependence of group members

TRANSLATING THE SCRIPT INTO AUDIO-VISUAL FORM

The pupils record sounds, make visuals and rehearse the live sequences. There are further discussions, giving of instructions and explanations of what is wanted. The activities include:

1. Preparation of the sound-track:

   Formal training in speaking for presenters, narrators, demonstrators and actors
   Preparation for recording speech, music and other sounds

2. Preparation of visuals:

   Painting and making still pictures
   Working on dramatic inserts
   Working on demonstrations and interviews
   Deciding on and filming telecine/portapack inserts

All these activities require co-ordination via oral communication: discussion, advice, explanation and teamwork.

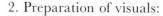
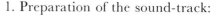

This develops:

Total discursive awareness
Openness to complex dialogue
Objective language
The ability to give and receive instructions
Shaping of narrative, etc.
Confidence in public utterance
Awareness of the interdependence of group
    members
Responsibility to the group for one's actions
The ability to accept and encourage modifi-
    cation of one's ideas

RECORDING SOUND AND VISION
Recording demands precise communication
and a high degree of social responsibility. The
procedure depends on the medium chosen.

1. Television
Groups of eight to sixteen pupils form to perform the necessary roles and to man the various pieces of equipment. These roles and
equipment will include some or all of the following:

Director
Vision-mixer
Sound-mixer

Tape-recorder
Record-player
Telecine/portapack

Cameramen
Caption-stand
Slide-projector

Floor manager
Actors
Narrator, etc.

All pupils work under critical performance
conditions which place a premium on effective
and clear communication.

This develops all abilities but particularly:

The ability to give and receive instructions
Awareness of the interdependence of group
    members

2. Tape-slide

Here the vision is simpler, allowing smaller groups.

Processing (colour slide) requires accurate group co-ordination.

Sound is similar to both film and television.

This develops all abilities but particularly:

The ability to give and receive instructions
Responsibility to the group for one's actions
(but in a simpler situation)

The Development of Social Skills and Analysis of Group Processes

Chapter 1 stresses the critical need for education to focus on the development of interactive and interpersonal skills among young people, and the last few pages will have shown how impossible it is to disentangle communication abilities from these. Nevertheless, in order to begin to clarify what was felt to be important in developing a supportive and cohesive group, the following list of empirical categories was made:

1. The ability to cope with rejection of one's ideas
2. The ability to accept and encourage modification of one's ideas
3. The ability to abide by a majority decision
4. An inclusionist attitude of encouraging and upgrading others
5. Awareness of the interdependence of group members
6. Awareness of the responsibility to the group for one's actions

Whilst these categories were found to be very helpful, they were rather general, and something more precise was needed in order to look more closely at the processes involved. One of the techniques used was a modified version of Flanders' interaction analysis, to see what was happening to the quality and nature of the interaction. The first point that stood out was that, unlike Flanders' findings (where teachers tend to dominate discussion to the extent of doing two-thirds of the talking), even with the teacher present the pupils did far more of the talking, and of course talked even more when the teacher was absent. What is more, again with the teacher present, there were far more unsolicited utterances from pupils, far more questioning of the teacher and far more interaction between pupils. Whether this necessarily means that more learning took place is not easy to answer, but it clearly indicates that a wider than normal variety of communication skills was being used.

Flanders' system has been very much criticized for various reasons, including the assumption that his categories are interpretive rather than objective. Clearly the assigning of particular interactions to particular categories involves a very considerable act of interpretation by the observer. In addition, Flanders' system contains a built-in model of the learning situation unsuited to the dynamic and creative processes being observed. It was therefore necessary to extend Flanders' system to make it more appropriate to the work of pupils in the Project. We next give an example of how a session was broken down on the lines of this extended analysis; it goes a good deal further than Flanders to try and describe what group processes were at work.

Discussion

First the pupils discuss the script:

Pupil D: You don't need that, John.

Pupil C: Yeah.

D: Frank, go and get the still picture, man.

Pupil A: What's it doing in here?

D: What do you want the still picture for, man?

C: Cos we need . . . that's the only picture we need.

Pupil B: In the studio.

Next they consider what pictures they need to draw:

A: Do 'British Breakfast'.

D: What else is there to do? Still picture. Is that all we've got to take up the studio?

C: Aye, just that still picture and that. . . .

A: Are you sure that's an inch?

D: Yes, I measured it right. We got to get the title done, got to get the title done. What else?

B: Like, get what we need next.

C: Get Michael on the screen first.

We need that poster.

Next, they consider the soundtrack:

D: We've got to get the music?

A: Got to plan out what we need next?

D: We need the poster, don't we?

B: From the country room?

E: I know, cos we get that when we're going home.

Analysis

Analysis of D's talk:

Trying to influence C's behaviour by giving information.

Requesting action.

Requesting information.

Examples of using oral language to influence the behaviour of others.

Analysis of the whole group:

Giving an instruction.
Requesting information.

Offering information.

Requesting information.
Offering information.
Trying to influence the behaviour of others by giving information.
Trying to influence the behaviour of others by offering information.
Trying to influence the behaviour of others by offering information.
Trying to influence the behaviour of others by offering information.

Deciding upon and organizing future activity necessitates using talk to influence the behaviour of others.

Although the preceding conversation has been interpreted as an attempt by individuals to influence the behaviour of others it may also be looked at as an exercise in self-clarification.

'Haven't we? I'm not sure.'
'Haven't we? I'm not sure.'

'Isn't it?'

A: Find out what we need next.

?: We've got one of those posters at home, Peter.

D: We start putting on a record, so that's all right.

?: *Food, Glorious Food*, wasn't it?

?: Ah.

?: Yeah.

C: We'll have to have Michael on the screen.

D: What for? Don't let him on.

'Shouldn't we?'

Testing out the idea.

Deciding upon and organizing future activity necessitates using talk to clarify the talker's ideas.

For any group to function, cohesion or a good working relationship must be maintained.

D: Yeah, so that's still picture. Record, title, what else is there?

A: Words. What are we going to say? Need to work out that.

?: Aye.

A: What's [inaudible] got to say?

?: Aye. Over the titles?

A: And what anybody else is going to say.

D: This is a film on 'British Breakfast', something like that, eh?

'We've done it, aren't we good?'
'We all need to think about it, we're all important.'
'You've got my support for that idea.'
'I think your opinion is important here.'
'I agree it's an important point to get together over.'

Deciding upon and organizing activity necessitates generating group cohesion.

They go back to the drawings:

A: We need more than one title, don't we?

C: Good idea. Now we've got a film.

A: That would be the main title. Then, like, some subtitles like how the egg comes about and how bacon comes.

?: How will the presenter sit and what will he do?

C: Best to see if he does sit down.

E: He'll draw a picture out.

A: No.

D: It's a canny idea, that.

Requesting agreement leads to cohesion.
Supporting a colleague leads to group cohesion.
Offering information: 'Do you agree?'

Requesting information: 'I think your opinion is worth getting.'
'Think about this possibility.'
'Perhaps this might be a solution. What do you think?'

Considering it again. Defending a colleague under attack.

| C: Or we can draw one after another, can't we?
D: Draw, draw a hen on one side and a pig on the other. | Attempt to get A to change his mind.
Trying to reach a unanimous decision.

When future activity is being decided and organized, talk is often used simultaneously to influence the activities of others, to clarify the talkers' ideas and to generate group cohesion. |

The final stage of evaluating the social/communication skills developed in the Project was to use an observation system based both on the discourse analysis method pioneered by Sinclair and Coulthard and on various other systems for observing and evaluating interactive behaviour in groups.[26] To summarize, it was found that, in the work of this Project, there was considerable behaviour which helped the group to fulfil its task, and also considerable behaviour which helped the members of the group to work well together with maximum use of the members' resources. There was very little behaviour which interfered with effective functioning of the group. Many of the traditional roles of the teacher (such as determining the boundaries of phases of the lesson, directing, eliciting, informing) were taken over by the pupils as a group, without strain. The pupils always seemed sensitive to each other, and decision-making was much more rapid than in normal lessons.

We now give two more extracts, the first of which is from a tape of a conscientious, well-respected further-education lecturer teaching students how to prepare and make capillary-soldered joints in copper.

Student 11: The adhesion of the molecules for glass is greater than their cohesion.

Lecturer: Therefore, consequently, the meniscus curves upwards and the liquid rises in the tube.

Student 12: Is a meniscus a curve in the liquid?

L: Yes, the curved upper surface of a liquid in a tube. Conversely, the cohesion of mercury molecules is greater than their adhesion to glass. The meniscus therefore curves downwards and this is accompanied by capillary depression. When might we use mercury?

Student 13: In a U-tube – a manometer containing water. We read the bottom of the meniscus, the vertical height between the bottoms of the meniscus, when recording pressure.

L: All right, a U-gauge. What about mercury meniscus?

Student 14: A U-gauge containing mercury for taking bigger pressures. You read the top of the meniscus, the top of the curve.

L: Why?

S14: Because of the reason you have just told us.

L: Why?

S14: I don't remember the technical stuff. I can read a gauge and I don't think I need any more.

[26]The Sinclair/Coulthard system offers the possibility of creating a descriptive continuum from the linguistic generalities of the sociolinguistic argument to forms of social behaviour that are only partially linguistic. The only element missing from this system is a method for looking closely at the processes of group interaction. Thus it was necessary to borrow from other systems to cover processes felt to be important.

L: Well, I think it's important you know the basic facts so that you can reason things out for yourself. If you can't you will be in great trouble with later parts of the course. I'll tell you again. The cohesion of mercury molecules is greater than their adhesion to glass. The meniscus therefore curves downwards. Right. What materials are required to make a capillary-solder joint?

Student 15: I don't know.

L: Because you are always late. Lessons have always started when you arrive. We talked about materials weeks ago. 'I don't know' gets no marks in the exam. Can you name the materials?

The emphasis here is very much on teacher control: he marks the boundaries of exchanges, elicits answers and informs the students. The students do a certain amount of informing and eliciting, but the mode of the lesson inhibits this. There is a preponderance of anti-group behaviour by the teacher and at least one student: for example, aggression ('Because you are always late.') and blocking ('I can read a gauge and I don't think I need any more.'). Although the lesson has pace, very little real internalization of learning appears to take place.

The second extract is from a tape of some sixth-form boys making a television programme about war-games.

Pupil A: Now this is going to be nasty because you are going to have to describe the periods: sort of like here we have the Indians . . .

Pupil B: Where?

A: . . . dated from 3000 B.C. to whenever they ended.

Pupil C: 600 A.D. is less; that's the time I've got.

A: Then should we stick some little, er, pictures in with them, fade some little pictures in with the soldiers?

C: I've a little soldier, phalanges and a cavalryman.

B: Well, will they be suitable?

A: Well, that's really finished that shot, hasn't it?

C: That's a problem.

B: Along there. Yeah, I think that's the best thing?

C: Could be, could be.

A: Just kind of . . . a bit more . . . leave trails.

B: That's if we can have a good crab.

C: Uh.

A: What if you can't have a good crab? Do you just shift them along, with your hand?

Here there are no teachers present, yet the pupils have no difficulty in recognizing and controlling just where the boundaries of verbal interchanges are. They move on efficiently and effortlessly. At the same time they elicit opinions and support from each other, inform each other, and make a real attempt at group cohesiveness in order to complete their task. They encourage each other, harmonize and compromise, and the session moves very rapidly, with a good deal of co-operative learning.

It is not being suggested that the further-education class is typical of traditional teaching, but it corresponds very closely to the approach of Flanders' dominative teacher. The war-games group is typical of the Project's work.

Although the aim of developing social skills in their pupils was new to most of the Project teachers they agreed that new forms of social interaction were taking place in the class-room. A significant number of the teachers were surprised by the degree of independent co-operative work that their pupils were able to develop and sustain. They all valued highly the aim of developing social skills.

Many pupils expressed enjoyment at working in groups and compared such co-operative work more than favourably with individual work. Observation confirmed this, pupils often being absorbed in the challenge of being effective in the group as well as frequently receiving positive feedback from colleagues on their discoveries and contributions. A number of the more academic pupils indicated that they found group work a pleasant and welcome change from the pressures of individual work. They felt that it was a necessary experience and should form one element of their education. A few rejected it as not serious learning.

It is also important to say briefly why these new social skills have a signifi-cant influence on intellectual development. Many workers in the field of socio-linguistics have emphasized the importance of role in determining ling-uistic performance. Tanner stresses that code choice is determined by a very subtle balance of situational tensions in which the setting, the content and the social distance of the speakers play major parts. The more sharply defined the elements of the setting and the clearer the role relationships, the more readily will the appropriate verbal and social skills be selected. Barnes[27] shows how for pupils there is often considerable confusion between the verbal/social skills required for handling subject-matter and those required for handling the role relationships of the setting. He shows also how these two sets of skills can contradict each other (if the teacher encourages pupils who report to him his own formulations of the subject then this prevents the pupils doing the explor-ing of the subject-matter which will eventually make it meaningful to them). In the work of the Project, teachers tended to become consultants, and pupils were forced to take responsibility for organizing, directing, selecting, and so on (teacher's skills). They also (very quickly, if jobs were to be completed in time) recognized just what their relations with the rest of the group were, and used the skills associated with these.[28]

We found that children shifted their roles very flexibly as the setting required. Chapter 2 comments on the young, non-academic director of a film taking over from a professional television production team in deciding on his set. This is typical of the kind of social-skills development the work is capable of generating.[29] We are very much in support of the work of Barnes and others who show that when working in co-operative autonomous groups children do in fact use a more varied and skilful repertoire of social and verbal behaviour. The Project bears that out fully, providing an adaptable method of achieving such gains across the curriculum and alongside, often, surprisingly significant gains in subject learning.

[27]D. Barnes *et al.*, op. cit., pp. 46–76.

[28]One of the very interesting aspects of the research has been the degree to which both teachers and pupils welcomed this change of teacher role and felt that it had contributed significantly to the high level of development of linguistic, social and technical competence in the pupils. The reader can readily see this by analysing the case studies. For example, see pp. 43–5.

[29]Whatever the outcome of the present technical and social changes may be, it has clearly become imperative that young people are educated for the development of high levels of social skill, since they are likely to need to change roles and directions suddenly and unpre-dictably. This requires that pupils be educated for autonomy yet also for adapting to chang-ing group relationships. Both of these requirements are necessarily covered by this work. What is more, it offers a very real opportunity, as several of the case studies reveal, for the pupils to work outside the school environment as a working group, thus carrying the social and language skills across the barrier between school and the outside world.

CHAPTER 11

Making Changes

The introduction of a new method of teaching inevitably brings problems and demands that may well be unforeseen at the outset. There are also, of course, problems that are clear from the outset. The task of this chapter is to outline the demands placed upon teachers and upon the organizational framework within which they work. These demands may be regarded as putting pressure on four areas of the teacher's operation: attitudes, resources, class organization and knowledge.

Attitudes

The Will to Change

If a teacher really wants to change his mode of working he will often find a way to do so. This was certainly the case with the Project teachers, all of whom developed and adapted the suggestions of the Project team to overcome their problems. Many were convinced from the outset about the value of the work, while with others conviction grew with initial success. It was this conviction that was central to the success of the work.

It was essential that the teachers believed that oral language is an important medium through which pupils can explore school subjects. Some teachers needed to be convinced of this; they held that writing was the only important medium of class-room work. It was also essential for teachers to feel that the development of social skills was an important function of the whole curriculum. For many this idea was new. Indeed, one educationalist displayed open hostility to the idea; he believed such training to be outside the brief of the school. Lastly, it was essential that the teachers looked upon the audio-visual domain as a serious complement to writing as a medium of communication for their pupils. Although all the Project teachers accepted this at the outset it was all too clear that in a number of cases colleagues of the Project teachers remained to be convinced. One teacher said that the lack of support that his work received within the school was due to this:

'They do not treat my work as serious or important. They tell me that writing and reading are all that is important yet as soon as they meet in the staffroom the first thing they discuss is last night's television.'

With time a number of those sceptical of the Project methods became convinced, usually as a result of viewing pupils' work, talking to the pupils or observing lessons in progress. However, a number were either unable or unwilling to find time for closer contact with the work so their attitudes tended to harden.

Attitudes in the Class-room

Within the class-room all the Project teachers had to adapt to new situations in which their activities and roles changed. With some the new situation presented an extension of methods of working already employed; with the majority, however, the changes were sufficiently dramatic to cause initial insecurities which took varying lengths of time to overcome. At the end of the two-year period there were at least two teachers who had still not fully adapted to the roles the new methods demanded of them, although they were thoroughly convinced of the value of the work and continued to plan courses involving audio-visual communications.

The majority of these changes occurred because pupils had to work in small groups and because some control of the learning activity had to pass from the teacher to the pupils.

All the teachers were encouraged to allow the pupils to decide how to approach the topic under investigation and to let them take greater responsibility for the direction of their research and what to include in their programmes. As a result the teachers had less detailed foreknowledge of the content of any one lesson. It proved inappropriate to plan each lesson in detail, allotting a certain amount of time to covering one section of the syllabus, or to note-taking, answering questions, etc. Rather than planning and teaching a small part of a syllabus at any one time, the teacher had to be prepared for questions on any part of his subject.

As pupils took advantage of this increased freedom to explore the discipline, they became the arbiters of when any element of an investigation was complete. In general the teachers were able to maintain control over the overall time spent in exploration by placing limits on the time spent on a particular activity. However, as the pupils felt that they must understand an idea or concept fully to be able to translate it into audio-visual terms to their own satisfaction, the time spent on a topic could be controlled only by encouraging them to shorten their coverage of the topic, or by offering further clarification of a point which was causing difficulty. Teachers had to adjust to the fact that, if they were going to allow pupils to go at a speed commensurate with complete understanding, the time spent on different aspects and ideas would often be very different from that spent in a more formal setting.

Much of the above resulted because the pupils worked in small groups, justifying their ideas to each other and satisfying themselves that each new idea or fact was fully understood by the whole group. (It was very rare for a group to move on without satisfying themselves of this.) At times the discussion would become quite animated, at others a gentle murmur of discussion from each group created an atmosphere very different from the one many of the teachers were used to. Initially teachers reported frequent discomfort at the lack of silence in their class-rooms, but as they became used to sampling the activity and progress of each group, they became reassured that learning was taking place.

The sampling techniques employed by teachers varied but the most favoured was to ask the group to identify the problem that they were engaged in solving or to request a verbal report of progress from the group. As the teachers developed confidence in exercising intervention in this way, the feeling of being out of control lessened, although they said that the need to accept not knowing what each individual was doing all of the time was extremely difficult to come to terms with. Confidence in accepting such a situation developed when teachers learned to assess learning periodically – at the time of examinations, for example. Some teachers worked with the class as a whole, feeling more in control in such circumstances. Although they divided the class into small groups at specific points in the process, they always felt that they could revert to working with the class as a whole if necessary.

Teacher intervention was identified as a crucial part of the teaching method. Apart from its role of assessing individual and group progress, it was seen as essential for feeding the children with ideas and facts and directing their developing work. Although teachers were often gratified by the degree to which their suggestions were accepted by the pupils, a number initially found it difficult to adjust to exchanges being initiated by pupils rather than by themselves.

In general the teacher's role became much more one of an advisor whose instructions resulted from pupils' requests. The teachers were often asked questions of the form 'Why is this important?', 'How can we "say" this?', 'What does this mean?', 'How can we show this?', or 'Do you think this or that should come first?'

Many teachers had to adjust to other new activities in the class-room: pupil-directed research, selecting pictures and listening to music were all symptomatic of the wider range of expressive arts that the pupils were encouraged to use in the organization of their audio-visual statements. It was at this point that a number of teachers called on colleagues specializing in the expressive arts for help. To some of these teachers team teaching, or indeed common exploration of a theme by a number of teachers at different times in the school week, was new. This presented problems of control and information-sharing among the teachers involved.

Pressure towards co-operative teaching also resulted from the increased control given to pupils over their learning. In numerous cases the pupils' approach to a topic led them to ask questions outside the discipline from which the topic was drawn. In one case, investigating coal-mining in a study of local industries led pupils to consider history, geography and chemistry, as well as drama, music and art. Many of the teachers felt the need to consult colleagues; some initiated team teaching, whilst others met the pupils' demands by explaining that they must limit themselves to the discipline in question.

All the teachers had to accept that the emphasis pupils placed on a certain aspect of a topic might be different from the emphasis they themselves would have given it, although most were able to use the increased pupil commitment that resulted from such a choice to good effect.

The use of audio-visual media meant that many of the teachers had to adapt to ideas being represented in visual form to a far greater extent than in their own training. Indeed, a few experienced some difficulty in recognizing the full meaning of these pictorial statements.

As the recording sessions neared the class became much more physically active. Pupils would produce drawings and paintings, and rehearse speeches, poems and in some cases dramas. The degree of movement around the class-room which was generated as pupils checked on each other's progress or consulted group members over problems was found quite disconcerting by a number of teachers.

Finally, two general points raised comment from teachers. The first was that the activity in general took longer to establish than did normal class-work, although opinion differed on speed of subject coverage once work had started. The second point concerned the general relationship between teachers and their pupils.

Initially teachers reported that when establishing the audio-visual methods they worried about the time it took for the groups to get off the mark. They often found it necessary to cover the whole topic in skeleton before groups could organize themselves into purposeful activity. They were also worried by the blind alleys pupils sometimes took, looking for information in inappropriate books or spending too much time discussing a point that was not crucial to their statement. Later, as teachers' intervention skills developed, such worries were reported less frequently, some teachers valuing the pupils' mistakes as the basis of valuable teaching. Also, pupils were willing to do a lot of preparation in their own time, which speeded up the class-room work.

Regarding relationships, a significant number of teachers reported the development of closer relationships with their pupils. These were universally valued but did cause some teachers to worry about meeting the new, more personal, commitment that their pupils were imposing on them.

It was evident throughout the Project that a great deal of training was necessary to help teachers adapt to many aspects of the work, not least the new skills required by changes of role. Nevertheless, it was felt to be important that the teachers should be helped to reconcile their view of themselves as transmitters of knowledge with these new requirements. This help is reflected in Appendix 1 (p. 188), which outlines the kinds of skill employed by pupils in various facets of the work, so that teachers can be more certain about what the pupils are doing in terms of skills relevant to normal school learning.

Resources

Provision of Recording Equipment

All the teachers selected the medium in which they worked according to the availability of equipment for that medium. A number of schools possessed their own equipment. All the schools had a still camera, slide-projector and tape-recorder; a number also owned Super 8 film equipment, two owned a television camera in addition to a videotape-recorder, and one had a three-camera television studio. All the schools had enough equipment to engage in the Project's work in at least one audio-visual medium.

In addition to the schools' own equipment a number of local authorities made some form of central provision. One authority loaned a two-camera portable television studio to schools on a termly basis, another provided a central television studio which schools could visit, and in a third an LEA college provided a similar facility and a loan facility.

Teachers preferred school-based equipment, feeling it to be more accessible, although the young teachers reported occasional difficulties in obtaining videotape-recorders owing to pressure of off-air recording. With non-video equipment – film and tape-slide – most teachers reported little competition for use. Unless there was a course on photography these items were often incarcerated in a locked cupboard.

Reliability of equipment was often a fear if not an actual problem. Reports of equipment failure were surprisingly few and were limited almost entirely to television equipment, and almost always to the video-recorder, although a number of schools were using extremely well-worn equipment. The average failure rate may be estimated as one occasion in twenty. This figure was considerably inflated by two particularly bad cases in one of which the machine was replaced. Even with the newest machine, although breakdowns were very rare (and even then usually due to operator error or incorrect wiring rather than to machine failure) a number of teachers felt it wise to have a contingency lesson prepared just in case. When a breakdown did occur pupils were often disappointed but almost always understanding.

Considering the reliability of the equipment and operators made many teachers feel that a centralized studio offered significant advantages. Both centralized studios used (one of which belonged to the local authority, one to a college) were maintained by a technician, and usually production advice was also at hand. Teachers felt a degree of relief that their responsibility was limited to the teaching aspect of the work, with the studio technicians responsible for providing the technology. There was a similar feeling about the equipment which was loaned in that there was always an adviser that could be called upon to offer help in the event of any difficulty.

In the school which owned its own three-camera television studio, the above did not apply as the school had appointed a television technician whose job it was to run and maintain the studio's equipment. Over a number of years the technician had gained a great deal of production experience and had, on more than one occasion, instructed a new teacher in television production methods.

In a number of schools with which the Project had contact, teachers overcame their problems by calling on a science technician for occasional help, although in at least one case the technician's own preference for audio-visual work did cause some inter-departmental strain. Finally, and most common, technical help was offered by pupils themselves. It was not uncommon to find that pupils were more at home with television equipment than were the teachers, and they soon became adept at coping with the assembly and connection of the various pieces of equipment. In one case a fifth-year pupil was brought in for precisely this task.

Not all arguments, however, were in favour of centralized facilities. The distance from the school to the studio was crucial. One teacher was faced with a difficult problem of transport as the school did not possess a bus of its own. She was very keen that the local authority should provide a special bus for the resources centre to be used by the growing number of schools using the studios. Where schools owned their own transport no such problem existed.

Although a number of teachers were initially worried that the number of visits to the studios required would lead to a lot of extra organization, the actual number of visits proved to be very small in comparison with the amount of class-room work that they generated. (Most television work consists of research, planning and preparation.)

Overall, the centralized loan or studio facility worked well for television work. With film and tape-slides there was less need for it as the Project schools possessed their own equipment, although one authority did have a general loan pool which included Super 8 equipment. Those teachers who used it found it invaluable although many teachers did not know of its existence.

Cost

All the Project teachers were asked on a number of occasions to identify problems that they faced or had to overcome in the course of their work. On a number of occasions cost was mentioned, but in no case was it considered prohibitive and it was rarely seen as the major difficulty.

Hardware

Hardware, the machinery used for recording, is costly but most middle and secondary schools have at least some hardware, if only a tape-recorder and still camera. The Project schools either had their own equipment or were able to use equipment provided by the local authority. Two schools had to use very old video equipment which needed replacing, but one of them was able to purchase new video equipment during the Project.

Maintenance was either carried out by a local-authority pooled maintenance service or paid for by the school. Such costs were relatively infrequent.

Software

It was expected that software – film, tape, videotape, paper, pens and paints, etc. – would be reported as a significant extra problem. In the event, although teachers always had to exercise some care (especially with film) and one had to limit the frequency of the activity, in no case did cost prevent audio-visual work from being carried out. A number of teachers thought that the establishment of a special extra fund for this work within the school would help tremendously. However, it was pointed out by teachers that the amount of film or tape used was very small in relation to the amount of time spent in preparation by pupils. Also, where the pupils were engaged in the production of teaching material for other classes, money was being saved by not buying 'professional', often less relevant, productions. Videotape and audiotape could be used over and over again, and teachers found that they could usually borrow from stock until their departments could provide their own. One teacher reported that the cost of film was less than that of the paper and other materials saved because pupils were working on a much smaller visual scale for animation. Those teachers who had access to records belonging to the school music department or costumes belonging to the school drama department found these very useful.

Overall, teachers experienced no more difficulty in finding resources for this area than for the whole range of school activities, although this was a time when all schools were suffering increasing problems with resources.[1]

Books

By far the biggest resource problem was the provision of books. Most of the teachers experienced some difficulty in providing a wide range of books to which the pupils could refer in their research. These books had to be clearly organized (for easy access), simply written and fairly heavily illustrated. It is clear that teachers had to change many of the exercises they would have liked to have developed because of the dire lack of books of the type described. In the initial stages of discussion and research, group progress was frequently severely hampered by the lack of material of this type. Also, for many specialist subjects there was no printed material that covered the wider range of questions that pupils asked. There was a great need for general readers and pictorial reference books (including packs, as well as prose and poetry related to the specialist subject).

[1]Here we have dealt exclusively with the ten Project schools. Books providing detailed information on equipment are mentioned in the Bibliography and agencies able to give advice are listed in Appendix 2.

Class Organization

Teachers found that they had to reorganize their classes in three main areas. They needed to develop ways of working with limited amounts of equipment with groups that ranged from fifteen to thirty-four in size, they needed to monitor work with small groups and they needed to develop ways of organizing access to books and materials that were sometimes new to their class-rooms.

Limited Equipment

All teachers were working with less equipment than would have been ideal given no financial restraints. Most teachers were working with one studio, one television camera, film camera or still camera, and one tape-recorder. They were also often working with several small groups who were developing individual themes simultaneously and might want to use the recording equipment at the same time.

When teachers worked with the class as a whole the problem became one of finding enough jobs to occupy all the pupils during recording. In a television studio a teacher could create between twelve and fifteen jobs but even when each member of a group could be allocated a specific role care had to be taken to ensure that individuals did not become bored. In many cases where commitment had been generated through contributions during the preparation stage, the degree of patience and interest shown by individual pupils in the recording session was extremely high, but when individual pupils had contributed little, care had to be taken to ensure that they were allocated active roles during recording. With film and tape-slide this proved more difficult. Where a teacher split the class into a number of smaller groups pursuing their own themes a far greater degree of involvement in both preparation and recording could be guaranteed.

Strategies for organizing recording varied. In some cases one group would record their programme while another would watch, reversing roles for the second half of the recording session. Where team teaching was used, one teacher could guide part of the group in recording while another continued preparation with the remainder.

A number of teachers were faced with the difficult task of organizing three or more groups in such a way as not to make simultaneous demands on equipment. In the case of film animation, telling the pupils the lessons during which they could have access to the equipment seemed to work well. A further advantage was that each small group could film small sequences to be edited together as one film when the film was returned from processing. One teacher used an evening animation class to finish films, to speed their sending away for processing.

In work with portable television cameras organization became a task of carefully choosing locations to satisfy a number of groups, with editing again separating the various sequences. A similar strategy was adopted with photography for slides.

With television and sound work in the class-room a number of strategies were developed. These relied on groups becoming ready to record at different times. This was usually achieved by giving pupils a clear idea of when equipment would become available to them, with the pupils adapting their work to these deadlines. Pupils were allowed to vary their time of production within certain limits. In one case (Chapter 2) the teacher integrated audio-visual work with more traditional work to overcome these problems.

Insufficient attention to this kind of planning led to decreased motivation on the part of the pupils in one case and the abandoning of an exercise in another. In the first a teacher held one group back from recording until the other groups were ready. He was working with four groups in a small class, which necessitated all the groups co-operating in the recording of any one production (in a three-camera television studio). The group in question chose a theme that was far less involved than those chosen by their colleagues and consequently completed their preparation a number of lessons ahead of the others. Being satisfied with their preparation and therefore not wishing to make any further modifications, the group became disgruntled when asked to wait for two lessons.

In the second case the teacher split the class into groups without giving sufficient attention to introducing the pupils to the activities and skills necessary. The consequence was that the groups found it difficult to work without detailed guidance from the teacher, and he could not cope with their simultaneous demands for help.

With a number of the smaller remedial groups teachers were able to avoid such problems by working with the class as a whole, although all teachers worked with smaller groups at some time.

Work with Small Groups

Having the class divided into a number of small groups working on individual topics or themes was a new experience for many of the Project teachers. As a result teachers reported that a whole host of demands was placed upon their ingenuity.

Teachers adopted a range of approaches to selecting group membership. In some cases it was left entirely to the pupils; in others various forms of structuring were employed. Where it was left to the pupils, groups of friends of varying sizes emerged, which after some weeks of work were re-formed at the pupils' request. It was interesting that, in one case that was observed quite closely over the two-year period, all but one of the pupils remained in groups as a matter of preference. This class was of mixed ability but the subject was a non-academic area.

Teachers who chose the groups themselves (the majority) commented on the importance of their selection to the groups' success. Some teachers appointed group leaders whom they felt to be capable of writing and directing the group activity. Others appointed no formal leaders but allowed them to emerge naturally. In this case the leadership sometimes changed at different stages of the activity, depending on individual strengths. With mixed-ability classes most of the teachers ensured a mix of ability in the groups in terms of both academic ability and ability in the various contributory skills — visual art, social organization, logic, etc. However, having structured groups in this way, most teachers needed to intervene in each group's work to encourage pupils to take on different aspects of the work as well as to ensure that each pupil had developed his own way of contributing to the group. Teachers stressed the importance of being successful in the first exercise and identified the careful structuring of groups as a key factor contributing to success.

It was essential that groups were fully aware of their tasks and how to perform them. In pointing this out, teachers stressed that careful preparation in which the class as a whole is introduced to the purpose and detail of each stage of activity must precede group work. The more carefully prepared the pupils were the less stress was placed upon the teacher by the group work.

All the teachers found it necessary to rearrange seating to facilitate group work, usually placing desks in fours in a rectangle. Many teachers found it useful to address the class as a whole at the beginning and end of each session, as it became more difficult to bring the pupils together during a flow of activity. (It was of course possible, and a number of teachers developed a special cough or call for this purpose.)

General Factors

All the teachers found it necessary to plan the use of equipment to facilitate internal or external working, visits and, in the case of film stock, to allow time for processing. In the case of tape-slide, difficulties arising from delays in processing were often reported.

Teachers often found it useful to allocate special areas of the room to the use of general books, drawing materials, tape-recorders, record-players, etc. Pupils then became used to moving to the resources when they were available without the necessity of teacher involvement.

It was also found useful to provide large folders or envelopes for collecting each group's work at the end of each session.

Integration of Audio-visual Work

Few teachers used audio-visual methods exclusively for the two-year period, and all developed a number of ways of integrating the work into their general courses. In some cases it was used as an occasional activity, slotted in when appropriate. Appropriateness was judged by the nature of the subject, the need to remotivate the pupils, the amount of time judged available at the outset of the course, and sometimes by the availability of equipment.

While some teachers favoured using the methods as a revision exercise, others used them for learning complete elements of a course. While some teachers devoted six or seven consecutive weeks to this work, others spaced out the work by inserting other, more traditional activities between Project lessons. All the teachers established a balance that suited their purposes and the priority they attached to the potential results of audio-visual work. No one strategy appeared to be outstandingly successful in comparison with the others.

Important amongst this variation was the amount of time available for recording in each session. All teachers preferred at least a double lesson (2 × 35 min) for recording, with some stating this as a definite necessity for such work. Many teachers found it possible to use single lessons for some of the preparation work.

Finally, the time which elapsed between the introduction of the methods to the pupils and the recording of the pupils' own work varied significantly. There was universal agreement that it was important to show pupils an example of a programme at the outset, but opinions on the time between introduction and recording differed. It was clear that this time could lengthen as the pupils gained experience but it is not possible to be specific except to say that it should be the minimum possible to do justice to the topic under study. It did seem useful to restrict the time to a period of only a few weeks with the least able in the first instance, but even here teachers were quite successful when they integrated the audio-visual work with other work and took a longer time. It was also found useful to take pupils through the production of a prepared script for television at the outset in order to introduce them to the sort of finished programme they were aiming at.

Knowledge, Skill and Sensitivity

In making any change in class-room practice the knowledge of the teacher is crucial, for it is the degree to which he has thought through a whole series of questions that will determine success or failure, whatever the learning objectives may be. In addition, and particularly in this work, the skill and sensitivity of the teacher will also play a large part. As a result of bringing together the experience of twenty teachers and that of the Project team itself, much was learned about these twin areas of knowledge and skill. We shall present some of this here to facilitate clarity when approaching this work, as well as to encourage development of the right kind of support for teachers from advisers and colleges and departments of education. Finally, it must be pointed out that there is space here to do no more than outline some of the more important areas of knowledge, skill and sensitivity.

Rationale

The most fundamental requirement of all those undertaking this work is to develop a clear rationale for its use. Although this may seem obvious, the rationale given in each case strongly influenced both the organization and the outcome of all subsequent activity. The case studies imply that there is a whole range of possible rationales for taking up this kind of work. Some of these are made explicit in Chapter 10, while other possible aims for the work are described in the first section of Chapter 12. Reading these three sections of the book will illustrate the wide range of choices open, from the development of social skills to better understanding of a scientific principle.

There is also a general issue concerned with the relationship of this kind of work to media studies. All the teachers except one regarded their work, consciously or subconsciously, as the use of a means of communication in order to communicate something specific and predetermined, in the same way as they would use writing. There was a well-defined subject to be studied and, like writing, audio-visual media were used as a means to this end: the pupils made audio-visual statements as an aid to organizing their thoughts and demonstrating understanding of the subject. The media themselves were secondary.

In media studies, however, the mass media constitute the subject. Thus the purpose of practical audio-visual work is to study particular aspects of the media themselves, which are therefore of primary importance. It is essential to recognize this distinction between media studies and the work of the Project, although we are not suggesting that this diminishes the value of either.

What Is Offered

The second essential requirement for using the methods described here is knowledge of the subject under study and of the means whereby it may be represented in recorded sound and vision. Knowledge of the subject was not a problem since most teachers chose a subject in which they had expertise and extensive knowledge, and thus knew what were the important facts, approaches and laws to be taught (as well as where learners most often experienced difficulties). It was what guidance to offer pupils on how to translate such concerns into recorded sound and vision that most often presented problems.

We have already mentioned the need for teachers to be familiar with basic recording techniques such as switching on, positioning tape, loading film and pointing microphones. Teachers trained more recently had usually covered this as part of their pre-service training, and others were able to acquire such knowledge from instruction books, a vast range of technically orientated publications, colleagues who were hi-fi enthusiasts or the Project team. Although all the Project teachers either had or acquired at least a working knowledge of these techniques, it is perfectly possible that some teachers will never feel comfortable with these new technologies. Such teachers may have to rely on pupil support, work in co-operation with other members of staff or technicians, or accept that, until the technologies are simplified further or adequate in-service training is available, the work may not be for them. However, it would be a rare school indeed where none of the above conditions could be met.

In addition to this basic knowledge, teachers needed information on sound-recording techniques and techniques, such as camera movement, for obtaining different results by using the equipment in different ways. Again there were found to be plenty of books and booklets relating to these aspects, and teachers found little difficulty in adapting the information to their own purposes, although sometimes the unnecessary technicality of these tracts made a simple physical demonstration necessary.

Beyond these fairly simple technical matters, information was not so readily available, and the Project team and teachers often had to work out answers to questions that were difficult to find in most of the published guides. The first area was discovering what may be placed in front of the camera and what may be recorded as sound. Except for highly specialized books on set design, lighting, etc., there seemed to be almost nothing easily adaptable to this kind of work. Thus the teachers and team had to find their own answers to such questions as 'What forms of expression could be useful in this work?', 'What is the importance of these in terms of learning gains, class and resource organization, and in relation to the recording medium being used?', or 'Which of these forms of expression are already developed in the school and what might be the effect of changing their context of use?'

The above may be regarded as questions about the different forms of language amenable to recording in sound and vision (for example, oral language, the language of music or the language of position and movement in dance or drama). The second type of information required was guidance on how these languages might be used to convey given meanings in the recorded forms of tape-slide, television or film. This seemed to be virtually unobtainable in printed form and there was a total absence of any indication of how such knowledge might be taught to pupils. The following are examples of the kinds of question to which answers were being sought:

'How do I begin to make pupils conscious of the range of sounds and sights that they regularly hear and see?'

'What sort of classification would aid this process?'

'How could such knowledge be used to develop the skills of manipulating sound and vision?'

'How would using different types of sound and vision affect what is seen as important in the subject under study?', and on the basis of this, 'What are the relationships between images and meaning?'

'Is there a more useful set of visual images for statements about science?'

'What constitutes useful music in developing historical consciousness?'

'How can various types and levels of thinking in a subject be translated into different types of visual and aural sequencing? For example, are there forms of visual sequence that reinforce a causal, temporal or dialectical form of statement? Does the film convention of flashback lend itself to causal and temporal organization of content? What sort of relationship between a general scene and a constituent of that scene can a "zoom" portray? How is the relationship held within a zoom transferred to the content being shown?'

Some teachers had already developed working answers to such questions, others were guided by members of the Project team, but whichever was the case, what was being developed was a series of rationales for developing sensitivities and transformational skills which allowed pupils to 'think' through sound and vision.[2]

How It Is Offered

Once a clear rationale has been developed and the main areas of skills and knowledge that must be offered to pupils have been decided, the best way to organize the work may also be determined. The previous sections have already mentioned such factors as resources and attitudes and some general conclusions have been drawn about class-room organization. There is one aspect of organization, however, that implies knowledge on the part of the teacher which is not directly related to knowledge of recording sound and vision but which is no less critical. We hope that it is clear that the pupils were engaged in a complex task of co-operative organization and learning and that within the various groups the pupils often developed a momentum and flow in their approach to their work which was one of the most pleasing aspects of the study. However, this placed enormous pressures on the sensitive teacher, for an awareness of these gains also led to an awareness of the critical nature of any intervention by the teacher in the groups' work. Careful thought about the overall task obviously led to a great deal of guidance being given at the beginning of the work, before the pupils began their group tasks, but however much guidance was given at the outset, there was always a need for the teacher to become involved with the later activity. This was relatively easy when the pupils themselves invited teacher intervention by asking a question about content or form but was far more difficult at those times when pupils should have been asking questions but were unaware of the need for them. These occasions, which often represented key learning points in the pupils' work, demanded a high degree of sensitivity and skill on the part of the teacher. The teacher had often to sense a difficulty, assess the cause, confirm and correct it by intervention but leave the pupils with the feeling that their control of their own work had not been usurped. Often the more the teacher had to offer, the more sensitive his approach had to be. There was always the danger of equating forced feeding with genuine understanding and learning.

Some teachers became quite adept at spotting appropriate moments to intervene, sampling activity and assessing progress. Various methods of feeding facts and feelings into a group's work emerged, confirming the complexity of this area. Teachers were seen spotting cues for intervention, sampling, withdrawing graciously, accepting being taught whilst at the same time teaching, using questioning techniques, accepting rejection of ideas and performing many other activities which betokened the high degree of skill and sensitivity they had developed. In terms of teacher knowledge such skills are crucial as, with knowledge of the media and subject chosen, they are directly related to the quality of the work the pupils achieve and as a result the learning gains made.

[2]Answers to some of these questions, at a simple working level, will be implicit in the materials mentioned in the Preface.

CHAPTER 12

Audio-visual Language and Learning

The most striking result of this study is the way in which the carefully guided creative use of audio-visual media by children enlarges our expectations of what they are able to achieve. This seems to be true across the whole ability range and in diverse subjects. This chapter attempts to explain this change of expectation and to show how, in the work of the Project, it arose as a result of changes in the communication medium through which pupils organized and expressed their learning.

First, we shall make generalizations based on the class-room work and attempt to show how many of these seem to tie in with differences in the educational process imposed by the different communication media used (words or audio-visual). Second, we shall make a theoretical analysis of the relationship between language, picture and thought as a way of explaining the changes observed. Finally, we shall summarize the main implications of this and the study as a whole and give our recommendations for education and training.

The Educational Process in Relation to Media

We first compare the effects upon learning of using words recorded as writing and using words and pictures recorded as television, film or tape-slide. We shall do this by looking at four aspects of audio-visual communication that seem to differentiate it from the use of writing alone. These are the collaborative nature of the process, the comprehensive nature of the medium, presentational differences, and the social relevance of audio-visual media.

The Collaborative Nature of the Process
None of the four factors just mentioned stood out as an explanation of the changes observed. Nevertheless, in terms of the Project's starting-point (communication and social skills) and in terms of some of the gaps in current educational practice, the social or co-operative work generated as a result of changing the medium in which children recorded their ideas and experiences certainly seemed to be of major importance. It plays a central role in developing social and language skills, providing social support for learning and also in changing some of the more negative relationships that develop within the class-room without wish or intent on the part of teacher or pupil.

In almost all the case studies (Chapters 2–9), which covered the work of twenty teachers, most of the audio-visual work was done in groups, which varied in size and organization. The pupils rarely felt that a programme was the brainchild of any one individual, but rather felt a common responsibility for the production. The final product was the property of all the pupils because tasks and responsibilities had not all been performed by one individual working alone but had been shared amongst the group. One teacher remarked, 'They worked in a co-ordinated way for a common goal.'

Except for television studio work, the production of audio-visual statements is not *essentially* a social process. It is quite possible, given the right equipment, to make films, television programmes or tape-slides as an individual enterprise. However, what the case studies clearly show is that producing audio-visual statements lends itself to group work and a co-operative atmosphere.

SOCIAL SKILLS

It follows from the collaborative nature of the production process that pupils have to become able to co-ordinate their individual contributions towards the production of an effective, and shared, end-product. In the early discussions in which the pupils explored and formulated their initial ideas, many suggestions were rejected or modified, and individual pupils had to come to terms with this curtailment of personal freedom. They were continually put into situations in which it would have been all too easy to feel a sense of personal rejection as the group rejected or modified suggestions, yet they very quickly came to accept this as a natural and necessary part of group work. Also, once they knew what it felt like to have an idea of their own rejected, they were more sensitive to the feelings of others within the group when discussing suggestions the others had made.

Pupils progressed from these early discussions on the basis of identifying a number of distinct tasks that they would need to perform (researching in books, obtaining information from teachers or other adults, selecting or preparing pictures, and so on). In taking up these individual tasks they developed a sense of responsibility to the group for the way in which they worked. They became responsible to the group for the quality of their activity, for the speed and thoroughness with which they approached it, for justifying their choices and decisions and for organizing an adequate presentation of their results to the group.

Throughout both the allocation and co-ordination of individual contributions and the group discussions about content it was of course necessary to organize and maintain the group itself. Pupils developed various ways of doing this. In some cases they would not continue until they had unanimous agreement within the group because they had 'learned that everybody's got to agree'. In other cases some form of democratic structure was erected to cope with disagreements. In others extra weight was given to the views of anyone who had particular expertise relating to the point under discussion or was going to do the work in question. Whatever form of organization they chose, coping with disagreements was something which each group had to consider. In almost all cases this was managed with remarkable skill, and some individuals demonstrated quite advanced organizational skills.

One such skill which deserves special mention is leadership. The first and most striking social result of the work was that very capable leaders emerged in many of the groups. These very quickly developed high levels of tolerance and guidance, so as to unite the activities of their colleagues.

The second, and even more interesting, development was that leadership changed as the activity changed. For example, one pupil would lead the theoretical discussions, another the visual planning and another the practical work of recording. The pupils became extremely adept at allocating leadership to various individuals from amongst their number at appropriate points.

These are only the more obvious social skills and situations that were evident as a result of the co-operative nature of the production of audio-visual statements.

LANGUAGE SKILLS

The wide range of social situations encountered by pupils working with audio-visual media also encouraged the development of language skills (which may, of course, also be regarded as social skills). As the activities of a group changed, so too did the relationships between members of the group and thus the demands placed upon the use of language by the group as a whole. This happened when, for example, discussion gave way to research and consequently speaking gave way to reading. Similarly, the language demands on each pupil changed in response to changes in the contribution that he was able to make. Once again, it may be useful to look at the various stages and types of activity in which the pupils engaged to examine this relationship between language use and its social context in more detail.

The first task of any group about to embark upon a piece of co-operative activity must be to define its aims and to generate an awareness of the views of each member. If the group members are motivated towards the goal (which was certainly the case in the class-rooms studied), each individual then tries to offer his own opinions on the details of the group's aims, in our case what the final programme should contain. Pupils experienced a need to present their ideas clearly and in a way that was readily understandable to the rest of the group. They backed up their suggestions with a combination of reasoned argument and concrete description of the way they felt about their ideas. They supported their arguments by predicting the response they thought would come from the audience, and often had to carry their arguments through challenges and interruptions. It was frequently necessary to concede the right to speak to a colleague who was forcefully following another direction. They would then take up their original line of reasoning at a later stage in the discussion or might concede the point completely, having recognized a better alternative. They might perhaps bow to pressure within the group or might give up because they had not managed to explain their points clearly enough. It was found that pupils relied heavily on oral language to negotiate these decisions and that this led them to exercise a wide range of language skills. These ranged from constructing and delivering coherent and convincing arguments, questioning for clarification and encouraging modifications to moving from the specialist language of a particular subject into a more familiar style and back again. It was clear that these diverse uses of language resulted from the need to share information and to agree upon a course of action, which in turn arose directly out of the co-operative nature of the whole exercise.

After the initial discussion to decide on the aims and overall content of the programme, the pupils usually moved on to identify what would need to be done in order to turn their ideas into a recorded statement. The specific nature of such tasks varied very widely as did the forms of social organization chosen to achieve them. What was common at this stage, however, was some form of planning discussion in which the emerging ideas were elaborated and individuals or smaller groups given responsibility for each element of the overall task. Consequently, new language skills were required since the pupils were no longer presenting ideas on programme content but were predicting future activity to determine what immediate tasks they would have to accomplish in order to reach their goal. Of course, this is a mental activity that we all frequently engage in, but what made it such a rich language experience for the pupils was the added dimension of working in a group, and the consequent need to articulate these thoughts.

The next task a group faced was to organize and allocate the various practical activities that had emerged. This again was most often negotiated through oral language but oral language of yet another type: language suitable for encouraging and convincing another person to act, which involved its own distinct set of intonations and phraseology. The most common activity decided upon and allocated at this stage was research, which often took the pupils into another language area, that of reading and writing. The pupils read mainly for information, however this information was affective as well as factual. A number of points can be made on the use to which the pupils put the printed word. First, unlike general project work, an individual's task was often quite closely defined by the group and a pupil quite clear about what he was looking for. As a result a number of pupils reported feeling able to discard unnecessary or unrelated material much more easily, and even indicated pleasure at finding books so useful. Pupils also often felt responsible to the group for the time spent gathering information and conscious of the imminence of reporting their findings to the group.

Another interesting social process involved was group-reading. In one form or another, each passage selected or identified as important by an individual had at some time to be presented to the group and a case made for its inclusion. Sometimes the grounds for its inclusion were its being the only relevant information available; at other times it would be sufficient simply to read the piece to the group to obtain approval. Sometimes, however, a stronger case had to be made because there was more than one piece competing for inclusion or because the group initially rejected the pupil's choice. In the latter situation the individual would spark off a dialogue in which he tried to justify his choice by reference to various passages of text, sentence analysis or interpretation of metaphor and so on. What one witnessed was not dissimilar to a conventional comprehension lesson except that it was being organized by the pupils themselves. In some instances this group-reading became even more accentuated as many pupils chose to do their reading as a team, with a pile of books in front of them from which each individual borrowed to make his case. As soon as a pupil felt that he had discovered a relevant passage it was presented to the group for consideration, and a process of analysis of content and clarification of interpretation led to a decision to accept, modify or reject it before the pupils read any further.

At this stage of the process, if not before, most pupils realized the need to write in order to improve and complete the work in which they were engaged. This often happened because the activity had become so complex that pupils experienced greater and greater difficulty in remembering all that had been decided and in relating present activity to their developing plans. Various forms of recording decisions were therefore readily adopted by pupils, and amongst these was writing. Writing was cheap, efficient and 'portable'. Each member of the group could have access to it or could make copies. It could be readily modified as decisions changed and it could even be used as a reference point to focus discussion. These examples of the ways in which pupils approached writing show how many reluctant writers rediscovered writing as a valuable communication medium. Writing became a valuable means to a desired end. Indeed some pupils discovered that it was a necessary means and others (see Chapter 8) even discovered the necessity of formal writing processes such as précis and punctuation.

This was not the only use to which writing was put by the pupils in their work, however. For example, in the research and reading stages of the process writing became a useful tool for noting down references, for summarizing, for copying useful passages and for recording the progress that was being made. Among these uses of writing perhaps summary deserves a special mention. In the same way as the purpose of reading was clear as a result of early exploratory discussions, the pupils' use of summary techniques was enhanced because they were clear about what information was needed by the group. As a result, they approached the task in a very business-like way. Certainly the group nature of the process did much to establish a clear purpose for summary of information gathered in research.

By this stage in the process the pupils had introduced various forms of oral language, reading and writing in response to the need to organize themselves to produce an audio-visual statement. They had engaged in discussions, allocated research tasks and begun to work their way through the various printed resources available to develop their ideas and to fill out their skeletal plans. All the information gathered (pictures, poetry, prose, summaries or ideas) now needed to be organized and adapted to their basic plans. For all but the most simple projects this led to a further detailed discussion in which the new information was assimilated and recorded in the written form of a script. The oral language used here was very similar to that of the earlier discussions. All the previously mentioned aspects of presenting, receiving and interpreting information by individuals in an attempt to relate to and influence the group's work occurred again but with a difference of commitment that raised the level of feeling accompanying each utterance. The pupils generally exhibited a greater sensitivity to having their own ideas recognized and discussed. They seemed to put more effort into the justification of their own ideas and handled more sensitively the modification of the ideas of others. Thus, although the discussions involved just as much factual information as the earlier ones (more, if anything), there was an increasing tendency for emphasis to be placed on the language of negotiation. This seemed to be due to the personal commitment that each individual felt towards the information or ideas he had discovered as a result of having put personal effort into the research.

At this stage also, as a result of the increased amount of information being presented within the group, many pupils resorted to making notes. Again, since they had a clear purpose in mind, aided by the discussions at various stages of the work, the pupils were able to identify important aspects as they were raised and able to make notes. In addition, when individual findings had been reported and the group began to organize and select some of these, individual note-taking tended to be replaced by group note-taking. Sometimes the whole group would decide on a point and make a note but more often one person was appointed as official note-taker. As each point was discussed and agreed, he would commit the results to paper. While this process was going on it was not unusual for other individuals to continue to make personal notes, but what was of far more interest was that the discussions at this stage often considered the method and status of note-taking itself as well as what was to be recorded. Groups would explore a piece of information offered and would then discuss the best way or reducing it to a note, suggesting and assessing alternatives. The following conversation is a fair illustration of this:

Pupil A: Get that down.
Pupil B: What shall I put?
A: Oh I dunno, the building, man.
Pupil C: How the buildings show the rich. . . .
B: Buildings show. . . ?
Pupil D: Buildings often show how rich people are.
B: Say that slowly.

As a set of organized notes emerged in a logical and temporal sequence the job of turning it into a script began. The balance between scripting and note-taking varied with different groups and at different times as did all the activities described, with some groups passing directly from discussion of research findings to scripting, but what was distinctive about the writing here was that the pupils were writing a set of instructions as well as a narrative. Pupils were writing words to be spoken, and detailing music or other sounds to be heard. The visual content (which for many pupils had been planned in the form of a series of simple sketches) was now transformed into a series of short written descriptions. The way in which the intended programme was to move from picture to picture and sound to sound had also to be written into the script. This had to be done in order to record the complex instructions and content in a form that would be available to all the group members at various future stages of activity. The script not only contained details of what had to be spoken (and rehearsed), of what had to be painted, drawn or made and of what drama had to be developed, but also provided an accessible set of instructions for the activity of recording. Once again, as a result of the need for the group to have a recorded plan from which to co-ordinate its individual activities, these various forms of writing were used as a necessary means to a valued end.

The need to organize and co-ordinate the group's work through oral language reasserted itself as the main focus of language use when the pupils reached the next stage of the work, which was to produce the various items detailed in their scripts. Notes had to be expanded into full statements to be read for recording, outlines of dialogue had to be elaborated, pictures had to be made or found, music had to be selected, the details of the recording strategy had to be finalized, and all these tasks had to be allocated and co-ordinated within the group. The most frequent strategy employed by the pupils was to identify each task, identify an individual or individuals to whom responsibility for the task would be given and then to outline the task in great detail until, as a group, they felt satisfied that those with particular responsibility were in no doubt about what was wanted. All this occurred through oral negotiation: a process that in individual work would take place inside the head was here an observable discussion in which it was possible for all to become quite clear through reasoning and logic. Once again, pupils were often found to be using note-taking, summary, essay skills and other writing skills to aid their work and, which was new, were beginning to read aloud various passages, statements or portions of dialogue in preparation for the next stage, which was recording.

For many of the pupils recording was a very exciting prospect, since now all the various activities were consolidated in a very practical way into one coherent product. From the language point of view it was also an exciting time, since most of the language activities observed at earlier stages were evident again but with an even greater premium on accuracy and clarity and in a context in which timing and efficiency were crucial. Pupils were reading instructions, reading aloud for recording, improvising speech and giving and responding to verbal instructions, but if there was a word out of place or read badly, an instruction not clearly articulated at the right moment, or if instructions in the script were not read and acted upon, then the whole recording activity broke down. Pupils very quickly became aware of this critical element whether they were making a sound recording for a tape-slide sequence or a studio television recording. This awareness was often easy to observe. Each pupil responsible for a particular job upon which every other job depended experienced a high degree of social pressure to do the job effectively, and at just the right moment. As a result pupils put great effort into being economical and accurate in all the language forms used.

One aspect of oral language used deserves special mention. Recording could not go on without some form of co-ordination of the individual activities contributing to it, and although the cues for action that the pupils used were of many types, the role of spoken instruction was very important. As a result, pupils became very careful listeners. Throughout the work, wherever oral language was used there was a consequent need to listen, but what was said could usually be repeated without causing too much damage. Here, however, if a cue was missed or an instruction only half heard, then the results could be disastrous. The premium on careful listening was thus high.

In addition to being verbal instructions, cues for activity were often contained within the sound of the programme itself. For example, the end of a sentence spoken for recording would be agreed upon as an appropriate cue for, say, the movement of a camera or the beginning of a speech. Here the pupils were alerted to the cues by appropriate words on their written scripts and had continually to monitor what they were hearing and relate it to their scripts.

Group listening was also observed. For example, three girls listened to a selection of pieces of music in order to choose the most appropriate for their programme. All listened intently until the end of each piece, then they exchanged their reactions, describing the merits of the piece for their specific purpose.

Yet another, and equally important, form of listening was the listening which many pupils did whilst recording speech. Many pupils reported that they became conscious of what they sounded like and found themselves monitoring their own speech in a way that was often new to them. For example, one pupil said, 'I listen to my own sound' (Chapter 5).

In the final stage, that of viewing and critically appraising the finished product, the effects of the social nature of the process were once again evident in the language pupils used. In their lively discussions each pupil had a stake as a result of the ideas, organizing, research, speaking and so on that he had contributed to the making of the programme. Pupils were able to identify weaknesses and strengths in technique, areas of new learning, success in organizing information and many other factors. They were able to share, once again through oral language, their individual views, this time on the overall success of the communication and the relation of that success to the way in which the programme was made. Sometimes this included consideration of the appropriateness of the various language forms used. The pupils ended their co-operative task as they had begun it, with a sharing of individual insight that might lead to more effective communication at a later time.

SOCIAL SUPPORT IN LEARNING

The social activity encouraged by the use of audio-visual media led directly to social support in learning. Although there is no adequate theory to explain why this aspect of human behaviour should be so central to human activity, we feel from our experience with the Project that this is nevertheless true. If education is to be a satisfying process then we need ways to encourage pupils to share their pride and their sense of difficulty in learning. It is quite clear that use by pupils of audio-visual media is one way of moving towards this. Such sharing in learning is an integral element of the work. We have already mentioned some of its specific effects within the groups (listening, speaking, reading and writing), but what is most important here is to describe certain relationships between the support that pupils were able to give each other and its effects on motivation.

The first area that impressed us when watching pupils working in the ways described in this book was the frequency with which they shared positive feelings of success. Whether this was the discovery of a relevant passage in a book, the writing of a necessary piece of prose or the drawing of a picture, as soon as it was achieved the next act was to share it with a friend. One fourth-year pupil said of his reading research, 'When you find something an' it's good, you feel, oh it's great and you've just got to show it to somebody; you've got to.'

The reaction of the person with whom success was shared was also interesting. We were able to compare situations in which this sharing took place among pupils involved on the same production and different productions respectively. It was noticeable that when the pupils came from the same group the reinforcing reaction of the person with whom the achievement was shared was in general much stronger. This was most probably because members of the same group had a shared purpose, so that an achievement by one member of a group was an achievement for the group as a whole.

Social support was also evident in the sharing of difficulties. If one individual was experiencing great difficulty with a particular task, other group members could be drafted in to help on the basis that the task was the group's responsibility since they had originally all decided upon it. Apart from this, the ability of a pupil simply to express his difficulty to a colleague enabled him to reaffirm the support of others for his efforts. Where this sharing did not lead to renewed clarity and through this to a solution to the problem, it seemed at least to result in renewed effort. One sixth former expressed this by saying, 'You can meet a problem and although you know you should keep at it it's very difficult to do so without a little bit of encouragement.'

Social support in learning, which arose directly out of the social nature of the learning process, was thus a major contribution to the increased motivation pupils exhibited when working in this way.

CHANGES IN THE RELATIONSHIPS IN THE CLASS-ROOM

The last of the four factors that arose as a result of the impetus given to social learning by this work was the change in relationships in the class-room. Teachers were often surprised by the maturity and seriousness of purpose that their pupils managed to display, and certainly observation was able to confirm unexpectedly high levels of professionalism. Pupils were usually able to plan their own programmes of work, organize their own activity, guide their group discussions and perform many other activities in a self-directed way, with the result that significant changes in the relationships among themselves and between them and their teachers occurred.

Concerning pupil–pupil relationships, we have already mentioned various activities and learning processes for which pupils took responsibility as a group. We have suggested that much of this probably resulted from the co-operative nature of the task of producing an audio-visual statement and have implied throughout that this increased degree of control and self-direction in learning was partly the result of pupils pooling their individual abilities. What we should like to concentrate briefly on here is the effect that this had upon teacher–pupil relationships.

With pupils taking more control of their own learning, both in being able to guide its direction and in being able better to understand the learning process, the immediate consequence was that the teacher took on a more advisory role compared with the traditional role of instructor. At all stages, teachers found themselves being invited to solve problems as they arose in the course of activity, with responsibility for the definition of problems shifting from the teachers to the pupils. Since the pupils worked out their own routes through the subject-matter, it was impossible for a teacher to dictate the speed and direction in the same way as might have happened in a more formal setting. As a result, by carefully sampling the activity, a teacher could learn a great deal more about how pupils were faring. For example, by listening to the pupils' early discussions he could easily find out a great deal about what particular aspects of his subject raised interest amongst his pupils. By noting the speed at which a group covered each aspect of a topic he could gain a fair picture of which parts of the subject the pupils found more difficult and which they could assimilate with relative ease. By listening carefully to the group's attempts to clarify its difficulties with those parts of his subject which they covered more slowly, he could obtain valuable knowledge about the specific nature of each pupil's problems. Also (as indeed the pupils were able to do) by careful observation he could learn a great deal more about the character and general development of his pupils.

This attempt to describe the changes emanating from the group nature of the activity may suggest that the teacher played a fairly passive role. This, however, was not the case. Teachers intervened quite skilfully at various stages of the activity, offering guidance and advice. Indeed the direction that the pupils took was strongly influenced by the introduction to the task that the teacher gave, the resources and books he provided, and many other factors within his control. However, the point we wish to make is that the group nature of the learning process allowed teachers to receive a lot more information directly from the pupils about their progress, with the result that it became easier to help pupils to achieve the various learning goals.

The Comprehensive Nature of the Medium

The second main difference between writing and audio-visual media is the relative comprehensiveness of audio-visual media. It became clear from watching pupils doing audio-visual work that they were including a far wider range of other communication media in their productions than they could with writing alone. Pupils were able *directly* to record paintings, drawings, diagrams, actual scenes or dramatic reconstructions; they were also able to record speech, music, sound effects and even writing. The fact that television, film and tape-slide provided a comprehensive medium for recording can be used to explain many other changes that were observed within the work.

MOTIVATION
The most immediately useful change in behaviour that may be explained, at

least in part, in this way is the increased motivation reported by so many teachers. It has been known for some time that ability is a complex combination of a great many specific skills and talents. It is also known that traditional class-room activities build on only a limited number of these, and that many pupils do not develop or even exercise many of their talents and potentialities until much later in their lives. A further factor is that there is probably nothing as motivating as successful, skilled and appropriate use of a talent or ability. These factors together provide a very plausible explanation for the increased motivation observed.

As a result of the more comprehensive nature of the recording media used, a very wide range of skills could be directly or indirectly incorporated into the pupils' final statements. We have already mentioned the skills of organizing, discussing, reading and writing embodied in the planning of their programmes. Added to these were the visual, oral and dramatic skills that formed the content of the recording. A pupil whose verbal ability was not strong might well be able to represent ideas graphically; another who was a weak organizer might well read for recording in a lively and exciting way. Others might be good at improvised speech, interviewing, acting, presenting, demonstrating, music making, the construction or design of sets, chosing locations, framing shots, drawing, writing, painting, etc. Where teachers were able to exploit the wide range of contributions allowed by audio-visual media in such a way as to match the special abilities of their pupils, the resultant feeling of well being on the part of the pupils was undoubtedly an important contributor to the increased motivation.

REACCESS TO SUBJECTS

Because of the opportunities for pupils to organize and articulate aspects of the subject under study in a variety of non-written as well as written forms, many who had previously found difficulty in gaining access to a subject as a result of weak literacy skills were able to approach the subject anew. Through various forms of non-written communication, pupils were able to exercise the language activity referred to by Britton as the 'expressive use of language', a term that refers to the ability of language to aid the sorting and ordering that must be done to make sense of the information and experience under consideration. That is, pupils were able to do this sorting and organizing through the design of a graphic, through talk or through planning sequences in picture form (the story-board), and hence were able to bypass the difficulties they had experienced in attempting to do it in written form alone.

A second factor that was aided by the new medium was that, as pupils could more effectively engage in expressive use of language and as a result produce a coherent statement of their reaction to the subject under study, teachers were presented with a more effective record of their progress through the subject than had been possible with writing alone.

TRANSLATION EFFECT

Chapter 10 suggested that when pupils translated ideas from one medium to another they were forced to give more careful consideration to meaning than when they repeated information in the medium in which it had been presented to them. Indeed a pupil may often recall a piece of information quite accurately in a written essay without understanding it at all. Also, the frequent translation of ideas among oral, visual and written forms might explain some of the increased thoroughness of understanding that was evident at times within the present work. Certainly, if this was the case the comprehensive nature of the medium of recorded sound and vision presented frequent opportunities for such translation.

DERIVATION AND APPLICATION OF KNOWLEDGE

One of the most interesting and possibly one of the most important effects of using new communication media concerned relating abstract concepts to the real world from which they are derived or to which they are applied. Pupils can often relate one abstract concept to another without knowing where it was originally derived or how it could be practically applied. However, it was repeatedly observed that when pupils had to express an abstract concept through audio-visual media they sought to illustrate or explain it by showing its application or derivation. For example, although some pupils who made a television programme about population and industrial changes in their local community first studied statistical records, they then interviewed old people about the changes they had seen and photographed many of the buildings, old and new, that reflected the changed patterns of industry. Similarly, in a study of changing employment in their area pupils interviewed a manager of a mine and a manager of a clothing factory as well as recording the inside of a typical factory. Also, two groups concerned with the concept of gravity and set theory in mathematics both sought concrete examples to illustrate the concepts being studied. In the case of the work on gravity, they illustrated the principle by showing various applications in building and in everyday life.

Numerous other examples were observed where pupils would study an aspect of a subject in a relatively abstract way (by examining statistical evidence in the social sciences and humanities, or laws and concepts in the natural sciences) then seek out concrete illustrations of the principle in the environment around them. Behind this shift towards the concrete lay the fact that audio-visual recording allows pupils to record their environment more directly than they can with writing alone. Thus the man-made environment could become an illustration of geometry and aesthetics. Likewise, interviews could be related to social statistics, the landscape to geography, machinery to physics, and so on, in such a way that pupils could be readily encouraged to relate abstract theories and concepts to the environment from which they are derived and in which they are applied.

THE DEVELOPMENT OF FEELING

Of no less importance were the opportunities that arose for the development of feeling and its application to primarily cognitive or academic concerns. Making audio-visual statements continually resulted in pupils giving serious consideration to what they felt about the subject under study. This was evident both in the observation of the process and in the results and was even confirmed in interviews in which pupils indicated a deliberate intention to include feeling as well as fact within their programmes. Some of the comments made by pupils indicating this desire included such phrases as 'make the programme interesting', 'move the audience', 'make them enjoy it and therefore remember', or 'pleasing to look at'. Pupils gave a great deal of attention to the feeling they were creating as early in the process as the first planning discussion and, of course, such considerations were clearly evident in their final programmes. This was not always as a result of conscious discussion but, in contrast with their essays, the final programmes were rich in feeling. There seem to be a number of reasons for this change, some to do with the nature of the media and their universality, others with the social expectation that surrounds their use.

If we take the universality of recorded sound and vision first, it is quite obvious that the range of media available to the pupils for use directly in their programmes was very wide indeed and that many of these media are very closely associated with the arts as expressive media. Of these perhaps music is the best example for it is an almost totally expressive medium. Thus its introduction into history or geography, science or English immediately signalled the introduction of affective concerns. It was not possible to give serious consideration to the appropriateness of a piece of music without relating to the subject being studied in an affective way, i.e. through feelings. Of course this does not imply that the written word is not also an affective medium. However, it is significant that this element of study is not sufficiently encouraged, and the use of only one style of written language in many subjects has come to symbolize this.

The second reason for the inclusion of feelings is bound up with the social expectation surrounding these media, particularly television. The pupils naturally expected, on the basis of many hours of viewing, that audio-visual media should be both informative and entertaining, and it is likely that this made them aim for an end-product that likewise combined information with a quality that would capture and hold the interest of an audience.

In the case of English the importance of feeling is more obvious. Language arises in a social context and there is no social situation which does not also have its own particular emotional structure. The different varieties of English used in a football game and in the class-room, the social superiority of Latinate English and the earthy roughness of an Anglo-Saxon brand demonstrate that use of a particular type of English expresses feelings as well as ideas. This, of course, is already recognized in the teaching of English, and great attention is paid to the feelings as well as the facts being conveyed by a written or spoken passage. So this was easy to harness with groups doing audio-visual work in the general area of English.

In the teaching of modern languages the same considerations generally apply. This was confirmed by the teacher of German, who more than once referred to the intense pride felt by many of her pupils in their work and frequently mentioned the degree of commitment that they felt towards what they were saying. The total number of pupils that learned modern languages in this way was very small (one hundred and fifty in all), yet it is tempting to suggest that some of the consistently higher levels of motivation were related to putting language into a more active social context, and as a result stimulating use of the pupils' emotional as well as their intellectual capabilities to learn and *experience* a modern language.

A further example which illustrates that the relationship between emotion and relevance is central to learning occurred in the teaching of history. As mentioned earlier, the introduction of music often signalled the conscious consideration of feelings created within a particular audio-visual statement. When pupils were offered a selection of music in history a similar effect was observed. Possibly as a result of this and possibly as a result of the use of pictures, pupils indicated very clearly their intention to express feelings in their final programmes. As a result they tried to use the information available to work out, for example, what it felt like to be a condemned person (in this case Queen Anne) or what was the mood of people faced with the devastation of the Great Fire of London or fear of the Plague. The pupils themselves were seeking ways of identifying with the predicament of people in former times.

They were creating relevance by applying what they knew – their own emotions – to an unfamiliar period, and in the process developing an ability to identify with other poeple. This ability is crucial because many historical facts make sense or indeed become significant only when one has a feeling for the period, and in particular for the attitudes and emotions of the people. This is also true in part of other social sciences, especially social geography and sociology. Although the Project work on science was not nearly so extensive, there was evidence to suggest that here too the pupils' search for emotional relevance aided learning. It was certainly sufficient to signal the need for further investigation.

The final aspect of the development of feeling in relation to the curriculum concerns subjective gains that may result from the creative use of audio-visual media. It was noted on a number of occasions that as pupils developed an affective relationship with the subject under study they became more aware of what they found pleasurable or distasteful within that subject. Although these responses can occur whatever the method of study, the use of audio-visual media allows such feelings to be expressed visually, musically and in words, and thus discussed.

Presentational Differences

The third major difference between written and audio-visual media significant to learning is the way in which statements were received by an audience. In many ways recorded sound and vision can be used in a far more public way than can writing. For example, most of the thousands of readers of a best seller will never knowingly meet, whereas filmgoers who attend the same performance of a popular film will share the atmosphere created in the cinema. Although this illustrates a very simple difference it has quite important implications in the class-room.

In the class-room pupils can plan for their work to be presented at a particular time, in a particular place and to a specific audience that they know will experience their communication together. The results of such knowledge are various and quite far reaching in their effect on learning. Knowing who the audience would be was often the main reason why pupils felt that working through audio-visual media was relevant. Certainly some audiences left pupils in no doubt about the value and success of their work, expressing variously disappointment, excitement, interest and enjoyment, etc., and many pupils had this culmination of their work clearly in mind throughout. Pupils frequently made references to their intended audience and often attempted to identify with them. They readily reacted to suggestions about what would particularly interest their audience, ways of presenting information and advice about the amount of knowledge an audience would bring with it. Pupils also showed a consciousness of the audience in the scripts they wrote. This clearly indicated a definite assumption about the relationship between themselves and their audience: sometimes they used very formal English to address an unfamiliar audience or much more lively and colloquial English for a peer-group audience.

Audiences could be drawn from the class itself, from other classes or from groups outside the school, and teachers were able to build on audience consciousness as a result. Presentations were often arranged with the producers present and they were thus able to feel the audience's reactions to their programme. It was quite clear that in many cases this was an extremely stressful situation which led to welcome release and pride if the programme was successful and sincerely felt sadness in the face of justified criticism.

The Social Relevance of Audio-visual Media

Many of the reasons we have given for the changes in motivation or the pupils' feeling that audio-visual media are more real are very much conditioned by social attitudes towards audio-visual media. Many young people have read very little but have watched thousands of hours of television. It is quite understandable that such a person would see great relevance in communicating audio-visually and little in writing. He may be quite familiar with the tape-recorder, telephone and television and yet relatively unfamiliar with books and writing.

Apart from the specific media of television, film and photography, other elements of audio-visual media also predominate within our culture. Music is pervasive, and we are constantly bombarded by all sorts of sounds. As soon as we open our eyes we are confronted by an abundance of visual images including man-made objects such as buildings and roads, cars and hoardings, newspapers and sweet wrappers, etc. It is not surprising, therefore, that many pupils are attracted to recorded sound and vision as another way or organizing and recording their reactions to what they are taught and the world they live in, and the educational gains that such work can lead to are, of course, very valuable.

Language, Picture and Thought

Here we look at the general relationship between thinking and the representation of ideas in words and pictures. Although this approach is far more speculative than the generalizations of the previous section it may offer further insight into the process at work in the class-rooms observed and again help to explain some of the changes witnessed by teachers and observers.

Of the forms of representation used within the work of the Project by far the most thoroughly explored (outside the Project) is language. From the many contributions to our knowledge of the connection between language and thinking we may draw out three central relationships. The first is that of concept-building. Evidence from many sources supports the view that the use of words plays a central part in the structuring of generalizations about the world in which we live. Both psychological research[1] and philosophical inquiry suggest this to be the case, support ranging from experiments which show that learning to recognize general categories of colour is speeded up by the use of associated words[2] to the reasonable argument that it is most probably through words that we pass on useful generalizations from one generation to the next.

The second way in which language is related to thinking is in some ways even more fundamental than the first in that it explains why generalization itself is of use to us. One of the key benefits of language is that it enables us to arrange and rearrange generalizations in the absence of the objects or relationships from which they are made.[3] We can thus predict future events and build up the scientific knowledge on which man's technological achievement is based.

The third contribution that language makes to thinking is that it allows

---

[1]See in particular A. R. Luria and F. I. Yudovich, *Speech and the Development of Mental Processes in the Child* (Penguin, 1971).
[2]Vigotsky, L. S., *Thought and Language* (M.I.T. Press, 1962).
[3]See A. R. Luria and F. I. Yudovich, op. cit. pp. 105–107.

mental generalizations to be matched with concrete experience. This completes the process of enabling us to act through thought.

Taking these three processes together gives us a model which explains how language helps us to generalize from specific concrete experiences, to manipulate those generalizations and then to move back to specific concrete experiences, only this time with a much sharper grasp of them:

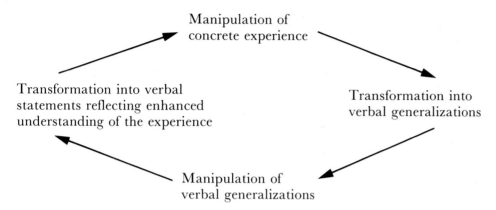

If the manipulation of verbal generalizations were the only form of thinking available to us (in other words, if thinking were synonymous with this verbal manipulation) then it would be impossible to explain the degree to which many children working on the Project were able to make more intelligent, logical and complex statements in audio-visual terms than they were able to do in words alone.

In order to understand what thinking is it is helpful to look at the way verbal generalizations themselves are manipulated. It seems to us that the rules for manipulating verbal generalizations are themselves generalizations but of a higher order of abstraction. At the highest level these rules are the processes of formal, propositional logic. M. Sinclair-De-Zwart[4] has argued strongly that Piaget's findings suggest that a higher level of development of logical thought exists among deaf children whose verbal development is impaired than would seem likely if language determined thought. Thus we might speculate that the principles of formal, deductive logic control the manipulation of both language generalizations and the generalizations of mental image, and that these two processes can be closely interactive or relatively separated (as with deaf children). Hence, for those youngsters who made more logical and complex audio-visual statements than verbal ones, there is perhaps also relative separation of the sort one sees in deaf children.

Assuming that propositional logic controls the manipulation of verbal generalizations and the generalizations of mental imagery, we have to explain what brings about new insight or generalizations (which are themselves usually the result of inductive or creative thought rather than propositional logic). At the level of pure language we have context-free manipulation of ideas by the limited rules of propositional logic, but at the level of actual experience we have real objects and relationships which are not limited but infinitely complex. As a result of the work of the Project we feel that new concepts and generalizations are brought about through the mental imagery stimulated by the sheer complexity of the real world; these then interact in the

[4]M. Sinclair-De-Zwart, 'Developmental psycholinguistics', *Language in Education* (ed. Cashden; Open University Press).

processes outlined in our model above to form the source of new ideas. So real creativity and new learning perhaps take place at the interface between verbal abstraction and concrete reality.

This is supported by the work of Bruner as well as that of Piaget. If we consider thinking as the context-free manipulation of ideas, then learning can be regarded as the generation of new imagery at the abstract/concrete interface through the iconic mode of thought. Many youngsters struggle at this point and may never achieve context-free manipulation because they have not fixed the new ideas in the iconic mode. The work of the Project is thus invaluable in that it offers an external form of recording (which can be manipulated by the rules of propositional logic) by which to fix and manipulate the new ideas emerging in the iconic mode. Thus the relationship between the enactive, iconic and symbolic modes is strengthened and deepened, and it becomes possible for creative ideas which could quickly die in a formal teaching situation to achieve considerable vitality.

The visual aspects of the Project's work exemplify the process. Consider the process of making a picture. First there is the enactive, real world in all its thisness, so the child puts a frame around part of it, which is the first stage of abstraction (and thence of generalization) – a piece of iconic imagery. He then puts frames around other parts, obtaining a series of images which he then rearranges in some logical sequence. While he is doing this he is talking and writing – in other words, setting up a series of language patterns which will ultimately enable him to free himself of the enactive context (through iconic imagery), then of the iconic context through the language that originally accompanied it. If he has manipulated the iconic imagery properly by propositional logic, then when he gets to the purely thinking or verbal stage he should be able to structure his ideas logically without any difficulty. This is exactly what we have found with the children in the Project. Hence, if one of our central aims is the development of context-free manipulation of ideas, it is important that this new recording medium encourages what goes on internally (transformations from the enactive, concrete world via the world of images to the world of words): that word and visual/auditory images exist side by side and interact at all stages.

An important phenomenon in the Project was the increased emotional content of statements made by the pupils, which everyone felt increased their ability to communicate successfully. It seems reasonable to assume that the ability to manipulate language to express feelings (as the O-level literature candidate does in Chapter 10) must be acquired in the same way as the ability to manipulate language to express ideas.[5] In other words, imaging has a key role in this area. Words are emotionally neutral but they generate images which are laden with value and emotions (hence perhaps Keats' attempt to 'load every rift with ore'). Perhaps, therefore, the whole business of valuing and responding to ideas and feelings takes place at the level of imaging. Since the work of the Project is so bound up with imaging this would help to explain the increased commitment, emotional involvement and valuing that went into the pupils' final statements. It would also support the role of the arts as necessary to all creative thinking.

[5]A. R. Luria, *Working Brain: Introduction to Neuropsychology* (Penguin, 1973). Luria is particularly concerned to attack the 'psychomorphological' approach of western experts who seek to pin down separate geographical areas of the brain to account for cognitive and affective functions. It is not clear how accurate Luria's claim is, but the empirical experience of many teachers suggests that when students are allowed to bring emotions and ideas together into the same learning experience, then the language development and the learning are much more powerful.

Of course, as well as pointing to the strength of the Project's work such a theory could also point to dangers. As the media can be used to aid learning by allowing logical manipulation of recorded images which helps fix concept-building, so too can they be used to hinder and even damage learning. If we return to the idea of recorded sound and vision being used as a reflection of the movement of thought from the enactive (concrete) to the symbolic or almost context free, we can see that it could offer too many abstract images with too many formal rules for their manipulation to the child and end up teaching clichés which prevent the child's own exploratory behaviour. This danger exists especially with a teacher who is interested in films or television for their own sake. It becomes essential to consider what is taught and how and why it is taught. If the aim is to develop greater flexibility in pupils' explorations towards understanding (by offering a recorded form for their imaging in the transformation from the concrete to the abstract), then teachers must develop their own imaginative skills. Indeed, the more complex and abstract the subject, the more developed the teachers' imaging skills must be, which leads us back to implications for teacher training.

Implications and Recommendations

Here we outline our main conclusions and make what we feel to be key recommendations. This is difficult as we need to relate the findings of this study to two rapidly changing areas of human endeavour. We are concerned on the one hand with the new media of recorded sound and vision – in themselves at least as important as the printed word – and on the other with the changing content and structure of formal education. We are thus describing one aspect of a potentially massive field. Only time will reveal the full effect of the recording of sound and vision on our knowledge about the world and, in particular, how we obtain that knowledge.

In a very few years video-recorders will be almost as common as audio cassette-recorders. Television-programme libraries already exist in education and industry and only a few years separate us from their inclusion in public libraries. The underlying technological progress is rapid, as the very short history of all audio-visual media testifies.

In a similarly short period education has also undergone massive changes. Technical colleges, technological universities and polytechnics have been born. Significant changes have occurred in the curriculum, and schools themselves have undergone a number of reorganizations.

Because of this speed of change, we are very conscious that in making our recommendations too specific we could well close as many avenues of exploration as we might open and the message from this study must be to face the future with a sense of excitement and an open mind.

It is quite clear that the creative use of audio-visual media provides an invaluable tool for teachers who regard the development of pupils' general communication and social skills as important. In particular, the work suggests itself very strongly as a means of developing oral language skills and, as a by-product of the social situation, providing peer-group support in learning. Also, the many aspects contributing to increased levels of motivation and involvement, success in communication, affective concerns, audience changes, etc., recommend the work to teachers who would like to develop a more lively and, for many pupils, a more fulfilling approach to learning in their class-rooms.

Teachers were able to develop aspects and possibilities within the work specifically related to their own subjects and we certainly feel that the study has shown that, with skilful management, work of this kind can bring quite substantial learning gains directly related to the subject under study. Whilst the work frequently led to pupils taking greater responsibility for their own learning (and this in turn led to teachers having to cope with a new set of relationships in the class-room), the wide range of learning gains fully repaid the extra effort.

Of the general learning gains, a number certainly warrant a second mention here. The first is that this kind of work makes the processes of learning visible, as opposed to being locked inside the head. This probably happened both as a result of social processes which encouraged pupils to discuss epistemological as well as factual concerns and because pupils were able to manipulate images instead of following an internal process. We suggest that making the processes of learning visible in this way will allow teachers to gauge far more accurately individuals' particular learning difficulties and strengths, which should make teaching more efficient. However, much more work needs to be done on understanding and developing appropriate responses to what has been observed.

The second of the general gains we restate here is the ability of this kind of work to develop a more applied attitude towards learning: that is, understanding derivations and applications as well as facts and laws.

The third gain is reaccess to learning, or bypassing literacy difficulties. Audio-visual media offer pupils the sorting power of language but in a way that is not so dependent on conventional literacy. This results for many pupils in increased access to traditional subjects, to building concepts and to understanding laws, whilst simultaneously encouraging fresh attempts at basic literacy skills.

In addition, there is the area of learning about communication itself. We have mentioned the relationship between doing and viewing and suggest that communicating through audio-visual media can act as a basis for a greater understanding of the processes, purposes and context of the use of electronic media and in particular broadcast television.

We also suggest that the wide range of subjects, aims, ages and abilities to which teachers adapted this work, taken in conjunction with work observed by the Project team with pupils aged six to students of mature years, indicates a potential role for these methods in all sectors of education.

Teacher Training

Chapter 11 describes some of the skills and knowledge teachers needed to reach the levels of competence described in the various case studies. In the case studies, particular examples of their application are given. Together these chapters describe starting-points for designing training for teachers in the use of recorded sound and vision. It would, of course, be ludicrous to consider them as more than starting-points when structuring courses. These chapters indicate possible directions, make first attempts at outlining skills and give a feeling for the sensitivities that will need to receive particular attention. In the longer term, training will have to be developed that adapts the high level of skills of those involved in day-to-day communication through audio-visual media (the professional fields of drama, television, writing, the visual arts, etc.) with the skills of teachers and others involved in education. Inter-professional work could aid this development, as indeed will the involvement of those directly concerned with teacher education.

Finally we emphasize the scale of change that is needed in teacher training.

We are now teaching the first generation of young people to be born in a world in which the use of recorded sound and vision is both commonplace and accepted. Their world is one in which the validity of finding out about that world through recorded sound and vision is unquestioned, yet many of those who teach them are members of a generation that did not grow up with these media, or were trained at a time when little credence was given to them in colleges and departments of education. It is therefore difficult to escape the conclusion that the work described in this book suggests the need for a major in-service programme as well as initial training.

Conclusion

We hope that by now it has become clear that the work undertaken for the Schools Council provides an exciting new direction to be further explored and developed. It was mentioned at the beginning of the book that young people at present receiving their secondary education will enter a complex and sophisticated world which will make heavy demands upon them. Among these demands will be the full range of communication and social skills. We believe that the evidence we have reported demonstrates that the use of audio-visual media offers a major contribution to the development of these skills.

In relation to the Project's aims of investigating general learning gains, we believe that the evidence indicates a valuable role for use by pupils of audio-visual media in the teaching of a wide range of subjects, ages and abilities.

Finally, we believe that the Project has challenged certain commonly held assumptions about the learning process. As we said in the Preface, almost all previous work on curriculum development has been shaped by a number of assumptions. One of these is the notion of the almost total supremacy in the learning process of verbal (particularly written) and numerical languages. Another is the view that learning proceeds most efficiently through over-whelming attention to logical thought, analysis, sequential reasoning and abstraction. The Project's use of audio-visual media, which allowed pupils to explore the world of learning through a wider range of modes of understanding, placed a premium on use of imagination by the pupils. Imagination was predominantly used in visualizing, creating structures in sound, and creating movement between these two as a way of coming to grips with a subject discipline. This involved the development of skills and sensitivities excluded by the assumptions mentioned above.

The evidence of the Project points strongly to the need to develop these additional skills: it may well be necessary for pupils to have imaginative interplay with the ideas and information offered them for these to be fully understood and for the pupils to be able to originate new ideas or apply established ones. Within much learning pupils' use of imagination clearly remains largely unrecognized. To recognize it and, as in the Project, provide a way of harnessing it in the service of the many aims of education would greatly increase the learning capacity and enrich the education given in schools. It is the combination of imagination and technique so central to this Project that at the most general level may account for the exciting gains observed.

Summary

1. The Method

Definition	1.1.	The method involves pupils responding to a topic as a group and expressing their joint findings as an audio-visual statement.
Relation to subject	1.2.	This method was used to introduce pupils to a new topic (pp. 31–2), as a technique for revising a previously studied topic (pp. 53–5, 57) or integrated with other teaching strategies (p. 79).
Media used	1.3.	Pupils used: *Television:* studio work in a central facility (pp. 91–101); studio work in the class-room (pp. 31–2, 101–111); one camera in the class-room (pp. 27–30). *Film:* documentary (ch. 7); animation (ch. 3). *Tape-slide* (pp. 56–7, 64–5, ch. 6) and *sound recording* (pp. 113–15).
Stages in process	1.4.	The method generally involved pupils in discussion of a topic, research, planning a programme in sketch and note form (a story-board), script-writing, producing visual material and rehearsing a script, recording, presenting and evaluating their finished product.
Group composition	1.5.	Pupils worked as a single group (pp. 63–6), in small groups allocated different parts of a single programme (pp. 31–2) or in small groups each with its own programme (pp. 53–6).
Audience	1.6.	Pupils made programmes for presentation to their own class (ch. 8), to other classes (p. 41, ch. 6) and to audiences outside the school (pp. 65, 87).

2. Language

General	2.1.	Pupils using the Project's methods developed reading, writing, listening and speaking skills.
	2.2.	The use of language to support the process of learning (exploratory language) was particularly in evidence.
	2.3.	A focus on language was created for subjects across the curriculum.
	2.4.	Pupils made extensive use of technical and formal language.
	2.5.	The range of language work encouraged was far wider than normal.
	2.6.	The use of language merely to repeat information was discouraged.
	2.7.	The work was particularly helpful in encouraging oral work.
	2.8.	The methods were particularly useful in encouraging language development with average and slow-learning pupils.
Oral language	2.9.	The quality and amount of pupil talk significantly increased both in general class discussion (p. 86) and in small groups (pp. 57, 163–4, 166).
	2.10.	Talk was usually purposeful and often unexpectedly succinct (pp. 98–9).
	2.11.	The methods encouraged exploratory talk: talking through ideas as they develop and testing individual insight against that of others (pp. 86, 103–104, 163–4).

2.12. Pupils used an unusually wide range of language codes and styles (pp. 65–6, 93, 111, 131, 133, 134–5).

2.13. Pupils were encouraged to expand, qualify and explore ideas in discussions in small groups (pp. 28, 40, 42, 43–6, 54, 55, 56, 86, 92, 100, 103, 163–4).

2.14. The methods encouraged discrimination of relevant from irrelevant talk (pp. 43, 47, 57, 66, 134–5).

2.15. Presentation of information for recording encouraged the development of vocal control (pp. 30, 53, 56, 65–6, 114).

2.16. Pupils were frequently encouraged to listen carefully to others in order to effect decisions or to co-ordinate actions (pp. 31, 32, 49–50, 55, 56–7, 67, 77, 93, 167).   **Listening**

2.17. Pupils were encouraged to listen to and monitor their own speech (pp. 65, 67, 76).

2.18. Pupils extended their range of reading (pp. 28, 96, 100).   **Reading**

2.19. Pupils were clearer as to the purpose of selecting books and other written information (pp. 30, 41, 42, 67, 96, 164).

2.20. Pupils found it necessary to analyse texts carefully (pp. 41, 42, 135, 164).

2.21. Reading across the curriculum occurred in order to gain information of many kinds (pp. 28, 42, 64, 85, 164).

2.22. Pupils were encouraged to read in a variety of situations and for a wide range of purposes (pp. 28, 53, 64, 101). This included reading to co-ordinate activity (pp. 50, 51, 53, 67, 93), reading aloud to record (pp. 28, 30–31, 64, 67, 68, 76, 116), individual reading in research (pp. 28, 42, 96, 100, 101, 109, 137), group-reading (pp. 30, 41, 64, 164) and reading at speed (pp. 30, 97).

2.23. The methods motivated many pupils to read who were previously reluctant to do so (pp. 30, 67–8, 81).

2.24. Motivation to write increased. This was particularly so with slow and reluctant learners (pp. 28, 30, 53, 57, 64, 67, 77, 84–5, 113).   **Writing**

2.25. Pupils' writing became more structured and coherent (pp. 31, 47, 54, 57, 78, 84–5, 103–104, 116).

2.26. Pupils paid greater attention to the need to redraft written work (pp. 28, 57, 77).

2.27. Attention was focused on the need for clear handwriting and appropriate punctuation (pp. 67, 116).

2.28. Pupils were encouraged to engage in a wide range of writing tasks. These included summary (pp. 56–7, 116), survey construction (p. 137), note-taking (pp. 28, 31, 56, 136–7, 165–6,), poetry (pp. 64, 67, 114) and prose (pp. 30, 65, 67, 68, 76, 115–16).

2.29. Pupils often discovered the purpose of various forms of writing from the activities they were engaged in (pp. 54, 64, 91–3, 113–14, 164–5).

3. Social Skills

3.1. Pupils worked successfully in groups and found the experience fulfilling (pp. 28–9, 40–41, 47, 53, 54–5, 57, 65, 96–7, 144–5, 162).

3.2. Pupils became aware of the value of team work (pp. 53, 66, 141–3, 167).

3.3. Pupils developed awareness of the interdependence of team members (pp. 53, 56, 97, 100, 116–17, 167).

3.4. The methods developed leadership skills (pp. 32, 40, 85, 97–9, 154), often unexpectedly (pp. 32, 57).

3.5.   Individual responsibility to the group was developed (pp. 29, 47, 54, 55, 97, 116–17, 162).

3.6.   Pupils developed sensitivity to each other's needs and styles of thinking (pp. 42, 54, 103, 124, 143, 162).

3.7.   Pupils learned how to take group decisions and abide by majority decisions (pp. 46, 55, 103, 116, 162, 168).

3.8.   Pupils learned to support each other's efforts and achieve group cohesion (pp. 45, 55, 76, 97, 124, 142, 144).

3.9.   Pupils developed skill in influencing the behaviour of their peers (pp. 55, 78, 98–9, 141).

3.10. Pupils learned to cope with rejection or modification of their ideas (pp. 110, 162).

3.11. Pupils were encouraged to talk with adults outside the class-room and to develop confidence in adult situations (pp. 56, 87, 137).

4. Subject Learning

4.1.   The methods encouraged learning in subjects right across the curriculum (for specific subjects see individual case studies).

4.2.   More thorough learning was encouraged, in terms of both memorizing facts (p. 79) and grasping concepts and ideas (pp. 41–3, 44, 46, 57).

4.3.   Pupils were encouraged to widen their understanding and knowledge of subjects under study (pp. 28, 79, 101, 149).

4.4.   Pupils increased their ability to structure their work (pp. 30–31, 41–3, 44, 57, 84–5, 86–7, 94–5, 103–104, 116, 124).

4.5.   Pupils displayed an enhanced ability to use technical language appropriate to the subject under study (pp. 41, 47, 64, 77–8, 98–9, 111, 132–4).

4.6.   Pupils were encouraged to explore connections between theoretical ideas and the practical world (pp. 31, 57, 128, 133–4, 171).

4.7.   Pupils were encouraged to explore their emotional reactions to subjects alongside cognitive learning (pp. 29–30, 95–7, 114–15, 126, 171–3).

4.8.   Reaccess to subject learning was provided for many pupils who had previously been hampered by weak literacy skills (pp. 126–7).

5. General Learning

5.1.   Motivation increased and remained at a high level (pp. 28, 56, 57, 63, 66, 78, 84, 88, 94, 101, 121–5).

5.2.   Conventional judgements of children's ability were often shown to be inappropriate in predicting success.

5.3.   Skills relating to the needs of adult life were developed (pp. 47, 110, 117).

5.4.   Emphasis was placed on the understanding of concepts and processes (pp. 42–3, 53–7, 124–5).

5.5.   Academic pupils were encouraged to extend themselves as part of the group activity (p. 40).

5.6.   Pupils developed their ability to use sophisticated technical equipment and valued the contribution of those most adept in this area (pp. 29, 42, 53, 94–5).

Self-concept   5.7.   The work often had a positive effect on pupils' valuation of their own abilities (pp. 32, 45, 55, 57, 65, 66, 78, 79, 85, 100).

5.8.   Pupils were encouraged to appraise their work critically to a degree that was not apparent previously (pp. 76, 91, 93–5, 110, 167–8).

5.9.   The work increased pupils' readiness and ability to apply analytical skills to their viewing of broadcast television (pp. 91, 94–5, 103, 108).

5.10. Many of the skills developed helped pupils to understand how to collect and organize information in order to guide future activity.

Learning how to learn

6. How the Methods Promote Learning

6.1.   The Project's methods build on the basic human need to understand, to communicate and to receive social support and approval. This is achieved in the following four ways.

6.2.   Pupils' efforts to understand subject-matter are encouraged by an enhanced desire to communicate clearly and effectively owing to the effect of the audience (pp. 41–3, 44, 56–7, 173–4), the relevance of the medium (pp. 94–5, 100, 125, 174) and emotional aspects of the situation (pp. 29–30, 114, 171–3).

6.3.   Success in the process of understanding is reinforced by peer-group approval, e.g. peer-group support (pp. 41–3, 45, 53, 76, 100, 168), individual responsibility to the group (pp. 92–3, 117, 162).

6.4.   A number of learning blocks are removed, e.g. there is reaccess to subject learning/bypassing problems of literacy (pp. 30, 47, 127, 170), visual support for logical structuring (pp. 41–4, 84–5, 116), clear feedback stages (pp. 41–4, 54, 101, 124–5), an improved self-image (pp. 32, 45, 55, 57, 66, 78, 84–5, 100, 128).

6.5.   A wider than normal range of learning methods is employed by the pupils, e.g. a wide range of pupil skills (pp. 28, 84–5, 96–7, 100–101, 117, 126, 169–70), group efforts at understanding (pp. 103–104, 164), varying speed according to difficulty (p. 148), translation effects (pp. 41, 42–3, 170), mastery learning (p. 125), iconic learning (pp. 125–6).

7. Audio-visual Language

7.1.   Pupils and teachers were helped to develop and use an audio-visual language. This involved the following four processes.

7.2.   Developing a knowledge of recording equipment and its adaptation to specific purposes (pp. 27–8, 29, 40, 45–6, 49–50, 53, 92–3, 101–102, 108).

7.3.   Translating specific subject content into visual and sound images (pp. 28, 31–2, 49, 53–7, 63–4, 81–4).

7.4.   Organizing visual and sound images into a coherent audio-visual statement (pp. 49, 53–7).

7.5.   Recognizing the power of audio-visual language to provide a recording medium for the mental imagery that mediates between experiencing the concrete world and the development of abstract reasoning (pp. 174–7).

8. Resources

8.1.   The range of equipment used varied widely from school to school, although all schools had enough to work in one or more of the media.

8.2.   In some cases centralized provision was made of more sophisticated equipment than was to be found in most schools (pp. 31, 49, 67, 91–2).

8.3.   Appropriate equipment in schools was often previously under-used.

8.4.   Equipment breakdown was not a major problem.

Cost

8.5.   The cost of consumables was less than for most other practical subjects and presented no difficulties (except in the case of live-action film).

8.6.   In the majority of cases costs were absorbed into normal subject allocations.

Books

8.7.   There was a dearth of appropriate visual and written resource material suitable for the very broad range of inquiry with which pupils became involved in the various subject areas (pp. 28, 152).

9. Changes in the Class-room

9.1.   The methods generated enthusiasm in both teachers and pupils.

9.2.   The work was readily integrated with a wide range of other teaching and learning styles.

9.3.   Teachers were able to vary the amount of time spent on Project methods.

9.4.   In some cases the Project's methods led to faster coverage of subject content (pp. 30, 79); in others coverage was slower (pp. 148–50). Some teachers offset time pressures by setting related homework (p. 150).

9.5.   The methods encouraged pupils to work in a self-directed way for unexpectedly long periods of time (p. 57), demonstrating previously unexpected abilities (pp. 32, 53).

9.6.   In consequence the teacher's role often changed to one of adviser, enabler and guide (pp. 29, 30–31, 40, 100, 109, 110, 149).

9.7.   Relationships between teacher and pupil dramatically improved (pp. 41, 47, 110).

9.8.   Increased demands were placed on teachers in terms of:

(a) Guiding and assessing pupils working in small groups.
(b) Ranging around subjects in response to pupils' inquiries.
(c) Helping pupils to represent subject-matter in terms of sound and vision.
(d) Planning resource provision and class organization.

9.9.   The learning styles and problems of pupils became more visible to teachers (pp. 43–4, 100, 114, 178).

Conclusions and Recommendations

1. Applications

1.1.   In respect of the outcomes listed in Summary points 2–5, the methods developed in the Project have been shown to be feasible and valuable right across the curriculum and across the whole ability range of pupils of secondary age.

1.2.   Observation of similar work in other contexts suggests its applicability in primary, further and higher education.

1.3.   There is much evidence to suggest that adaptations of the methods could be fruitful in areas of behaviour modification and in the training of personnel for management and other occupations requiring a high degree of interpersonal skills.

2. Standards

2.1.   Although much of the work developed in the Project was of a high standard, wider observation confirmed that such standards were not automatic outcomes of use by pupils of audio-visual media, but depended also on teachers' skills, organization, and so on.

2.2.   Further work needs to be undertaken to simplify and make available means of assessing the overall quality of such work.

3. Assessment and Examinations

3.1.   For teachers specifically concerned with generating an understanding of communication processes, a number of formal examinations are available at CSE, O- and A-level (see Appendix 3).

3.2.   Although these methods are eminently suitable for use during the learning process even for very formal examinations, where teachers are concerned primarily with subject learning there is less scope. There needs to be greater acceptance by schools and those responsible for formal examinations of audio-visual presentations as evidence of learning.

3.3.   Where teachers are primarily concerned with the development of communication and social skills, profile reporting may offer a valuable means of assessment.

3.4.   Concern with examinations should not be allowed to detract from the value of the work as a *general method of teaching and learning*.

4. Resource Provision

4.1.   Where local authorities and colleges provided centralized facilities for television and sound recording, this worked well.

4.2.   This practice, as well as the loan of simple studio equipment to schools, should be encouraged wherever possible.

4.3.   The most significant resource problem concerned books. School departments were frequently unable to provide sufficient general reading material at appropriate levels of complexity to enable pupils to take full advantage of their willingness to research and read around specific subject areas.

5. Support for Teachers

5.1.   The fact that such programmes as these are more concerned with method than with content does not mean that training is not important.

5.2.   Standards in this work will suffer if adequate training is not provided.

5.3.   Training for this work should involve methods that increase:

> Perceptiveness towards sound and vision
> The ability to use vision and sound to represent ideas and feelings
> The ability to use dramatic forms and structures
> Knowledge and skill in work with small groups
> Knowledge of communication skills
> Knowledge of media production skills
> Knowledge of evaluation and assessment procedures
> The ability to apply the above to the teaching of specific subjects

The last skill will be helped by the development of:

> The ability to organize pupils' audio-visual work in small groups
> The ability to translate subject ideas into vision and sound
> Skills appropriate to teacher intervention in small-group work

5.4.   Although most of the above skills are best developed through exposure to those who are already highly proficient (in combination with guided practice), there is a need for a broad approach to training involving the five points which follow.

5.5.   Class-room materials and teachers' guides for practising teachers wishing to start using the methods.

5.6.   Training courses for those most likely to be called upon to support the work of practising teachers.

5.7.   A nucleus of highly trained teachers who can support the work of colleagues. This can be achieved only through a long course and may be most appropriate at pre-service level and in extended periods of school-based training.

5.8.   Schools television could aid training by producing a series on communication and social skills based on the work of the Project.

5.9.   A centre should be established to co-ordinate development by providing a regular newsletter, a loan library of typical audio-visual programmes produced by pupils, and a register of agencies able to offer specific help, courses, advice and research.

6. Research and Development

6.1.   The Project introduces a new language and approach which can be applied to the whole curriculum. It also suggests both practical and theoretical questions for future research and development.

6.2.   There is a need for further development of the methods in schools and other institutions. This would be best performed in conjunction with practising teachers as action research.

6.3. Such research could also explore various aspects of the methods including small-group work, visualization, resource provision, teacher skills, assessment, language and gains in social skills, relations with specific subject learning, etc.

6.4. Much of this could benefit from the application of quantitative research methods to explore learning gains in greater detail.

6.5. Particular attention could be given to further exploration of the way these methods can modify behaviour and can develop pupils' awareness of their own abilities and needs. Attention could also be given to the relationship between producing audio-visual media and attitudes towards broadcast television.

6.6. Further work needs to be done on adapting the audio-visual methods to a wide range of subjects, including mathematics and science. The production of class-room materials would be valuable.

6.7. The methods need to be explored further in relation to primary and tertiary education and to a wider spectrum of educational aims.

6.8. A number of hypotheses relating audio-visual language and learning have been developed:

(a) that iconic and enactive styles are necessary at all levels of learning for that learning to be thorough in respect of generating new understanding or being applied to new situations;

(b) that formal reasoning is far less important than imaginative manipulation of visual and other symbolic forms in generating insight and conceptual learning;

(c) that aspects of these inferred processes are externalized in audio-visual work.

These and other questions about the relationship of an audio-visual language to learning and thought signal major directions for future research.

7. Terminology

There is a need for terminology to distinguish between the use of audio-visual media as an aid in teaching (audio-visual aids) and their use as an aid in creative learning. It is suggested that the latter might be referred to as *audio-visual statements*.

APPENDIX 1: Activity and Learning Gain

Process	Communication		
	Oral Language (speaking and listening)	Writing	Reading
1. Discussion 1.1. Discovering the specific interests of each group member in the topic given	Questioning and cross-questioning Expressing ideas clearly Explaining and developing a rationale Discovering skills and attitudes through accurate interpretation Exploratory talk to develop a rounded understanding of ideas, and as an aid to group cohesion	Note-taking: to record suggestions – aid to summarizing ideas rather than copying verbatim Establishing a *need* for writing	
1.2. Deciding on the approach and what should be included in the programme	Defining aims, presenting ideas clearly, supported by reasoned argument Negotiating, reasoning logically, evaluating individual contributions, recalling points made in 1.1, organizing thoughts and developing generalizations, expressing intentions and needs, interpreting information, ideas and meaning Anticipating actions and intentions Relating associated contributions Distinguishing relevancy Predicting response of audience Coping with challenges and interruptions Identifying problems Understanding another's point of view and taking it into account in developing argument and counter-argument	Note-taking: to record decisions, reinforcing need for writing	Pre-reading preparation: creating a place for different kinds of reading in the overall plan; locating the need for specific books, articles, etc. (establishing a *need* for reading); locating reference sources

n Producing Audio-visual Statements

Visual Language	Social Skills	Subject-learning Skills	Audio-visual Aspects
(including both 'body language' and the manipulation of visual signs and symbols) Facial expression, gestures, body position and movement, hand, finger and arm movements – supporting or replacing verbal contribution Indicating interest Displaying feelings (nervousness, anxiety, excitement, enthusiasm, etc.) These areas occur throughout all the stages with the addition of specific hand signals in 'quiet' situations	Developing a flexible group – one leader may emerge or control of the group may be shared at this stage Agreeing on first task Encouraging participation Upgrading a member's contribution Clarifying points for uncertain group members Listening to others' ideas Remembering all the areas covered Coping with the hostility of someone against one's personality and/or ideas Coping with frustration when having difficulty in 'getting a word in' Keeping a contribution succinct so that there is time for others	Developing less rigid 'mental sets' and 'learning styles' through group tolerance and seeing that a subject can be approached in many ways	Defining target audience – considering their previous knowledge, interests and expectations Defining aims of programme
Seeing swiftly and comprehensively, often simultaneously analytically and synthetically Understanding visual media and the ability to express ideas in visual terminology This covers the following components of visual intelligence: basic elements syntactical structures perceptual mechanisms technique styles systems (medium)	Analysing what exactly needs to be said to weld the group together and give direction Assessing the viability, given the strengths and weaknesses of the group, of the ideas suggested Persuading someone to expand their ideas Accepting rejection of an idea Preventing a dominant personality from taking over Being inspired by another's initial idea Responding creatively to develop or modify another's idea Listening to others and waiting for the right moment to speak or intervene Rejecting an idea without being destructive Praising a good point Feeling excitement at the possibilities and harnessing this feeling within a contribution Overcoming diffidence when trying to suggest something Letting off steam when frustrated or annoyed, without offence Developing confidence to contribute ideas and ask for clarification Using 'acceptable' vocabulary which all members of the group can understand Trying to win someone over to one's own point of view Trying to understand other people's point of view Showing empathy and sympathy with others' positions Deferring to a majority decision Drawing out group members who might by shy or nervous Developing a supportive group environment Extending viewpoints by being made aware of others	Developing awareness of most appropriate learning styles and strategies for specific problems Exercising intellectual operation of evaluation in relation to a variety of intellectual contexts Encouraging divergent thought	Deciding roughly what audio-visual elements should be used Initial discussion on audio-visual formats to use with 'content' and 'approach' Visual considerations: still pictures (captions) studio sequences location shots Sound considerations: speech music sound effects

Process	Communication		
	Oral Language	Writing	Reading
1.3. Organizing the activities of group members so that relevant material can be obtained	Deciding, persuading, explaining, directing, taking initiative, setting conditions, projecting needs, predicting and anticipating, organizing tasks and people, contributing skills Co-ordinating activities so that they are complementary and not competing with each other	Note-taking: list activities to be organized and carried out	Purposeful reading of annotated list of decisions in order that all members of group take responsibility for a task

2. Research
2.1. Book-based research
	Developing library information retrieval skills:
	  asking questions
	  seeking advice
	  obtaining experts' opinions
	Giving verbal reports of progress
	Investigating topic
	Constructing and delivering coherent and convincing arguments
	Encouraging modifications
	Moving from specialist language into more familiar language and back
	Sharing information
	Agreeing on mutual selection
	Developing understanding of when task is complete
	Receiving ideas and facts
	Integrating information from different sources
		Note-taking:
		  collecting findings
		  collating results
		  annotating assessments
		Using précis: summarizing passages from books, journals and magazines, newspapers and information sheets in preparation for scripting stage and in relation to needs of task
			Planning research strategy: between general impression and detailed attention
			Determining main theme and sequences of ideas
			Reading to answer questions and find relevant facts
			Locating, selecting and evaluating material
			Developing ability to define areas of search by using subject indexes, classified catalogues, abstracts and bibliographies
			Checking reliability of source material
			Referring to other sources for comparison and illustration
			Tackling difficult books because of commitment to end-product
			Using comprehension skills – literal, inferential and evaluative
			Using reason, existing knowledge and imagination

2.2. Other research	Defining objectives: information and/or visits and/or interviews Requesting guidance: an appropriate person or place, obtaining addresses, etc. Compiling questions, judging approach, indicating areas to be covered, considering reliability, constructing format – appropriate sample size and population, etc. – postulating response, urging participants, scrutinizing returns, indicating trends, observing changes, grading responses, organizing results, revealing prejudices Establishing, arguing, justifying area, examining material, compiling data, identifying important criteria, analysing and collating results	Letter writing: requesting interviews, visits or information Constructing surveys to collect relevant data Writing reports to organize and clarify information for inclusion in final script	Setting up hypotheses and testing them Reading letters, survey results and reports – interpreting meaning, deciding on action

Visual Language	Social Skills	Subject-learning Skills	Audio-visual Aspects
	Remembering what has been covered Summarizing what one wants to achieve Discovering individual talents within the group Requesting action of a group member Encouraging action by a diffident member Being clear and specific on what a task covers Feeling enthusiastic at the prospect of what one's task entails Understanding the group's aims	Recognizing that personalities, etc., have close relationships with learning styles and strategies – increasing objectivity towards one's own learning	

Developing the means for seeing, and sharing meaning with some level of predictable universality
Perceiving, watching, observing, discovering, recognizing, visualizing, examining, 'reading', looking
Considering the use of fine art, applied art, subjective expression and functional purpose
 	
Visual input:
    symbols systems
    representational material
    abstract understructure (the form of everything we see, natural or man-made)
Analysing and defining visually
Considering the relationships between visual stimuli and human organization
 	
Pre-visualization:
    careful planning
    intellectual probing
    technical knowledge
    considering function/aesthetics and form/content
	The following applies to 2.1 and 2.2:
	Taking methodical approach
	Receiving instructions (where to find material)
	Deciding practicality (whether or not one piece of information is worth the time and/or effort required)
	Showing courtesy in requesting information or help
	Being persistent in discovering relevant material
	Deciding what to keep or discard, taking group needs into account
	Being patient and coping with frustration
	Being aware of the needs of others – librarians, others in the library, the group
	Using perception in interpreting human condition – responding and reacting (internally from text research, externally through surveys, visits, interviews, etc.)
	Persuading people to assist with task
	Overcoming fear of dominant personality or authority figures
	Being careful not to antagonize someone by a thoughtless approach
	Developing critical faculties
	Thanking people for their help (advice, time, effort, etc.)
	Coping with hostility (in interview)
	Apologizing if a mistake is made
	Learning to interact positively with adults
	Taking responsibility for task and its completion
	Getting job completed within time constraint and framework
	Coping with new situations
	Using initiative
	Developing confidence to handle retrieval situations
	Questioning and interpreting instructions skilfully
	Developing pride in job
	Reporting problems and difficulties
	Coping with personnel at local council offices, social services, police force, etc., as part of search for material, speakers, visits, etc.
		The following applies to 2.1 and 2.2:
		
		Cognitive Theory
		Learning importance of sharp, but multi-dimensioned, definition of 'goals'
		Developing cognitive maps and general strategies for dealing with masses of data
		
		S.R. Theory
		Using trial and error in exploration
		Experiencing patterns of reinforcement and feedback
		Becoming familiar with, and acquiring skill over, verbal medium
			Visual Research
			
			Still Pictures
			Locating pictorial resources
			Considering fine art, graphic representation, etc.
			Finding stimulus for pupil-produced still pictures
			Considering possibilities of 'real objects', models and animated captions
			Creating collages
			
			Studio Sequences
			Speculating on set design, background screens, furniture
			
			Location Shots
			Selecting suitable places for location work
			
			Sound Research
			
			Speech
			Linking with written research material
			
			Music
			Considering appropriate music
			
			Sound Effects
			Developing initially appropriate sound effects

Process	Communication		
	Oral Language	Writing	Reading
3. Story-boarding 3.1. Analysing the printed and visual material from research	Establishing original intentions Comparing material Balancing contributions Quantifying amounts of material required Analysing methodically and exercising logic Devising direction of use of material Speculating Deducing conclusions Integrating information from different sources	Note-taking: listing decisions taken on research material	Reading selectively Summarizing information Paraphrasing Using topic cards and flow diagrams
3.2. Deciding what material should be included	Identifying relevancy, specifying objectives, promoting positive selection and rejection Debating, demonstrating, justifying disagreeing, qualifying, appealing against decisions, reasoning, implying Quoting from findings, giving opinions Intervening and interjecting	Note-taking: listing material to be included in script Using précis: summarizing conclusions of interviews, surveys, research findings, etc.	Skimming Picking out important features Identifying general structures and relationships Identifying function of structure and relationships Evaluating initial research reading strategy by justifying effectiveness in terms of outcomes and information in response to questions asked
3.3. Creating the initial shape of the statement in both vision and sound	Combining various inputs, divulging interests, rejecting material Understanding, appeasing and pacifying members whose materials are rejected Involving all members in comment Leading group to focus, discriminate and take necessary decisions Identifying problems Reporting progress verbally Planning the structure, outlining the main theme, devising, imagining, relating, connecting, adapting, adjusting, combining various inputs, constructing whole from parts, focusing on	Reshaping and formulating first annotated draft of script Integrating information into coherent, shaped whole	Determining personal prejudice and opinion in colouring research reading to material representative of group

	Social Skills	Subject-learning Skills	Audio-visual Aspects
Visual Language			
	Telephoning for information or appointments Developing individual responsibility for own contribution to a collective task Taking personal decisions and being responsible for own effort Being consistent and reliable Understanding the structure and who to refer to Relating to peers and adults in authority Working without supervision Being responsible to group for quality of the activity, speed of delivery, thoroughness and accuracy Justifying choices and decisions Organizing adequate presentation of results to group		
xpressing ideas in sketches, drawings and diagrams aking decisions on range of visual material found einforcing knowledge and information visually Understanding the closeness of visual material to 'real' experience dentifying simple objects sing symbols eveloping language to conceptualize onsidering: utility (basic need) and aesthetics (emotional need) eporting, interpreting and expressing topic through visual sources sing pictures to convey information, express a specific message, express feeling, tell a story	The following applies to 3.1–3.4: Taking decisions as group on order and content: democratic vote extra weighting to 'expert' extra weighting to person carrying out the task Clarifying suggestions in light of group's strengths Trying to be fair to all individual contributions in terms of selection and rejection Carrying a group member with the group when his contribution is rejected Defending contribution, by both contributor and others, when split over its inclusion Accepting rejection and continuing to give positive suggestions Being firm and decisive as a group Modifying and adapting individual contributions to needs of group end-product Holding back hurtful criticism and offering constructive changes Intervening to focus group on to relevant areas Being aware of time constraint and the need to work within time limits Coping with frustration or hostility	The following applies to 3.1 and 3.2: Thinking convergently and divergently Distinguishing figure from ground (field independence) Developing perceptual and cognitive discrimination Developing flexible patterns of logic, i.e. recognizing that the different goals of each communicative situation require subtly different logical orderings of material	Taking major decisions on audio-visual shape Deciding combinations of: still pictures narrator presenter interview demonstration dramatic sequences location shots
nderstanding, controlling and using visual language reating a visual message: sequencing rough sketches probing for solutions increasingly refining versions exercising choice taking decisions raming, changing and making concrete the pre-imagined image, considering different types of image: factual, atmospheric, realistic, fantastic onsidering functions of images: factual (information) environmental (establishing location)	Evaluating and influencing contributions Responding and reacting creatively Being the driving force to stimulate others Encouraging a flourish of ideas which can be pruned selectively as the group gains awareness of the whole area and what they specifically want to contribute Accepting necessary compromises Developing determination which ensures a thorough completion of the task Recognizing skills in others and appreciating their contribution Solving problems as a group Having a positive attitude to others	Exercising pupils' capacities for seeing intellectual transformations (how particular data can be transformed into some other form – a very complex aspect of intelligence) and implications (i.e. what is not apparent in the surface form of the data, but must be abstracted from it) Developing capacity for grasping the overall system or structure of a piece of learning and the importance of getting a 'fix' on it (i.e. recognition that meaningful learning occurs when a personally meaningful pattern has been formed)	Deciding whether speech should be live or voice over, male or female, natural or characterized Deciding what music should be used and where Deciding what sound effects should be used and where

Process	Communication		
	Oral Language	Writing	Reading
	main points, checking and clarifying that all decisions in 3.2 are incorporated into work of 3.3		
3.4. Organizing which team member will be responsible for the various aspects of translating the story-board into a script (a) Summarizing the research material to fit into the script (b) Script-writing (c) Deciding on the technical aspects of recording the script (numbering shots, camera positions and operations such as zoom, pan, etc.; planning the recording of captions, scenes and location shots)	Evaluating future activity and negotiating tasks Formalizing group responsibility Discovering individual skills and abilities Setting deadlines for work to be completed Announcing job roster Delegating responsibility Gaining co-operation	Note-taking: formulating list of jobs with personnel	
4. Scripting			
4.1. Revising and reshaping structure of story-board suggestions	Assessing work on story-board Making final decisions and comments Analysing content and clarifying interpretation Using a vocabulary to describe, develop and manipulate visual aspects	Revising and reshaping material on story-board: introduction establishing topic logical sequencing conclusion	Evaluating style in relation to original script for programme and various styles offered by research material
4.2. Making précis and adapting research material to fit script concept	Confirming rationale and purpose for summarizing research material	Using précis to shorten and adapt specific passages to be used in script	Scanning research material for revision and final selection and inclusion into script
4.3. Redrafting script.		Handwriting must be clear as all members of group must be able to read it Punctuation must be correct as all members of group must be able to read the script. Some members will have to read aloud	Reading the draft individually and as a group

Visual Language	**Social Skills**	**Subject-learning Skills**	**Audio-visual Aspects**
interpretive (of ideas, thoughts and feelings) symbolic (of places, moods events) representative/imitative (of action, appearance) identifying (association with particular people, events) recapitulative (recalling) sequencing (linking events, themes) montage (interplay between a succession of images or a juxtaposition of objects)	Being aware of interdependency – others are relying on one's precision, quality of work, timing, punctuality and seriousness of application Developing self-image – confidence to perform a job well		
	Extending individual perspectives by being made aware of others Developing experience in being able to take other people's feelings into account Providing social support: sharing positive feelings of success, difficulties and achievement	The following applies to 3.4 (a) and (b): Making abstractions concrete (reinforcement of concepts) Generalizing concrete experiences in concrete form (important in concept development) Developing capacity for intellectual 'transformation' and seeing the overall 'system' of a piece of learning Developing evaluation The following applies to 3.4 (c): Reinforcing ideas by finding technical correlations 'Translating' ideas into concrete technical form (seeing how ideas should 'look' in print and/or visual form) – using capacity for making 'transformations'	
Scanning visual material for revision and additional work	Making sure everyone knows the precise nature of the task Analysing the group's intentions Questioning the interpretation	The following applies to 4.1 and 4.3: Thinking convergently Developing important understanding of the painstaking revision necessary to genuine intellectual exploration Realizing that no statement, no knowledge is ever *final* Using intelligence evaluatively and for making transformations Developing, possibly, symbolic thought Learning the extreme importance of basic theoretical perspectives on the cognition, interpretation and communication of data	Considering: shape style pacing audio-visual balance development of climaxes dramatic impetus, etc.
Numbering pictures carefully and deciding which camera should carry each picture Discussing visual sequencing and continuity Considering distance and movement Discussing length of shot Varying viewpoints Matching scenes (position, movement, direction of attention) Considering visual action and reaction Considering title (to identify places and time; can be written, printed, pictorial, diagrammatic, designed)			

Process	Communication		
	Oral Language	Writing	Reading
4.4. Discussing the draft from various viewpoints: 　content 　style 　audio-visual balance 　initial intentions 　audience	Evaluating draft script Appraising critically Suggesting constructive 　improvements Making supportive comments Affirming decisions Conceding minor changes Resolving final contributions	Scripting in: 　factual writing 　technical description 　imaginative writing 　documentary writing 　linking research findings or 　　interviews 　adapting writing to suit audience	Speculating on experience 　beyond one's own, projecting, 　trying out alternative 　explanations
4.5. Redrafting script (adding technical dimensions)		Redrafting for final script	Handling new data Providing group support for 　tentative, discursive, inexplicit, 　unsure direction and second 　thoughts – feeding progress into 　second draft Considering material for the benefit 　of a variety of listeners whose 　attention pupils must try and 　hold
5. Producing Visuals and Rehearsing Script 5.1. Deciding on final requirements for still pictures, studio sequences and location shots and allocating specific tasks to group members	Creating expressive conditions Devising audio-visual continuity Designing artistically enabling 　structures Inventing, suggesting, sustaining, 　maintaining, urging, influencing, 　confirming	Note-taking: 　recording decisions 　producing a floor plan 　producing camera cards	Reading aloud specific tasks Reading instructions Reading floor plans and captions
5.2. Producing or finding still pictures	Identifying sources Evaluating appropriateness Evaluating aesthetic qualities	Handwriting: preparing graphics	Reading catalogues, etc., for visual 　material or music

Visual Language	Social Skills	Subject-learning Skills	Audio-visual Aspects
	Handling carefully group reaction to first draft Praising writers' efforts Evaluating results in terms of previous work and decisions Questioning choice of style or audio-visual balance, or reaffirming if correct Handling individual diversity of opinion positively to enable satisfactory progress to a final script Gaining general agreement and enthusiasm before undertaking final scripting Developing pride in work Coping with change Being efficient, consistent and reliable Developing responsibility for individual written contribution to a collective task Being able to work without supervision Finding personal freedom curtailed in working to group objectives	Learning the different relationships between content and the medium for perceiving it and transmitting it Being aware of the significance of the audience in communicating ideas	
Applying logical, analytical thought process to selective visual ideas Becoming aware of how attention might be held by visual means		Developing capacity for using intellectual systems (i.e. not experiencing learning as fragmented or compartmentalized) and classes (i.e. classifying) Realizing the sharpness of understanding generated by the multi-dimensionality of the media	Developing script into shooting script Allocating shot numbers Deciding which camera takes which shot Describing camera instructions (long shot, mid shot, close-up, zooming, panning and tilting, tracking and crabbing) Deciding visual continuity (fade-up, cutting, mixing, superimposing, special effects, fade to black)
Taking final visual decisions before still pictures (captions), set designs, costumes, masks, etc. are produced	The following applies to 5.1 – 5.8: Ascertaining aesthetic perception of the group Taking decisions on artistic ability and technical knowledge Encouraging imaginative and creative contributions Developing patience for emotional situations Being persistent on quality of activity Developing manual dexterity Understanding nervousness when recording perfomances Persuading reluctant contributors	Deepening cognitive/perceptual understanding through group exploration of ideas	
Reviewing pictures found in research Deciding on use Backing and framing if necessary Adapting and modifying if necessary Considering all still pictures to be made – these must be designed, made, sketched, painted, drawn, scratched, constructed or sculpted Using knowledge from fine art, three-dimensional design, graphic design, architecture and photography	Supporting individuals' performance or art work Checking all work and planning for quality control Accepting constructive criticism and improving presentation Being adaptable and coping with flexible situations Developing a positive attitude to others' efforts as they practise and develop presentation Developing versatility – offering various talents where needed (organizing, lettering, presenting etc.)	The following applies also to 5.2 – 5.4: Sharpening grasp of concepts through finding equivalents in another medium Using faculty for seeing implications and for making transformations Developing divergent thinking and evaluation	Producing still pictures (captions)

Process	Communication		
	Oral Language	Writing	Reading
5.3. Producing or finding relevant music	Co-ordinating music making or finding music Discussing purpose	Note-taking: recording decisions, adding to working script	Reading record sleeves
5.4. Producing or finding sound effects	Co-ordinating sound effects Discussing quality and quantity	Note-taking to record results, adding to working script	
5.5. Planning technical aspects			
5.6. Rehearsing live performances, whether narrator, presenter, interview, demonstration or dramatic sequences	Speaking for performance Stimulating dramatic activity Attending to vocal control and range	Note-taking: making alterations, adding movement, etc., to working script and floor plan	Reading script
5.7. Rehearsing voice over and recording if applicable	As above, adding technical instructions for recording purposes		Reading scripts and instruction cards for pre-recording audio
5.8. Planning and checking any location shots	Organizing schedules	Note-taking to record results to be acted upon in recording stage	Reading organizational plans for location shooting

Visual Language	Social Skills	Subject-learning Skills	Audio-visual Aspects
e following applies to 5.2, 5.3, .5 and 5.8 sidering: *Basic Visual Elements* , line, shape, direction, tone, olour, texture, scale or roportion, dimension and otion ving between contrast and armony *Syntactical Structures* ince, stress, levelling and arpening, attraction and rouping, positive and negative *Perceptual Mechanisms* resentation, symbolism, bstraction *Techniques* ance/instability metry/asymmetry ularity/irregularity ty/fragmentation derstatement/exaggeration dictability/spontaneity veness/stasis tlety/boldness trality/accent nsparency/opacity sistency/variation uracy/distortion ness/depth gularity/juxtaposition uentiality/randomness rpness/diffusion etition/episodicity *tyles* synthesis of elements, chniques, syntax, inspiration, xpression and basic purpose tural styles and conventions mitivism, expressionism, assicism, the embellished style, nctionality *ystems (medium)* pture, architecture, painting, ustration, graphic design, dustrial design, photography es, film, television ure composition (tone, balance, nity, visual rhythm, proportion, ale) ning, subject importance, shape ity of meaning and intention using visual attention (subject titude, movement, contrasting bject/background/surroundings, mera control) tinuity of composition ice of composition ial effects (superimposition, pes, split screen, etc.) elaboration of many of the ove terms, see Donis A. ondis, *A Primer of Visual teracy*)	Reporting problems and faults and remedying them Coping with changes Developing efficient working techniques Taking responsibility for individual contribution to group end-product Being consistent in performance and reliable Understanding the structure of activity and who to refer to	Further reshaping and refining of cognitive/perceptual understanding through detailed evaluation of adequacy of live presentations to represent underlying ideas Reinforcing ideas Reshaping through successive approximations (development of a sense of probabilistic rather than absolute truth) Further reshaping and refinement from yet another standpoint Developing reinforcement contingencies on a probabilistic basis	Producing music Producing sound effects Sorting out the technical requirements: cameras lenses microphones film slides records audio tapes special lighting effects Devising a studio floor plan showing layout of sets, background screens, furniture, display material, caption stands, the position, height, movement and field of view of each camera, the positions of any studio monitors Rehearsing dramatic sequences Rehearsing demonstrations

Process	Communication		
	Oral Language	Writing	Reading
6. Recording 6.1. Setting up studio: referring to floor plan, organizing positioning of sets, background screens, furniture, display material, caption stands	Interpreting information Directing activity Controlling movement Deciding on final positions		Referring to floor plan
6.2. Lighting			
6.3. Rehearsing with cameras	Giving and taking instructions Interpreting requests Questioning action Reporting problems Offering suggestions Taking final decisions	Making alterations to script or camera cards	Referring to scripts and camera cards Reading instructions
6.4. Recording	Requirements for critical performance element: accuracy clarity split-second timing and decision-making efficiency giving and responding to verbal instructions		Referring to scripts and camera cards Reading instructions Reading aloud for recording Improvising speech
7. Presentation and Evaluation 7.1. Viewing programme: (a) organizing an audience (b) introducing the programme (c) handling technical presentation		Note-taking for raising points in discussion	
7.2. Evaluating programme: (a) eliciting response from an audience (b) assessing accuracy, clarity, impact (c) relating weaknesses and strengths to activities in the process (d) noting implications for future audio-visual and other work	Using evaluative language: assessing achievement in terms of intention and communication success of end-product		

Visual Language	Social Skills	Subject-learning Skills	Audio-visual Aspects

Checking visual aspects:
  camera positions
  captions
  dramatic scenes
  sets
	The following applies to 6.1 – 6.4:
	
	Generating group awareness of critical performance activity
	Developing quiet confidence
	Ensuring group control
	Reassuring each other over difficulties or mistakes
	Encouraging group concentration and discipline
		The following applies to 6.1 – 6.4:
		
		Further deepening of awareness of significance of communicator's/ learner's *standpoint* in determining the selection and synthesis of data
		Reinforcement of learning
		Extending skill in making intellectual transformations and grasping systems of ideas
			Television
			
			Allocating roles:
			  director
			  vision-mixer
			  sound-mixer
			  shot-caller
			  floor manager
			  caption-pullers
			  personnel in front of cameras
			  narrator
			  presenter
			  demonstration
			  interviewer
			  interviewee
			  actors
			
			Carrying out tasks associated with above roles

Checking camera compositions and movement, vision mixing Using hand signals (usually by floor manager controlling activity in studio in silent conditions)	Giving and receiving instructions efficiently Split-second decision-making Acting immediately on decisions without discussion or negotiation Timing accuracy (including punctuality) Taking individual responsibility (for own task) for group effort Assessing quality of technical activity, presentation and performance as programme is recorded Being adaptable in stepping in to rescue the situation Being responsible for individual role in team activity Relating to peers and adults in authority		
Evaluating visual effectiveness Reflecting on the parts which work visually and those which do not Offering constructive alternative visual treatments in light of critically analysing end-product	The following applies to 7.1 and 7.2: Assessing the group's ability to co-ordinate individual contributions towards the production of an effective, shared end-product Sharing positive feelings of successful achievement Sharing disappointment that end-product failed in some way and constructively deciding on what could be done, and how, to improve the statement Developing positive self-image – confidence to perform a job well Testing good social relations Developing confidence in personal abilities	Developing social (behavioural) intelligence Defining subject further (a) Sharpening cognitive/ affective awareness through feedback (b) and (c) Developing self-criticism, behaving objectively in relation to content (c) Developing capacity for seeing implications, seeing ideas as part of a continuum (a), (b) and (c) Seeing relationships, grasping systems and evaluating	Checking effectiveness of audio-visual dimensions

APPENDIX 2: Useful Addresses

Schools Council Communication and Social Skills Project, Faculty of Educational Studies, Brighton Polytechnic, Falmer, Brighton, Sussex BN1 9PH

British Film Institute, 127 Charing Cross Road, London WC2H 0EA
The Education Advisory Service provides advice and information on media studies

Council for Educational Technology, 3 Devonshire Street, London W1N 2BA
Advice and information on full range of educational technology

Educational Television Association, 80 Micklegate, York YO1 1JZ
Forum for those concerned with media in teaching and training

Institute of Amateur Cinematographers, 63 Woodfield Lane, Ashtead, Surrey KT21 2BT
Film and tape library, copyright schemes

London Co-operative Society
Biannual festival of films produced by children

National Committee for Audio-visual Aids in Education, 254 Belsize Road, London NW6 4BY
Advice and information on all aspects of audio-visual aids

Royal Photographic Society, The Octagon, Milson Street, Bath, Avon
Education group on education and photography

Schools Council, 160 Great Portland Street, London W1N 6LL
Many related projects whose materials and ideas could be usefully incorporated into this project's methods

Scottish Council for Educational Technology, 16 Woodside Terrace, Glasgow G3 7XN
Advice and information on full range of educational technology

Local Authority Advisers for Audio-visual Aids or Educational Technology
Address from Local Authority
Provide support and advice, and in a number of areas supplement school resources

APPENDIX 3: Examinations

For teachers wishing to develop the Project's methods alongside an academic study of modern communications, the following boards provide formal examinations:

ASSOCIATED EXAMINING BOARD
GCE A-level Communication Studies: 30% of marks are awarded for a practical project which could be an audio-visual statement.
A-level Graphic Communication.

LONDON
Elements of modern communication in various social-science A-levels.

OXFORD
GCE O-level Modern Communications (television):

Paper 1: historical, economic and social aspects;
Paper 2: techniques and evaluation;
Paper 3: practical.

WELSH JOINT BOARD
GCE O-level Mode 2 Film Studies.
GCE O-level Mode 2 Mass Media Studies.

For those teachers wishing to use the Project's methods as a means of studying mainstream curriculum subjects, the following boards provide formal examinations:

LONDON
Environmental Studies A and Geography AO could involve pupils in projects with practical media elements for examination purposes.

JOINT MATRICULATION BOARD
GCE O-level Integrated Humanities: pupils study five topics chosen from ten, one of which may be designed by teachers for local needs; methods of teaching and assessment are the responsibility of schools, subject to general criteria given by the Board. The Project's methods would integrate well with this approach.

CSE boards provide a wide range of courses in modern communications, media studies, film and television. Details are available in local areas. In addition, audio-visual presentations have been accepted as evidence of learning by a number of boards. Teachers wishing to develop such methods would be advised to contact their local boards.

Bibliography

Language

Barnes, D. *From Communication to Curriculum.* Penguin
——, Britton, J. and Rosen, H. *Language, the Learner and the School.* Penguin
Bell, R. T. *Sociolinguistics.* Batsford
Bullock Committee *A Language for Life.* H.M.S.O.
Cazden, C., John, V. and Hynes, D. (eds) *Functions of Language in the Classroom.* Columbia: Teachers College Press
Chanan, G. and Delamont, S. (eds) *Frontiers of Classroom Research.* N.F.E.R.
Delamont, S. *Interaction in the Classroom.* Methuen
Labov, W. *Language in the Inner City: Studies in the Black English Vernacular.* Blackwell
Lyons, J. H. (ed.) *New Horizons in Linguistics.* Penguin
Open University *Language and Learning E262.* Open University Press
Pride, J. R. and Holmes, J. (eds) *Sociolinguistics.* Penguin
Sinclair, J. Mc. H. and Coulthard, R. M. *Towards an Analysis of Discourse: the English used by Teachers and Pupils.* Open University Press
Smith, N. and Wilson, D. *Modern Linguistics: the Results of Chomsky's Revolution.* Penguin
Stork, F. C. and Widdowson, J. D. A. *Learning about Linguistics.* Hutchinson
Stubbs, M. *Language, Schools and Classrooms.* Methuen
——, and Delamont, S. (eds) *Explorations in Classroom Observation.* Wiley
Trudgill, P. *Accent, Dialect and the School.* Edward Arnold
——, *Sociolinguistics: an Introduction.* Penguin
Walker, R. and Adelman, C. *A Guide to Classroom Observation.* Methuen
Webb, C. *Communication Skills: an Approach to Personal Development.* Macmillan

Social Skills

Argyle, M. *The Psychology of Interpersonal Behaviour.* Penguin
Association for Liberal Education *Teaching Social and Life Skills.* Association for Liberal Education
Becdar, R. J. *Skills for Effective Communication.* Wiley
Berger, M. L. and Berger, P. J. (eds) *Group Training Techniques.* Gower Press
Blaumberg, A. and Golembiewski, R. *Learning and Change in Groups.* Penguin
Cartwright, D. and Zander, A. (eds) *Group Dynamics: Research and Theory.* Harper & Row
Cathcart, R. and Samovar, L. *Small Group Communication.* W. C. Brown
Dyar, D. A. and Giles, W. J. *Improving Skills in Working with People: Interaction Analysis.* T.S.A. Training Paper 7, H.M.S.O.
Hargraves, D. H. *Interpersonal Relations and Education.* Routledge & Kegan-Paul
Hinde, R. (ed.) *Non-Verbal Communication.* Cambridge University Press
Hollander, E. and Hunt, R. (eds) *Current Perspectives in Social Psychology.* Oxford University Press

Johnson, D.   *Reaching Out: Interpersonal Effectiveness and Self Actualisation.* Prentice-Hall

Kelvin, P.   *The Bases of Social Behaviour.* Holt, Rhinehart & Winston

Ottaway, A. K. C.   *Learning Through Group Experience.* Routledge & Kegan-Paul

Rackham, N. *et al.*   *Developing Interactive Skills.* Welkens

Turner, C. M.   *Interpersonal Skills in Further Education.* Further Education Staff College, Coombe Lodge

Visual Language

Arnheim, R.   *Visual Thinking.* Faber & Faber

——,   *Art and Visual Perception.* University of California Press

Berenson, Bernard   *Seeing and Knowing.* Chapman & Hall

Berger, J.   *Ways of Seeing.* Penguin

Dondis, Donis A.   *A Primer of Visual Literacy.* M.I.T. Press

Gattegno, C.   *Towards a Visual Culture.* New York: Outerbridge & Dienstfrey

Gregory, R. L.   *The Intelligent Eye.* Weidenfeld & Nicolson

Ivins, William   *Prints and Visual Communication.* M.I.T. Press

Klee, Paul   *Notebooks Vol. I: the Thinking Eye.* Lund Humphries

Koestler, A.   *The Act of Creation.* Hutchinson

McKim, R. H.   *Experiences in Visual Thinking.* Brooks-Cole

Miller, G. A.   *Psychology of Communication.* Penguin

Ornstein, R.   *Psychology of Consciousness.* Freeman

Palmer, F.   *Visual Awareness.* Batsford

Read, Herbert   *The Meaning of Art.* Penguin

Samuels, Mike and Samuels, Nancy   *Seeing with the Mind's Eye.* Random House

Sheikh and Shaffer (eds)   *The Potential of Fantasy and Imagination.* Brandon House

Television Production

Alkin, G.   *Television Sound Operations.* Focal Press

Davies, D.   *A Grammar of Television Production.* Barries & Rockliff

Gibson, Tony   *The Practice of E.T.V.* Hutchinson

King, Gordon J.   *Beginners Guide to Television.* Butterworths

Millerson, Gerald   *Basic Television Staging.* Focal Press

——,   *Effective Television Production.* Focal Press

——,   *Television Camera Operation.* Focal Press

——,   *Television Lighting Methods.* Focal Press

Turner, Peter   *Television in the Service of the School.* National Committee for Audio-visual Aids in Education

——, and Atkinson, C. R. M.   *An Experiment in Closed-circuit Television at Millfield School.* National Committee for Audio-visual Aids in Education

Wilson, Alistair J.   *Television Guidelines: Writing, Directing and Presenting.* Hutchinson

Film

Anderson, Yvonne   *Teaching Film Animation to Children.* Van Nostrand Reinhold

Arijon, Daniel   *Grammar of the Film Language.* Focal Press

Beal, J. D. *Cine Craft.* Focal Press
——, *How to Make Films at School.* Focal Press
Cheshire, David *The Book of Movie Photography.* Ebury Press
Halas, John and Manvell, Roger *The Technique of Film Animation.* Focal Press
Hayward, Stan *Scriptwriting for Animation.* Focal Press
Kennedy, Keith *Film Making in Teaching.* Batsford
Linder *Film Making: a Practical Guide.* Prentice-Hall
Lowndes, Douglas *Film Making in Schools.* Batsford
Matzin, Myton A. *The Super 8 Film Makers' Handbook.* Focal Press
Perisic, Zoran *Focal Guide to Shooting Animation.* Focal Press
Rose, Tony *The Complete Book of Movie Making.* Fountain Press

Tape-slide

Beaumont-Cragg, R. *Slide Tape and Dual Projection.* Focal Press
Duncalf, Brian *Focal Guide to Slide-Tape.* Focal Press

Photography

Gaunt, Leonard *Commonsense Photography.* Focal Press
Hedgecoe, John *The Photographer's Handbook.* Ebury Press
Langford, Michael *Basic Photography.* Focal Press
——, *The Step by Step Guide to Photography.* Ebury Press
Leggat, Robert *Photography in School.* Fountain Press
Pickering, John *Photography for Children.* Batsford
Saxby, Graham *Focal Guide to Slides.* Focal Press

Audio

Capel, Vivian *Creative Tape Recording.* Fountain Press
Jessel, J. *D'Arblay Sound Studio Workshop.* Cobiron Ltd
Jones, J. Graham *Teaching with Tape.* Focal Press
Lloyd, Joseph M. *The All in One Tape Recorder Book.* Focal Press
Staab, Joachim G. *Fun with Tape.* Focal Press
Western, John *The Tape Recorder in the Classroom.* National Committee for Audio-visual Aids in Education
Wood, D. Neville *On Tape: the Creative Use of the Tape Recorder.* Ward Lock

Organizing Resources

Besinck, Norman W. *Schools Resources Centre.* Schools Council Working Paper no. 43
Malcolm, Adam H. *The Setting Up of a Resources Centre: 1. Basic Ideas.* Scottish Educational Film Association
——, *The Setting Up of a Resources Centre: 3. Retrieval Systems.* Scottish Educational Film Association
Tucker, R. N. *The Setting Up of a Resources Centre: 2. Planning and Staffing.* Scottish Educational Film Association